Legal Challenges of AI Across Interdisciplinary Sectors

Konstantinos Kouroupis
https://orcid.org/0000-0003-1193-8224
Frederick University, Cyprus

Iris-Panagiota Efthymiou
https://orcid.org/0000-0001-9656-8378
University of Greenwich, UK

IGI Global
Scientific Publishing
Publishing Tomorrow's Research Today

Vice President of Editorial Melissa Wagner
Director of Acquisitions Mikaela Felty
Director of Book Development Jocelynn Hessler
Production Manager Mike Brehm
Cover Design Jose Rosado

Published in the United States of America by
IGI Global Scientific Publishing
701 East Chocolate Avenue
Hershey, PA, 17033, USA
Tel: 717-533-8845 | Fax: 717-533-7115
Website: https://www.igi-global.com E-mail: cust@igi-global.com

Library of Congress Cataloging-in-Publication Data

Names: Kouroupēs, Kōnstantinos editor | Efthymiou, Iris-Panagiota, 1967- editor
Title: Legal challenges of AI across interdisciplinary sectors / edited by Konstantinos Kouroupis, Iris-Panagiota Efthymiou.
Other titles: Legal challenges of artificial intelligence across interdisciplinary sectors
Description: Hershey : IGI Global Scientific Publishing, 2026. | Includes bibliographical references and index. | Summary: "This book aims to offer a holistic and interdisciplinary approach of the legal challenges arising from the extensive use of Artificial Intelligence across various sectors of public and private life"-- Provided by publisher.
Identifiers: LCCN 2025034545 (print) | LCCN 2025034546 (ebook) | ISBN 9798337354521 hardcover | ISBN 9798337354538 paperback | ISBN 9798337354545 ebook
Subjects: LCSH: Artificial intelligence--Law and legislation
Classification: LCC K564.C6 L439 2026 (print) | LCC K564.C6 (ebook) | DDC 340.0285/63--dc23/eng/20250912
LC record available at https://lccn.loc.gov/2025034545
LC ebook record available at https://lccn.loc.gov/2025034546
British Cataloguing in Publication Data
A Cataloguing in Publication record for this book is available from the British Library.

Table of Contents

Detailed Table of Contents

about who is responsible when things go wrong, how to protect patient data, and how to properly regulate AI use. This paper examines the challenges and possible solutions for controlling AI in healthcare, with a special focus on the legal changes happening in the European Union. It discusses how the EU AI Act, the General Data Protection Regulation (GDPR), and the Medical Device Regulation (MDR) work together to manage high-risk AI systems in hospitals and clinics. The paper also looks at key issues like who is to blame when AI makes decisions, how to safely handle private health information, and the difficulties developers face in meeting these rules. The study suggests a transparent, open, and fair way to regulate AI that supports new ideas.

As AI technologies become increasingly integrated into long-term care settings, they are not only transforming service delivery but also influencing the quality of human relationships within these environments. This chapter delves into the evolving dynamics of human-AI interaction from a Social Work perspective, emphasizing ethical considerations, relational aspects, and person-centered care in long-term care contexts. Grounded in core Social Work values – dignity and worth of the individual, the importance of human relationships, and social justice – this chapter critically examines how AI technologies (e.g., robotic companions, predictive analytics, and ambient monitoring systems) intersect with the daily lives of older adults, care workers, and social workers. This chapter presents a compelling case for a Social Work-driven framework to guide the development and implementation of AI in long-term care. It underscores the importance of ensuring that technology serves as a tool to enhance, rather than replace, human connection, while upholding individuals' dignity and rights.

The American criminal justice system is undergoing a rapid transformation with the introduction of artificial intelligence (AI). Proponents support these technologies as an efficient, objective, and data-driven solution to the problems of human error. The use of AI, ranging from predictive policing and facial recognition to algorithmic risk assessments, is creating a new form of discrimination. AI systems are trained on datasets with decades of human bias. This chapter details the operational mechanics of these tools, their reliance on biased data, and their obscure "black box" nature. These tools, from street-level policing and detective work, through federal counter-

Preface

INTRODUCTION

Artificial intelligence (AI) has moved rapidly from the margins of technological innovation to the center of legal, economic, and social transformation. Its deployment across corporate governance, creative industries, healthcare, social services, and criminal justice systems has introduced unprecedented efficiencies while simultaneously exposing profound legal and ethical uncertainties. Law, as both a regulatory mechanism and a normative framework, is now confronted with questions that transcend traditional doctrinal boundaries—questions of accountability, authorship, transparency, human dignity, and the distribution of power between humans and intelligent systems.

The legal challenges posed by AI are inherently interdisciplinary. They do not arise solely from technological novelty, but from the interaction of algorithmic systems with existing institutional structures, cultural norms, and regulatory traditions. As AI systems increasingly mediate decision-making processes—whether in hiring, healthcare diagnostics, policing, or creative production—the limitations of current legal frameworks become evident. Fragmented regulatory approaches, jurisdictional divergence, and gaps between ethical aspirations and enforceable rules complicate efforts to govern AI in a manner that is both innovation-friendly and rights-protective.

This edited volume, *Legal Challenges of AI Across Interdisciplinary Sectors*, is conceived as a timely and critical contribution to these ongoing debates. Bringing together scholars from law, social sciences, healthcare governance, and technology policy, the book offers comparative, sector-specific, and normative perspectives on how AI is reshaping legal responsibility and institutional accountability. Rather than treating AI as a purely technical phenomenon, the chapters collectively emphasize its social embeddedness and the need for legal responses that are anticipatory, context-sensitive, and grounded in fundamental principles of justice and human rights.

OVERVIEW OF THE CHAPTERS

Chapter 1 examines AI corporate governance and legal accountability through a comparative analysis of Indian and international regulatory frameworks. By exploring how AI-driven decision-making affects corporate responsibility, liability, and transparency, the authors propose a hybrid governance model that integrates statutory reform, ethical oversight, and regulatory experimentation.

Chapter 2 turns to the field of copyright law within the European Union, focusing on the hybrid nature of AI-assisted creative works. It distinguishes between AI training, autonomous outputs, and human-led AI-assisted creation, offering a layered understanding of originality that aligns existing copyright principles with emerging creative practices.

Chapter 3 extends the copyright discussion by focusing on moral rights, particularly attribution and integrity, in the context of AI-generated and AI-assisted creations. The chapter highlights how AI disrupts traditional notions of authorship and argues for the preservation of human-centered values within evolving copyright regimes.

Chapter 4 explores the regulation of AI in healthcare, with particular emphasis on legal accountability, data protection, and the practical application of the EU AI Act. It analyzes how the EU's regulatory ecosystem—including the GDPR and Medical Device Regulation—addresses high-risk AI systems while balancing innovation and patient safety.

Chapter 5 approaches AI from a social work perspective, focusing on human–AI interaction and the ethics of care in long-term care settings.

Grounded in core social work values, the chapter argues for relational and person-centered frameworks that ensure AI enhances, rather than diminishes, human dignity and relationships.

Chapter 6 analyzes the use of AI in law enforcement and the criminal justice system, particularly within the United States. It critically examines predictive policing, facial recognition, and risk assessment tools, highlighting issues of bias, opacity, and democratic accountability, while proposing legal and institutional reforms.

Chapter 7 concludes the substantive contributions with a comparative analysis of facial recognition technology as a form of algorithmic governance. By examining regulatory approaches in India, the United States, and the European Union, the chapter underscores the human rights implications of surveillance technologies and advocates for safeguards that protect civil liberties.

CONCLUSION

Taken together, the chapters in this volume illustrate that the legal challenges of AI cannot be resolved through isolated regulatory interventions or purely technical solutions. Across sectors, recurring themes emerge: the diffusion of responsibility, the opacity of algorithmic decision-making, the persistence of bias, and the tension between efficiency and fundamental rights. These challenges demand legal frameworks that are adaptive, coherent, and capable of engaging with the social realities in which AI systems operate.

This volume also highlights the importance of comparative and interdisciplinary approaches to AI governance. Differences in regulatory philosophy—whether risk-based, sectoral, or principles-driven—shape how societies balance innovation with accountability. By placing jurisdictions, sectors, and normative traditions in dialogue, the contributions demonstrate that no single legal model can adequately address all dimensions of AI regulation, yet shared principles can guide context-specific solutions.

Ultimately, *Legal Challenges of AI Across Interdisciplinary Sectors* seeks to inform scholars, policymakers, legal practitioners, and technologists who are grappling with the implications of intelligent systems in law and society. The editors hope that this book will not only clarify existing legal tensions but also contribute to the development of governance frameworks that ensure AI serves the public interest, respects human dignity, and reinforces—rather than undermines—the rule of law.

Chapter 1

AI Corporate Governance and Legal Accountability:
Comparative Indian-International Frameworks

Shashank Solanki
https://orcid.org/0009-0002-5923-0516
Christ University, India

Rituraj Sinha
https://orcid.org/0000-0001-5790-9571
Christ University, India

Kalpna Sharma
https://orcid.org/0000-0002-4511-7988
University of Delhi, India

Sheetal Singh
https://orcid.org/0000-0002-7266-8910
Christ University, India

Vijaishree Dubey Pandey
https://orcid.org/0000-0003-3207-7814
Christ University, India

Vijeta Verma
https://orcid.org/0000-0001-9255-9132
Christ University, India

Mayank Kapila
https://orcid.org/0009-0001-4874-8283
Babasaheb Bhimrao Ambedkar Bihar University, India

DOI: 10.4018/979-8-3373-5452-1.ch001

ABSTRACT

This chapter examines the intersection of Artificial Intelligence, corporate governance, and legal accountability through a comparative analysis of Indian and international regulatory frameworks. It evaluates how AI's integration into corporate decision-making—across finance, hiring, compliance, and supply chains—raises challenges of opacity, bias, and liability diffusion. Internationally, frameworks such as the EU AI Act (2024), OECD AI Principles, and U.S. sectoral regulations impose varying degrees of oversight, transparency, and risk classification, while India's evolving regime, shaped by the Digital Personal Data Protection Act, 2023, the IT Act, 2000, and the Companies Act, 2013, remains fragmented. Using case studies from India, the EU, and the U.S., the chapter identifies governance gaps and proposes a hybrid model combining statutory reform, mandated algorithmic transparency, board-level AI Ethics Committees, enhanced disclosures, and regulatory sandboxes. It argues for anticipatory and ethically grounded corporate governance that balances innovation with legal safeguards.

1. INTRODUCTION

1.1 Background and Motivation

The affiliate marketing system works on a very simple concept, and that is to earn incentives for telling people about certain products, which are either digital or tangible. Artificial intelligence (AI), however, is a paradigm shift in the behaviour, planning and management of today's businesses. Today, artificial intelligence systems are increasingly used to automate the hiring process, to track credit risk, to make sure companies comply with regulations and to make financial projections. These tools are starting to take operational and strategic positions previously held only by a human decision-maker. As such, the legal and moral consequences of delegating decisions to AI require careful attention by scholars (De Almeida, Santos, & Farias, 2021).

The uncertainty of AI systems, especially the black box models, is an important concern. These models are not transparent and make it challenging for the corporate actors, the regulators, and other stakeholders who may want to trace or question the automated decisions. The problem is complicated by the problem of algorithmic bias, which poses a risk of perpetuating and institutionalizing discriminatory practices such as hiring, lending and consumer profiling.

AI's autonomy is a further challenge because systems are self-learning and adaptive without constant human oversight. This development results in urgent questions of responsibility and liability in corporate governance. Traditional company law principles (e.g. fiduciary duties, business judgment rule, liability of directors) were constructed on the presumption of human will and control. These doctrines are unsettled by the use of algorithms in decision making which reveals lack of accountability, due diligence, and risk management (Abhilash, Shenoy, & Shetty, 2023).Much of the speech has focused on European and US regulatory models, with relatively little scholarship on Indian and greater Asian approaches. This imbalance highlights a significant research gap. The case of India as one of the most rapidly growing digital economies is particularly relevant from the perspective of its dual commitment to promoting the development of AI innovation and the need for protecting through regulation. Recent initiatives like the Digital Personal Data Protection Act, 2023, sectoral guidance from SEBI and RBI, and ethical frameworks from NITI Aayog and ICMR indicate the evolving governance scenario in India.

The comparative perspective is thus necessary. In addition to analysing the established frameworks of the European Union and the United States, this chapter takes into account some emerging approaches from around the world, such as Canada's Artificial Intelligence and Data Act (AIDA, 2022) and Singapore's Model AI Governance Framework. Such an analysis allows the identification of convergences and divergences across jurisdictions and in this way contributes to a richer debate around the relationship of AI, corporate responsibility and ethics governance across the world.

1.2 Research Objectives

This chapter provides a critical analysis of the legal, regulatory and ethical implications of incorporating AI in corporate governance, with a specific focus on accountability. Its main objectives are:

- To conduct a comparative legal analysis of the responses of India, European Union and United States to the adoption of AI in corporate context especially with respect to regulatory requirements, responsibility of directors and risk management practices.
- To examine if current corporate law doctrines adequately address the challenges posed by algorithmic decision-making, and to identify emerging areas of legal principles that can provide a sense of accountability where it will otherwise be lacking.
- In order to take a look at the overlap between data protection legislation, sector-specific legislation and soft law instruments (e.g., AI ethics frameworks and Environmental, Social, and Governance codes), as well as assess how this affects legal responsibility in AI-driven contexts.
- To propose a theorized governance model balancing the imperatives of innovation, legal accountability and ethical responsibility.

By seeking these objectives, the chapter fills a major research gap. The bulk of previous research has treated AI governance and corporate law as two distinct fields; however, this research shows that the two are interdependent and suggests that regulation should be formulated with these two interdependencies in mind (Ulnicane, 2024).

1.3 Methodology

The paper uses a doctrinal approach to law, depending on comparative analysis of statute and policy. It relies, mainly, on the first-hand legal sources such as statutes, regulations and case law, which are obtained in India, European Union, and the United States, as well as the secondary sources, such as judicial commentary, policy documents, and regulatory guidance (Chen & Gao, 2022). To ensure depth as well, the analysis goes to corporate actors that deploy AI within accountability frameworks (Efthymiou, 2024).

Case studies (including denial of credit by Indian NBFCs, Amazon's AI based hiring practices, the German SCHUFA credit scoring controversy and applications of AI in healthcare) have been chosen to highlight enforcement issues, allocation of liability and governance practices, in real life situations. These case studies are practical evidence of how regulatory principles are operationalized and tested in different jurisdictions.

The major regulatory frameworks discussed, being EU Artificial Intelligence Act (2024), Digital Personal Data Protection Act, 2023, Companies Act, 2013 & Sectoral Guidelines issued by SEBI, RBI, ICMR etc. In addition, the paper takes into account influential soft law instruments, such as the set of principles on artificial intelligence developed by the Organisation for Economic Cooperation and Development (known as the "OEA Principles") and the Responsible Artificial Intelligence framework developed by the National Talmud-Katzir Committee on Artificial Intelligence (known as the "NITI Aayog Responsible AI framework"). The methodology also includes a cross-jurisdictional comparative approach and policy analysis, which will allow for the derivation of a hybrid governance approach that engages legal, regulatory and technical perspectives.

Consequently, the chapter is a multi-dimensional, multi-disciplinary understanding of AI, corporate governance and AI accountability, both theoretically and practically (Batra, Sannegadu, & Mehta, 2022).

2. CONCEPTUAL FRAMEWORK

2.1 Defining Corporate Governance in the AI Era

The forces behind regulation and corporate accountability have been pegged on corporate governance which has traditionally been considered as the mechanism by which corporations are guided and controlled (Efthymiou, and Egleton, 2025). As artificial intelligence (AI) becomes the trend, there is a massive change in this landscape. The classical model focuses on the division of powers between directors, management, and shareholders, the fiduciary duty, the presence of stakeholders, and an organized risk management approach (Radanliev, 2025). Nevertheless, the growing dependence on AI, especially when it comes to decision-making, has broadened the role of these actors (Efthymiou, 2025b).

It is the most basic principles that boards and top management should act according to the law, and with due diligence, good faith, and protection of corporate and stakeholder interests. These obligations are enshrined in the Companies Act, 2013 in India, especially in Sections 166 and 134 that introduce the responsibilities of care, expertise and informed supervision. Conversely, American corporate governance is based on the judicial doctrines that include the business judgment rule and are supplemented by the statutory law, whereas the European Union is based on the explicit codification in the form of the AI Act or GDPR (Lane, 2022).

One of the most important questions that arise in the field of corporate law scholarship is whether AI management might be regarded as an explicit fiduciary obligation. There are researchers, who claim that current fiduciary duties are also adequate and do not need changes, and there are researchers, who state that the transparency and systemic risks of AI will demand new transparency and technological accountability (Peng et al., 2023). Therefore, the corporate governance in the AI age should no longer be based on the usual fiduciary watchfulness, but rather active, focusing on the risks that can potentially be posed by technology and ethical questions (Efthymiou, 2025a). Concepts of transparency, monitoring, and accountability should be reconsidered as far as AI-driven changes in the functioning of corporations and regulatory frameworks (Sharma and Haralayya, 2025).

2.2 Core Legal and Ethical Concerns with AI in Corporate Use

Implementing AI into the corporate frameworks presents a myriad of legal and ethical issues that place strain on both compliance and risk management frameworks. Mistakes, prejudice, and obscurity in the decision-making process of AI may culminate in serious economic losses, negative publicity, and lawsuits. Prejudice, specifically, is also a chronic problem, with AI systems tending to either recreate or increase the disparities in the society that exist in training data. This is seen in areas relating to hiring, credit scoring, insurance and predictive policing. As an illustration, the recruitment tool at Amazon discriminated against some candidates in a systematic way that led to ethical and legal issues and breached the anti-discrimination legislation and provisions of Article 14 and 15 of Indian Constitution, U.S. Civil Rights Act, and EU Charter of Fundamental Rights (Zhao and Fariñas, 2022).

The other difficulty is explainability. Complex deep learning networks can be considered black boxes, and it is hard to trace or explain their outputs. Such non-transparency will diffuse due process, consumer rights and legal defenses. The rights structures, including Article 22 of GDPR and Article VII of ICCPR, therefore, declare the right of individuals not being exposed to purely automatic decisions (Shaban and Omoush, 2025). Such rights can be addressed through the use of algorithmic explainability tools, which will provide the necessary compliance therewith and augment the fiduciary responsibilities of informed supervision of directors.

Governance is also complicated by regulatory arbitrage and distributed liability. With companies shifting to third-party providers or AI-as-a-Service (AIaaS) companies progressively relying on them, responsibility in incidents of harm becomes decentralized. In India, the Digital Personal Data Protection Act, 2023 as well as the Information Technology Act, 2000 does not contain specifications about how to work out the liability apportionment within AI supply chains (Saheb & Saheb, 2023). This provides the prospects of forum shopping and offshoring the data to less strict jurisdictions. The harmonization of standards is getting urgent since AI is transnational. The attempts to fill these gaps can be traced in international initiatives like the OECD AI Principles, the White House AI Bill of Rights, or the Council of Europe Convention on AI, Human Rights, Democracy, and the Rule of Law.

Lastly, outside of the implementation of laws, it is also questioned whether the application of AI within corporations needs radically new frameworks of accountability. In this case, ethical control, external audit, and increased involvement of the stakeholders can be as important as legal conformity (Radanliev, 2025). Sustainable corporate AI governance will probably require a hybrid approach involving the combination of law, ethics, and technical safeguards.

Table 1. Comparative Table: Fiduciary Duty Obligations in AI Oversight

Jurisdiction	Legal Framework	Fiduciary Obligations in AI Context	Enforcement Mechanisms
European Union	AI Act (2024), GDPR	Explicit emphasis on AI risk management, transparency, and individual rights (Article 22 GDPR).	National supervisory authorities; cross-border EU enforcement mechanisms.
India	Companies Act, 2013 (Sections 134, 166); SEBI Guidelines	Duties of care, informed decision-making, and stakeholder protection; no explicit AI oversight, but fiduciary duties can extend to technology risks.	SEBI enforcement actions; judicial interpretation under company law.
United States	Business Judgment Rule; FTC Enforcement	Deference to directors' discretion unless gross negligence; emerging focus on algorithmic accountability through FTC investigations.	Courts applying business judgment rule; FTC enforcement powers.

This comparative model shows the diverse focus: whereas the EU implements the direct AI-related commitments, India modifies the fiduciary principling by interpreting the law in statutes and the U.S. depends more on judicial deference and agency supervision.

In addition, the interconnection of technical mechanisms with these legal doctrines is necessary. Statutory due diligence and transparency requirements by the statute can be operationalized with the help of algorithmic auditing, and the explainability techniques support the compliance with the data protection rights under GDPR directly and the fiduciary duty of informed oversight in both the U.S. and India. Technical safeguards in this sense can be seen as the linking points between the changing legal doctrines and the realities of AI governance.

Figure 1. AI in Corporate Decision-Making Ecosystem

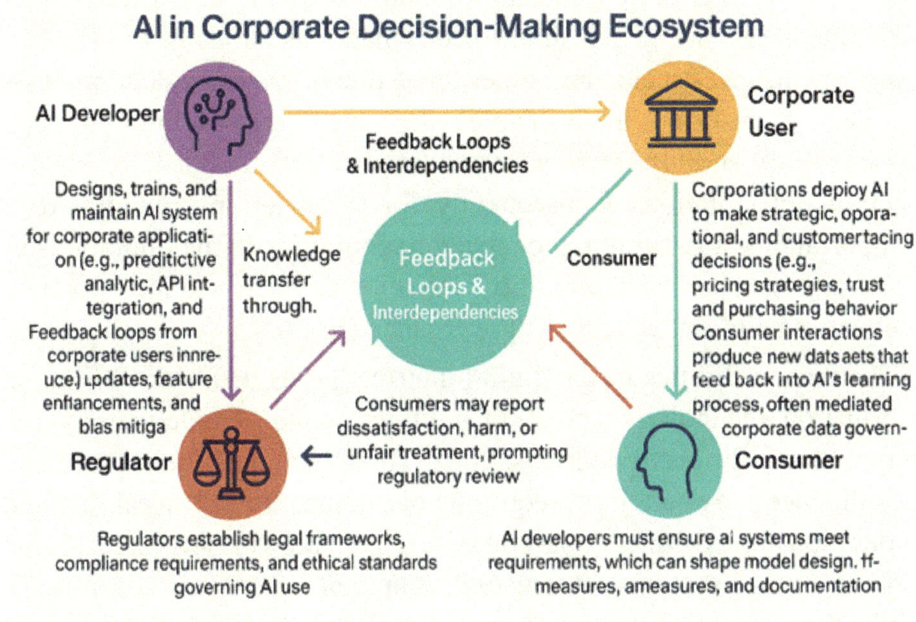

Influence direction is charted between AI developers, corporate users, consumers, and regulators. It points to the way in which AI systems inform decision-making, create feedback loops, and enact regulatory scrutiny. This ecosystem is dynamic and whatever is done by one stakeholder will have its effects on the other-this is why ethical transparent and accountable AI governance is needed.

3. INDIAN LEGAL AND REGULATORY LANDSCAPE

3.1 Key Statutes and Regulatory Frameworks

The regulation of artificial intelligence (AI) in India particularly in the form of corporate governance is around a pre-existing legal structure that include data protection, information technology and corporate law. The Digital Personal Data Protection Act, 2023 (DPDPA) has been a paradigm shift in the data governance regime in India. While the statute does not deal directly with the topic of AI, it has a specular impact on the governance elements by imposing obligations upon "data fiduciaries." Such fiduciaries are responsible for the made decisions in the field of employment, investments and other areas due to personal data processing. The Act enshrines the principles of consent, purpose limitation and accountability and also empower an administrative authority to impose sanctions for violations. Consequently, for organizations to adopt AI, it is important for algorithmic processing to comply with the limitations of processing data and accountability which forces boards to incorporate a fiduciary type of duties with AI governance (K, 2025).

The responsibilities of the digital intermediaries had been defined in Information Technology Act, 2000 and Intermediary Guidelines and the Digital Media Ethics Code Rules, 2021. These include duties of care and due diligence and operational requirements, for example: Traceability and moderation, have a direct impact on AI-driven platforms (e.g. algorithmic trade execution systems, automated compliance, content moderation). Whilst the majority of these rules apply to digital platforms there are spill over effects for business AI systems which process massive amounts of user generated and third party data.

The Companies Act, 2013 also have some significant corporate governance anchors which makes it relevant to AI. Provisions requiring due care, skill and diligence of the directors, disclosure requirements under Section 134 means that boards will have to treat with these risks related to AI such as algorithmic bias, model robustness and cybersecurity vulnerabilities are material governance issues. Risk management and also audit committees have also been asked to integrate reporting of AI risks in their once-a-year reporting and audit processes than ever before (K, 2025). Not to miss out on case, a fintech company being fined by the SEBI in 2024 for not disclosing the information properly about the algorithmic trading shows the extent to which boards are being held responsible for AI-related risks in the real corporate world.

3.2 Emerging Soft Law, Sectoral Guidance, and Regulatory Signals

AI governance in India is slowly coming in terms of soft law, policy directives and regulatory measures on a sector-by-sector basis. NITI Aayog's Responsible AI strategy and discussion papers has laid down normative expectations on certain principles like transparency, accountability, safety and inclusiveness. Although these documents are not binding but the result is that the firms fall into the line with the ethical standards globally (Ratnawat, 2025).

Sectoral regulators have also begun to come out with A.I related guides. For example, some of the expectations set by the financial regulators in the area of algorithmic trading are auditability and pre-trade validations. The regulatory sandbox pilots of the Reserve Bank of India has taken a few forays with financial products based on AI/ML and generated insights on the risks and benefits of their operation. Similarly the securities exchange board of india (SEBI) has issued consultation papers and advisories with respect to algorithmic trading and model risk including pre-deployment checks audit trails and market conduct. In the medical field, there has been some recommendations by the professional bodies on AI validation and ethics in medical devices and clinical practice with an emphasis on accuracy, patient consent and safety (John, Smiju, Thampi, & Joseph, 2024). Collectively these instruments are, however, a piecemeal practical benchmarks and there is the possibility of cross sectoral learning.

3.3 Key Regulatory and Enforcement Challenges

Despite these developments though, the Indian AI regulatory environment is fragmented and under developed. The current framework is founded to a large extent upon adapting laws which have been existing for some time now (e.g., the IT Act, the Companies Act, and the DPDPA) to solve the novel harms posed by AI. This piecemeal, sectoral approach means that there are some gaps in the coverage as well as inconsistencies when it comes to enforcement. In addition, there is no coherent and risk based law in India on systemic risks emanating from AI. Key concepts such as "autonomous decision-making systems" are also yet to be defined which is a problem in generating uncertainty for both regulated entities as well as adjudicatory bodies (Nadella, Meduri, Maturi, & Whig, 2024).

One of the most important is a problem of enforcement capacity. Regulatory bodies and adjudicative bodies tend not to have what is needed to assess complicated models and the origin of the data used to train them, or any robustness whatsoever: technical expertise, AI auditing tools and skilled people. For example, while the SEBI have taken action in misuse of algorithms and RBI have gone ahead with their experiments on sandbox, it is still tough for the regulators to scale technical oversight in different sectors. The lack of standardised auditing frameworks in conjunction with certified AI experts is a factor in lack of compliance monitoring. These gaps provide a regulatory environment within which it can be said that sophisticated AI systems can operate with little oversight, particularly in cases of high stakes (for example, algorithmic credit scoring, automated manipulation of markets).

Collectively, non-existence of statutory gaps, incompleteness and patchy soft law and poor institutional capacity implies the need of a holistic and risk-based regulatory framework. International models, like the EU Act on Artificial Intelligence is a model that India could customise to Indian requirements, but with provisions for flexibility for sectoral regulators (Sklavos, Theodossiou, Papanikolaou, Karelakis, & Ragazou, 2024).

3.4 Practical Toolkit for Corporate Governance: a Compliance Checklist for Indian Boards

In order to translate the requirements for legal and policy compliance to effective governance which can be managed, Indian boards should adopt compliance toolkit which is auditable and operable and is context specific. The table below is a summary of some of the important elements in an organised table of checklists at board-level:

Table 2. Compliance Toolkit of Artificial Intelligence Government of Boards, India

Governance Area	Board-Level Actions
Inventory & Risk Typing	Maintain an inventory of AI systems; classify as low/medium/high risk based on potential legal, financial, or reputational impact.
Pre-deployment Validation	Require model cards (architecture, training data, performance metrics); conduct fairness, accuracy, and security audits.
Data Governance & DPDP	Ensure lawful processing under DPDPA; adopt privacy-by-design and purpose limitation principles.
Human Oversight Protocols	Integrate human-in-the-loop mechanisms for high-risk AI decisions; establish escalation procedures.
Independent Audit & Review	Conduct periodic independent audits for high-risk systems; maintain audit trails for reproducibility.
Ethics & Board Reporting	Establish an AI Ethics Committee; mandate regular board reporting on AI risks, incidents, and remediation.
Incident Response	Implement AI incident response plans; provide grievance redressal mechanisms for affected stakeholders.
Training & Capacity Building	Train directors and senior management in AI fundamentals, regulatory obligations, and interpretation of technical evidence.
Regulatory Collaboration	Engage with SEBI, RBI, and other regulators through consultations and sandbox participation.
Openness & Communication	Disclose AI use in corporate reports; explain automated decision-making processes to stakeholders.

While the regulatory framework in India is still fragmented, this compliance toolkit helps the boards to lose the hard work of operationalizing the fiduciary duties of proactively managing the risk around AI. Moreover, amalgamation of the sandbox learnings (RBI) and regulatory actions (SEBI fintech penalties, 2024) as precedents in real life which board can use to benefit from the difference between law and practices (Ratnawat, 2025; John, Smiju, Thampi, & Joseph, 2024; Nadella, Meduri, Maturi, & Whig, 2024; Sklavos, Theodossiou, Papanikolaou, Karelakis, & Ragazou, 2024).

4. LEGAL FRAMEWORKS AT THE INTERNATIONAL LEVEL

4.1 European Union

The European Union (EU) has become a world leader in regulation of Artificial intelligence (AI) especially with the AI Act (2024) which takes a holistic, risk-based approach. This Act assigns risk levels to AI systems with the highest obligations to be placed on systems which are being deployed in critical infrastructure, law enforcement, education and employment. Providers of high-risk AI will be required to undergo conformity assessments in order to ensure adherence to standards for safety, transparency and accountability. Human oversight mechanisms are also required to facilitate the management of possible illegal/discriminatory outcomes (Rajagopal et al., 2022).

A special issue in the EU context is the interaction of the AI Act and the General Data Protection Regulation (GDPR). Given the fact that AI systems involve the use of a large amount of personal data, consideration of the GDPR principles (lawfulness, fairness, transparency, purpose limitation and data minimization) must be adhered to. This is complicated by article 22 GDPR that gives individuals the right not to be subject to solely automated decisions with significant legal consequences high-risk AI applications (Shandilya, Datta, Kartik, & Nagar, 2024). This dual compliance structure is in line with the EU's approach to the harmonisation of innovation with fundamental rights which is based on a rights approach, as enshrined in the Charter of Fundamental Rights of the European Union.

4.2 United States

Unlike the EU, the United States (US) has a fragmented and sectoral regulatory approach (vs. one and overall AI statute). Federal agencies govern AI according to their mandates with the Federal Trade Commission (FTC) addressing the risks of deception, bias and unfair practices with the principles of explainability, truthful marketing and good data governance (Samuel, K, Rajesh, M, & A, 2023).

Draft legislation like the Algorithmic Accountability Act aim at placing some requirements for impact assessment on AI driven systems especially on the topics of discrimination, bias, and data quality (Eroğlu & Kaya, 2022). However, a lack of coherent and unified law is complicated by state-level initiatives - California, Colorado and New York have each implemented sector-specific advances in AI laws in employment and consumer law arena (Walter, 2024; Almaqtari et al., 2020). The result is a patchwork system which makes compliance difficult for the firms operating in more than one jurisdiction.

4.3 Principles of The Organization of Economic Cooperation and Council of Europe

At the multilateral level, the principles of Organization for Economic Cooperation and Development (OECD) on Artificial Intelligence (2019) emphasize trustworthy, human rights-based and innovation-friendly Artificial Intelligence with the key aspects of transparency, accountability and proportionality in governance (Choi, Han, & Lee, 2024). Similarly, the Council of Europe, following its human rights mandate, promotes the principle of proportionality in public sector AI, in particular in order to prevent the risks of mass surveillance, discrimination and privacy violations. Current endeavor is being made to include these standards in legally binding instrument which are tied to the European convention on human rights (ECHR). Collectively, these frameworks form benchmarks and soft law recommendations for national regimes even if the enforceability of the recommendations differs (Burström et al., 2021).

4.4 Canada

One of the first broad national level frameworks outside of the EU is Canada's Artificial Intelligence and Data Act (AIDA) (proposed under Bill C-27 (2022)). AIDA includes introducing obligations for “high-impact” AI systems such as risk assessments, accountability and harm minimization mechanisms. Although not in full force AIDA states that Canada's intent is to create the right balance between innovation and consumer protection and fundamental rights. Its risk oriented structure is of course in line with EU principles, but is still in an emerging phase of development in comparison to the binding structure of the EU.

4.5 Singapore

Singapore has done well in the Asia-Pacific region with its Model AI Governance Framework (2019) with practical toolkits. Rather than prescriptive regulation Singapore focuses on industry-led and voluntary compliance with an emphasis on being transparent, explicable and accountable and human overseen. One notable innovation is the fact that the government has issued compliance toolkits for firms as well which are in line with international best standards. Importantly, enforcement mechanisms have also developed through the sectoral regulators - Infocomm Media Development Authority (IMDA) promoting adoption of auditing AI governance practices.

4.6 Japan

Japan has a jurisprudence-based and hybrid model which brings in AI governance in the framework of its overall Societe 5.0 initiative focussing on human-centric innovation. Regulatory efforts are based on AI R&D Guidelines and existing institutional frameworks of law in data protection and consumer law rather than an AI-specific statute. Japanese courts and regulators have started to develop an AI jurisprudence through case law and administrative practice, which deals with and fills in gaps discovered in normative laws and constitute a Lex Japan, which is said to be a crossroad between Western versions based on rights and Asia-Pacific versions based on industry.

4.7 India

India has this patchwork and underdeveloped artificial intelligence governance. While tremendous progress has been achieved with the Digital Personal Data Protection Act, 2023 and by regulatory sandbox efforts of Reserve Bank of India (RBI) and Securities and Exchange Board of India (SEBI) there is no comprehensive AI Act yet. Current measures are still fragmented between data protection, consumer protection and sector specific regulations. Courts and regulators have been concerned with issues of data accountability and algorithmic fairness, but institutional mechanisms for controlling AI are weak. India's framework is also in an early stage and needs to be better enforced and harmonised with global best practices.

4.8 Global South Perspectives

AI governance debates are not just for Europe, North America or Asia. In the Global South, the practices taken up with the help of AI have demonstrated problematic regulatory gaps particularly in the area of fintech. For example, predatory practices, algorithmic transparency and abuse of personal data of African lending apps suggest the risks of inadequate oversight. These examples indicate how risks of discrimination, exploitation and consumer harm can be enhanced by weak enforcement capacity in developing economies and the need for globally inclusive standards of governance.

4.9 Comparative Outlook

Three major models of regulating AI can be seen in the international path of regulation of AI at:

1. Rights-based and binding frameworks - e.g. European union, Canada (AIDA, emerging) and Council of Europe instruments.
2. Fragmented and sectoral approaches - e.g. United States, Japan and India.
3. Operational, industry-led governance models - e.g. Singapore, the soft law in form of the Organization for Economic Cooperation and Development.

A comparative synthesis finds the EU has a leading regime of binding rights-based, the US is patchy sector-based regime, India is in process of building a patchwork of sector based initiatives, Canada has a nascent rights-based model, Singapore has practical industry-based tool kits, Japan is jurisprudence and human-centred principles and Global South reveal gaps in governance are urgent for attention.

Table 3. Comparative Table of International AI Regulatory Approaches

Jurisdiction	Key Law/ Instrument	Scope	Enforcement	Relevance to Corporates
EU	AI Act (2024)	Binding, risk-based	Yes	High
India	DPDP Act, IT Act	Partially binding	Limited	Medium
US	Sector-specific	Fragmented	Medium	Variable
OECD	Soft law	Non-binding	No	Advisory

5. CORPORATE LIABILITY AND RESPONSIBILITIES IN THE EXECUTION OF AI

5.1 Fiduciary Duties and AI

Fiduciary duties of directors are related to the utilization of care, skill and diligence. The introduction of AI adds to the complexity as a result of the 'black box' nature of the machine learning and deep learning applications. Such opacity may hamper good decision-making as the directors may trust the outputs of algorithms that cannot be fully explained even to the technically capable stakeholders. This is a challenge that hampers on achievement of duty of care (Anthuvan & Maheshwari, 2025). Directors who are not technologically enough may however still have to assess AI generated recommendations as well as to consider hidden dangers embedded within the technology.

Comparative jurisdictions put emphasis on the obligation of the directors to educate themselves about the material risks. For example the U.S. Caremark doctrine, and the U.K. Companies Act 2006 section 174 both put an emphasis on diligence with respect to supervision. Similarly

Indian Companies Act 2013 has also directed the directors to exercise reasonable care and diligence. In reality, unless directors are proactive in upskilling or getting independent audits of AI, directors are exposing themselves to breaching their duties (Petrin, 2024). This risk is often high when the incidences that are associated with AI result in either financial or reputational damage (Hossain, Hasan, & Hasan, 2024).

To help overcome this challenge, boards should make enforcement-based governance tools, including:

1. A believable set of clauses in an AI Oversight Policy on transparency, accountability and mechanisms for escalation; and
2. An AI Impact Assessment Template to support directors in approaching risk and benefit in a systematic manner in deployment; and
3. A.I. Audit Checklist which will ensure regular and independent A.I. behaviour, data quality and compliance with regulation audit.

These measures not only operationalize fiduciary duties but they also result in an evidentiary record of diligence that is subject to scrutiny by regulators, courts and investors. Importantly, investor and shareholder activism is also an increasing source of change - as exemplified in the US and Indian cases where activist shareholders have call for the disclosure of AI related risks in board reports, and sustainability filings. Such developments suggest that it is not only up to the authorities to regulate the exercise of fiduciary duties in the governance of AI, but the mechanisms of accountability in the markets are equally enforceable too.

5.2 Allocation of Liability

Assigning liability for the harm done by AI is a contentious issue especially insofar as misuse by third parties. Corporate legislation are complicated with the distributed nature of AI systems where responsibility may be shared between developers, data providers and end-users, and each with different levels of control (Jain, Balakrishnan, Beeram, Najana, & Chintale, 2024). Without any specific safeguards in a contract (indemnities, warranties, etc), corporations are susceptible to direct and indirect liability, either to the consumer or stakeholder or regulatory agency or by class action for algorithmic misbehavior.

Internationally, there are attempts like the draft AI Liability Directive of EU, to harmonize the evidentiary standards, and create some clarity in the divide of fault. India by contrast has a patchwork of laws either industry specific or a general contract law resulting in uncertainty and holes in governance. Best practices dictate that purchase contracts and licensing agreements made by boards provide for liability limits, means of dispute resolution and risk sharing clauses (Meduri, Podicheti, Satish, & Whig, 2024).

A governance-based response for Indian firms would be to adopt AI liability mapping at the board-level which would give clear responsibility to each of the stakeholders and review periodically. Such mapping beyond the fostering elimination of the diffuse liabilities, corporate is put in a publicity position in anticipation of the future codified standards. Furthermore, there are experiences from the Global South which testify to the urgency of such measures: controversies around the application of AI-based lending solutions in Africa, which illustrate gaps in accountability and consumer protection, and controversies around fintech governance in Latin America and South East Asia, which illustrate how the allocation of liability is often not well developed in emerging economies. Inclusion of these examples are a good way to create-up a more balanced comparative perspective outside of the EU/US contexts.

5.3 ESG and AI

AI implementation is beginning to cross over with Environmental, Social and Governance (ESG) imperatives. Governance aspects include a focus on transparency, accountability, fairness and reducing bias, and is more than compliance with current data protection and anti-discrimination laws. Corporations are now being held accountable to these global frameworks such as the following: the OECD AI Principles and the UNESCO AI Ethics Recommendations. Alongside ethical and security issues, the environment

- and the carbon-intensive process of training large-scale AI models, in particular - is having an impact on ESG ratings (Okuno, & Okuno, 2025).

Boards should therefore make their disclosures around AI governance a form of ESG reporting. In India, Business Responsibility and Sustainability Reporting (BRSR) framework of Security and Exchange Board of India is a mechanism of embedding AI specific governance. For example, BRSR disclosures could be:

1. Specifications on the AI governance charters compatible with the principles of the 'OE' (Organization of Economic Cooperation and Development) on Artificial Intelligence;
2. Reporting on training AI models carbon footprint, as well as mitigation measures;
3. Documentation of the bias testing and corrective actions before being deployed; and
4. Stand alone results of audit of artificial intelligence are published.

Such disclosures serve two purposes: to comply with the regulatory requirements, and to demonstrate corporate leadership in responsible AI governance. Globally, investors are spelling up the pressure on the companies to be considering AI-related risks in ESG strategies. In the U.S as well as India, shareholder proposals have begun to push boards to ensure that algorithmic bias gets addressed and explainability is incorporated as part of the ESG disclosure. Alignment of the corporate reporting in India with international standards like the EU Corporate Sustainability Reporting Directive (CSRD) will help in the continuity of the investor confidence and ensure that the AI deployments are under sustainable corporate frameworks.

Figure 2. Legal Risk Spectrum of AI in Corporate Governance

The hypothetical graphical display of how the degree of legal liability scales with a spectrum of an increasing risk of automation (e.g. optimisation of routinised processes with few regulatory interconnections on one extreme and the application of autonomous decision-making with a high-cost regulatory and reputational liability on the other). Fiduciary vigilance, contractual protection, and ESG compliance come in a sequence of interventions by the figure as more important governance interventions on this scale of activity.

6. CASE LAWS AND REAL-LIFE EXAMPLES

6.1 Indian Context

Case Study: Artificial Intelligence Lending stranglehold: NBFC Lending & Discrimination in Credit Denial

In India, the utilization of AI based credit scoring models by Non-Banking Financial Companies (NBFCs) has been quite unbelievable and this has allowed them to process their credits much faster, enhance their operational efficiency and penetrate underserved markets. However, these opaque systems of algorithms have raised some concerns about the discriminatory practices, particularly vis-a-vis applicants from certain socio-economic, linguistic or regional backgrounds. A notable one being that of an NBFC who had relied on a credit model which was trained using historical lending data using artificial intelligence (AI) and perpetrated and magnified existing human biases. As a result, applicants that were similar in terms of their creditworthiness but were in demographically similar groups were disproportionately rejected more (Singhania & Saini, 2021).

From a legal point of view, such practices are inviting scrutiny in the light of Digital Personal Data Protection Act, 2023 (DPDP Act) which give a focus on statistical compliance of the principles of lawfulness, transparency and purpose limitation with respect to processing of personal data (Sections 4-6). The use of sensitive personal data such as caste, religion or biometric data without the express consent of the user can be a violation of the Act. Further, the lack of human oversight in any meaningful way through the algorithmic process of making credit decisions kills accountability and fairness (Chowdhury, Budhwar, & Wood, 2024).

There is also other complementary legislation in place. The Information Technology (IT) Rules, 2011 provide for accuracy and security of personal information, and Rule 5(6) provide for a right to access and correct of individuals to their data, which become practically ineffective in "black box" AI systems. Failure to exercise due diligence can render the directors liable for Section 43A of Information Technology Act, 2000. Similarly, according to the Companies Act, 2013, it is compulsory for the directors to sensibly manage the risks (Dhongde, Kumar, Patra, & Mishra, 2025).

The Securities Exchange Board of India (SEBI) also has initiated consultations for fintech regulation which aims at, inter alia, algorithm audit trails, explainability logs and transparent disclosures for firms that use AI in processes that are faced by consumers (Hasan, Aly, & Hussainey, 2022). Importantly, however, Indian shareholder activism is starting to cross over with AI governance. Shareholders have raised issues relating to issues around transparency in algorithmic credit processes in responses to the SEBI consultations and litigation with some activist investors calling for boards to set up independent AI oversight committees. Such developments indicate a departure from passive acceptance of complacency and towards ethical active supervision of the AI risks in consumer finance.

Supplementary Case: Artificial Intelligence In Healthcare Diagnostics

Similar challenges are there in the Indian Healthcare industry where AI tools are being implemented in more numbers in the field of radiology, oncology, and pathology. While the applications of these have shown promise for early and efficient detection of medical conditions, diagnostic errors have been found because of use of non-representative datasets - for example, under-representation of rural and female patients. Such errors can constitute medical negligence under the Consumer Protection Act, 2019 apart from the possible compliance issues under the ambit of India's Digital Health Mission. Importantly, errors of healthcare AI have a direct link with the constitutional guarantee of protection of the Right to Life as per Article 21. This is all to highlight the need of the hour to integrate the principles of auditability, fairness and explainability in AI enabled healthcare systems.

6.2 International Case Law

Case Study: European Court of Justice (ECJ): SCHUFA Algorithmical Scoring

The case of SCHUFA before the European Court of Justice (ECJ) was about algorithmic profiling in the field of the area of credit scoring in the context of the General Data Protection Regulation (GDPR). The Court ruled out the possibility that fully automated decision-making can be within the scope of Article 22 of the GDPR and restricts the decision solely based on processing that is automated (Giannini & Kwik, 2023). The ruling reinforced the concept of meaningful transparency, by forcing companies to explain how algorithmic models work and it also allowed people to objectify negative results. This precedent shows the incompatibility of the principles of opaque AI systems with rights-based approaches to regulation, and is a useful precedent for jurisdictions like India where the protection of discriminatory outcomes goes beyond data protection regimes.

Case Study: Amazon's Abandoned AI Recruitment Tool

In the United States, Amazon's artificial intelligence (AI) based recruitment system was removed when it was discovered to be discriminating against women. The tool, which was trained on historically male-dominated hiring data, penalized resumes which mention women's college or having a female affiliation (D, E, & E, 2021). While no lawsuit was taken, what the system did do was violate Title VII of the Civil Rights Act of 1964, which prohibits discrimination because of gender. Amazon took off the cord off the tool, after it was criticised by the public and its reputation was damaged and a realisation of the power shareholder pressure and corporate reputation has to compliance despite a lack of direct regulatory action (Horneber & Laumer, 2023; Roundy, 2022).

Asian By Example: Japan's Activities Regarding AI Governance

In Japan, the government is very forward looking in terms of AI governance. Enforcement measures to enhance fairness and transparency of AI driven financial services have been introduced as well as the 2022 AI Strategy and Governance Guidelines by the Japanese Personal Information Protection Commission (PPC). For example, the PPC issued compliance directions on a major Japanese credit scoring company who had failed to disclose the grounds for the automated decisions including a need to integrate explanations of the decisions and improve consumer redress mechanisms. This is one case which brings into focus Asia's still developing jurisprudence around the balancing of innovation and responsibility in complement to comparative lessons from the EU and US.

FinTech Example: Experiences of Singapore and South

Singapore's Monetary Authority of Singapore (MAS) has set the standard in fintech regulation by way of its Sandbox Express regime and require AI models in credit scoring to be explainable, quantifiable and non-discriminatory. Providers are also under an obligation to show that they mitigate risks, governance audits are conducted and transparency disclosures are made. This proactive regulatory approach is quite opposite to India which is more reactive in approach.

In the Global South, countries like Kenya, Nigeria and South Africa have witnessed the exponential growth of apps to micro-lend on a basis of artificial intelligence with or without any robust regulatory frameworks in place. These apps have been criticised for privacy violations, exploitative collection practices and debt shaming compromising consumer protection in the name of achieving the objectives of financial inclusion. The Nigerian National Information Technology Development Agency (NITDA), for example, has received several complaints of abusive lending practices and this has led to more calls for proper oversight. These experiences illustrate the two-edged sword that AI can play in the financial inclusion space: While AI can provide access to populations that need it, there is no governance in place to stop consumers from being exposed to new forms of harm.

6.3 Lessons for Comparison: Enforcement

The cases reviewed highlight three important compliance and enforcement lessons, these will be synthesized in Table 2 (Comparative Case Law Analysis) of this chapter:

1. Explainability and Transparency as non-Negotiables The SCHUFA decision of the ECJ and the requirements of MAS's sandboxes demonstrate that "black-box" AI models are not compatible with legality and fairness.
2. Director and Board Liability Beyond Compliance with Statute Case for Indian NBFC and Healthcare shows that liability is not limited to compliance with laws on data protection and information technology laws and is defined under more general concepts of business and medical negligence as well (Chowdhury, Budhwar, & Wood, 2024; Dhongde, Kumar, Patra, & Mishra, 2025). Shareholder litigation and activism in India also helps to strengthen the board level accountability.
3. Reputation and Market Pressures as De Facto Regulators The Amazon case has shown that compliance can happen much faster due to corpo-

rate reputation, shareholder activism and consumer trust than formal regulation Horneber & Laumer (2023).

Thus, in different jurisdictions, AI governance enforcement is not limited to data protection compliance. This also depends on the procedural fairness, corporate governance culture, shareholder oversight and societal accountability mechanisms.

Table 4. Legal Outcomes and Responses in Key Cases

Case	Jurisdiction	AI Use	Legal Issue	Outcome	Corporate Liability
Amazon AI Hiring	US	Recruitment	Bias	Tool withdrawn	Non-binding
SCHUFA Scoring	EU	Creditworthiness	Lack of explainability	Under ECJ review	Medium
Indian NBFC case	India	Lending	Data misuse/ discrimination	Regulatory warning	Low

7. ANALYSIS: GAPS AND NEW TRENDS

7.1 Limitations of the Existing Criminal Law Instruments

The prevailing corporate law regime breaks down in the context of the growing artificial intelligence (AI) that is being inculcated in major industries like fintech and healthcare in India. As per SEBI (2023), in 2023, 23 per cent of bigger Indian fintech companies and 23 per cent of healthcare listed companies have made their decision making with the help of AI. This fast speed of uptake results in a great deal of legal uncertainty because the current corporate statutes (e.g. the Companies Act, 2013 (India), the Companies Act, 2006 (UK), and the Delaware General Corporation Law) is based on decision-making processes that are linearly traceable to identifiable human actors. Such assumptions are gravely compromised by deep learning models, sometimes referred to as "black boxes" because it is hard to know what the causal chain of decisions is. This opacity is a challenge to the application of such basic legal doctrines as the mens rea in corporate criminal liability, the duty of care due by directors and scope of vicarious liability (Sklavos, Theodossiou, Papanikolaou, Karelakis, & Ragazou, 2024).

7.2 Risk for Diffusion of Accountability

The advent of AI in the corporate governance has also resulted in diffused accountability. Developers, vendors and management, compliance officers and end-users have a collective role in the outcome; which results in the allocation of liability becoming a blur. This problem is affected by the practice of outsourcing and off-the-shelf AI tools. SEBI's Annual AI Report (2024) mentions the instances of the Indian listed companies that failed to name and shame the guilty parties after losing due to AI in the market. The EU's proposed AI Liability Directive is one attempt to solve this issue, by apportioning liability to participants, but the Canadian Organisation for Economic Cooperation and Development (OECD) AI Principles are not binding and fail to provide any enforceable standards. Indian regulatory mechanisms are quite feeble and put the firms under severe governance risks (Vettriselvan et al., 2025).

A further challenge is the lack of focus on the Environmental, Social and Governance (ESG) frameworks in terms of regulation of AI. At the moment, Indian companies are not bound by any law, which has them disclose AI-related risks in their ESG reports. As of 2024, only 16 per cent of the companies on the NIFTY 50 index have mentioned AI related risks like algorithmic bias in their ESG disclosure. Strengthening of the integration of AI ethics in ESG reporting could help to increase stakeholders trust and support responsible innovation.

Investor Activism and Litigation Trends: An increased attention from shareholders is making boards to be more powerful in their AI management. Cases of shareholder litigation against healthcare corporations both in India and the United States for poor AI disclosures, is on the increase. This trend suggests the way there is a move towards more board-level oversight of for example the establishment of formal committees that are tasked with auditing algorithms and governance (Roundy, 2022).

Global South Comparative Example: Algorithmic impact assessments and explainability requirements have been introduced as a part of its model of AI governance by Singapore in its fintech sector especially in the regulation of digital payments. On the other hand, there has been judicial resistance against algorithmic lending activities leading to discriminatory outcomes in Nigeria and this is highlighting the need for clarity on the statute and pre-emptive governance.

7.3 Significance of Pro-Active Governance

Current enforcement mechanisms which rely heavily on reactive litigation are not well-suited to deal with the rapidly-evolving risks of AI. Post-harm remedies are simply not always addressing systemic risks as a result of data-driven decision making (Sharma & Haralayya, 2025). There is hence a need for an approach with a future goal. Recommended measures include mandatory auditing of AI, explainability and algorithmic bias checks before putting a system to work. Singapore's Model AI Governance Framework and Canada's Algorithmic Impact Assessment tool are good examples of this on an international level.

In India, proactive governance, relating to AI risk management obligation, could be improved by relating it to Section 166 of the Companies Act, 2013 which requires the directors to act in the best interests of the company in good faith and in the best interests of the company. Boards may be made to undertake forward looking artificial intelligence risk assessments and public disclosures of artificial intelligence related risks exposures. Not only would this ensure better compliance but make sure the value of the shareholders and enhance the credibility of the governance (Jain, Balakrishnan, Beeram, Najana, & Chintale, 2024).

7.4 Lessons Learned on Enforcement and Institutions Capacity

A comparative analysis does provide some important lessons of enforcement. In the EU, there are the AI Act and the AI Liability Directive that are supposed to provide a clear channel of liability and duty of preventive compliance. The US has been more sector specific in their enforcement with agencies like FTC, and have often taken aim at the focus on consumer protection and algorithmic bias. Singapore has been a pioneer in the algorithmic impact assessments with the involvement of the regulators while India is at an early stage with primary reliance on the general corporate and data protection statutes.

One of the most important challenges in India is institutional capacity. Courts and Regulatory authorities like SEBI and RBI are not equipped with expert knowledge of auditing AI, explainability of algorithms and checking the compliance of technical on day to day basis. Without capacity building - through technical training programs and dedicated units for AI oversight and partnerships with academic or technical institutions - enforcement of AI-related governance standards will remain weak. Stronger institutional expertise is therefore equally important as law reforming to guarantee effective AI in the corporate context.

Table 5. Enforcement Outcomes and Compliance Lessons

Jurisdiction	Recent Enforcement Outcome	Compliance Lesson
India	SEBI fined fintech for non-disclosure of algorithmic bias (2024)	Mandatory AI audits required
Singapore	Successful implementation of algorithmic risk management (2023)	Pre-deployment impact assessment crucial
USA (Delaware)	Litigation driven board reforms in AI oversight (2024)	Investor activism accelerates governance
Nigeria	Court-mandated compensation for AI lending bias (2023)	Statutory clarity is essential

8. PROPOSED FRAMEWORK OF HYBRID GOVERNANCE

The regulation of Artificial Intelligence (AI) in business environment require the development of hybrid regulatory system: outside-in and inside-out regulation. Such an integrated approach is one which brings together statutory requirements, internal corporate governance processes, the disclosure and accountability regimes, regulatory sandboxes and collaborative alliances between government, industry and civil society. This framework recognises the disruptive nature of AI, as well as potential risks of AI, but assures that governance is geared towards transparency, fairness, privacy protection and minimising harm. By using the practices from both the Indian and international experiences, it has been attempted in this framework to provide a balanced model to protect the interests of the society at large while facilitating innovation (Anthuvan & Maheshwari, 2025).

8.1 Legislative Reforms

For AI governance to be a success, legislations are a must. Fiduciary duties of the directors and key managerial personnel should be expanded under Companies Act, 2013 to specifically include the responsibilities relating to the deployment of AI, monitoring and oversight. Such reforms would ensure that the directors would be legally required to verify that AIs systems are trained on non-discriminatory data, are still explainable and adhered to legal and ethical norms whenever their output significantly affect shareholders, employees, consumers or the public (Chen & Gao, 2022). Similarly, the Digital Personal Data Protection Act, 2023 (DPDP Act) will have to be modified to include liabilities for harm arising out of automated decision making such as service denial, privacy invasion or discriminatory outcomes. Current ambiguities in the distribution of liability between developers, vendors and corporate users, risks creation of doctrinal loopholes (Nadella, Meduri, Maturi, & Whig, 2024). In contrast, European Union AI Act provides a model of how clear and precise statutory language on accountability in high-risk AI systems eliminates the ambiguity of interpretation as well as introduces greater enforceability, and will be a legislative model for India to adapt (Salako et al., 2024).

8.2 Board-Level Interventions

In order to make legislative requirements workable, there must be embedded in corporate structures, board level mechanisms. The establishment of compulsory AI Ethics Committees is a very important step. These committees, it is suggested, should be cross-functional, comprising compliance officers, technologists, legal experts, independent directors and sectoral specialists and be given the responsibility to audit the procurement and implementation of AI, to ensure compliance with regulatory and ethical requirements and to oversee the periodic auditing of AI, which they should report directly to the board (Rajagopal et al., 2022). Regulatory authorities can exercise their enforcement power by asking companies to report an annual AI compliance report to ensure the compliance of companies with the mechanisms of AI governance. A practical compliance checklist which boards should adopt are regular internal and third-party artificial intelligence (AI) audits, formal adoption of an artificial intelligence (AI) ethics policy, testing of algorithmic bias and fairness, use of standardised disclosure templates for shareholders and regulators, documentation of explainability protocols for critical artificial intelligence (AI) decisions and implementation of artificial intelligence (AI) ethics training modules for employees. The international experiences offer valuable lessons that can be compared: Canada's Algorithmic Impact Assessments (AIAs)- which require ex-ante evaluation of AI systems, and Singapore's Model AI Governance Framework which offers sector neutral and practical guidance on explainability, fairness and accountability (Hasan, Aly, and Hussainey, 2022). These best practices is reflective of concrete mechanisms for taking into account oversight in corporate governance.

8.3 Requirements for disclosure and reporting

Transparency and disclosure is the necessary part of AI governance. Corporate annual reports and CSR disclosure should be accompanied with a special section devoted to AI governance where it is defined what kind of AI systems are used, what risk assessments are carried out, what strategies are implemented for risk mitigation and what are the disclosures regarding malfunctions or breaches of ethical principles (Batra, Sannegadu, & Mehta, 2022). Taking the cues of the integrated reporting models of the UK and EU, the corporate reports of India should fit in the AI governance under the Environmental, Social and Governance (ESG) models, thereby bringing the AI ethics into the sustainability goals as well. To increase the comparability of the different companies, regulators should require standardised disclosure templates that will promote consistency, transparency and market discipline.

8.4 Regulatory Sandboxes

The adoption of regulatory sandboxes is one approach to establishing a safe mechanism to test AI innovations without a large risk. Building on the Reserve Bank of India's model of sandboxes, it would be possible to create sector-specific sandboxes in high risk sectors such as healthcare, insurance, transport and critical infrastructure (Giannini & Kwik, 2023). Participation should be conditional on demonstrating evidence of data-protection commitments, oversight by ethics committees and submission of outcome reports to regulators. The eligibility criteria should consider innovation potential, industry relevance and sensitivity of risk. Lessons can also be learnt in the case of efforts in the sandbox approach in Singapore with emphasis on iterative evaluation and sector wide learnings as well as that in the Society 5.0 framework in Japan which embeds AI governance and sustainable development goals. These examples from Asia highlight the importance of sandboxes in striking the right balance between innovation and accountability and provide India with replicable models on responsible experimentation.

8.5 Public Private Partnerships

Finally, public-private partnership is a key part to creating an adaptive governance model. Effective co-regulation then requires the participation of government regulators, corporate organizations and academic institutions as well as civil society organisations. While the regulators might provide the standard by which standards for their industries are to be set, industry associations can create sector specific codes of governance apart from the statutory requirements (Chowdhury, Budhwar, & Wood, 2024). Active engagement with universities and research institutions to ensure that governance policies are based on evidence-based knowledge and technological advancements with civil society organisations being able to provide oversight, advocate for inclusion and equity and highlight emerging risks (Dhongde, Kumar, Patra, & Mishra, 2025). Importantly, India has a unique advantage of playing a leadership role in the Global South. With its sound digital infrastructure and regulatory innovation, India is in a position to set the parameters in the governance of innovation and equity and lead other countries in the Global South by example. Such leadership would not only boost India's regional influence, but it will also be a part of the efforts to create global norms for AI governance to be inclusive.

9. CONCLUSION AND SUGGESTION

The comparative analysis helps bring out the growing consensus of the acute need for clear and enforceable legal frameworks of accountability in the management of artificial intelligence (AI) in corporate governance. This regulatory responses Indian and international are an attempt to carefully balance the need to promote innovation but at the same time reduce the risk. Recent efforts such as the proposed AI Act in European Union and the US sectoral regulatory guidance are some of the examples of this trend. In India, however, despite the promising steps, which include, for example, the National Strategy on Artificial Intelligence (2018), corporate governance reforms, data protection and an amendment of the intellectual property legislation, the regulatory framework is fragmented. The lack of clear rules associated with corporate responsibility specific to AI implies lack of sectoral coherence (Lane, 2022).

The result of this research show that interdependent regimes of accountability (from corporate law to data protection, intellectual property and liability law) will have to meet in order to build corporate liabilities on the one hand and obligation in respect of algorithmic integrity, ethical compliance and harm prevention on the other. Without such alignment, technology agnostic strategies have risked allowing regulatory arbitrage, where companies take advantage of areas of gaps in oversight jurisdiction to avoid oversight.

In view of the fact, that the AI-driven decision making knows more and more no national boundaries, the importance of international regulation cannot be overestimated. Present frameworks under the theudication of the OED, G20 and UN under digital cooperation are very first building blocks however tend to be non-binding and get to develop into enforceable mechanism to guarantee consensus between nations on corporate accountability globally. Such convergent shouldn't be in Euro-American perspectives but also have Asia-Pacific integration wherein rates of adoption of AI are high and where capacities to govern is different. As a nation, India need legal reforms to be contextualised to the domestic corporate realities and the socio-economic requirements as well as the patterns of technology utilisation (Burström, Parida, Lahti, & Wincent, 2021). Some of the practical measures may include:

(i) making provision with respect to requirements of AI governance in Companies Act, 2013;
(ii) amending the SEBI (LODR) Regulations for making it mandatory to introduce the provisions of auditing and AI risk disclosures; and
(iii) introducing liability and consumer protection provisions specific to AI into civil and consumer law and Equally critical is capacity-building, ensuring that the institutions and courts have the technical expertise to adjudicate issues of accountability related to AI well.

Indian corporate governance boards should pro-actively take their responsibility to take forward looking mechanism to operationalise these reforms. These mechanisms include setting-up dedicated AI Ethics Committees, AI auditing policies, mandatory disclosure of risk in annual reports and the use of regulatory sandboxes to control the experimentation process. Such measures would not just result in better compliance, but a higher degree of confidence from stakeholders on AI enabled decision making.

The way forward is, therefore, two-fold: (i) increase international legal harmonisation so that there is no fragmented regulatory environment and (ii) come up with the specific regulatory architecture that suits Indian conditions and is compatible with transparency, ethical protections and accountability in corporate governance, especially related to AI. The implication for management is obvious: boards need to make AI governance an integral part of corporate strategy, be proactively transparent about risks and create internal mechanisms for oversight. Absent such a coherent strategy - spanning law and management - the risks and opportunities of AI in corporate governance will continue to be unevenly regulated, leaving the legal frameworks in a reactive, rather than anticipatory position.

Key Takeaways

For Policymakers

The inclusion of the provisions of sector-specific AI under Companies Act, SEBI (LODR) Regulations and consumer protection laws with an option of international harmonisation of laws.

For Boards

Establish artificial intelligence ethics committees, Artificial intelligence compliance to checklists, Artificial intelligence risks communication capability, artificial intelligence compliance in company strategy.

For Regulators

Invest in capacity-building and technical expertise to be able to effectively monitor, enforce and adjudicate AI-related accountability mechanisms; and This Chapter makes a contribution to the debates on global governance in proposing a hybrid model of accountability, which bridges legal doctrines and technical tools of auditing.

REFERENCES

Abhilash, A., Shenoy, S. S., & Shetty, D. K. (2023). Overview of Corporate governance research in India: A bibliometric analysis. *Cogent Business & Management, 10*(1), 2182361. Advance online publication. DOI: 10.1080/23311975.2023.2182361

Almaqtari, F. A., Hashid, A., Farhan, N. H. S., Tabash, M. I., & Al-ahdal, W. M. (2020). An empirical examination of the impact of country-level corporate governance on profitability of Indian banks. *International Journal of Finance & Economics, 27*(2), 1912–1932. DOI: 10.1002/ijfe.2250

Anthuvan, T., & Maheshwari, K. (2025). AI-C2C (conscious to conscience): A governance framework for ethical AI integration. *AI and Ethics, 5*(4), 4241–4253. Advance online publication. DOI: 10.1007/s43681-025-00736-2

Batra, B., Sannegadu, R., & Mehta, K. (2022). Gender diversity on the board and corporate social responsibility disclosure in the digitalisation era. In *Advances in human resources management and organizational development book series* (pp. 174–197). DOI: 10.4018/978-1-7998-8594-8.ch009

Burström, T., Parida, V., Lahti, T., & Wincent, J. (2021a). AI-enabled business-model innovation and transformation in industrial ecosystems: A framework, model and outline for further research. *Journal of Business Research, 127*, 85–95. DOI: 10.1016/j.jbusres.2021.01.016

Chen, Y., & Gao, Y. (2022). Comparative analysis of digital trade development strategies and governance approaches. *Journal of Digital Economy, 1*(3), 227–238. DOI: 10.1016/j.jdec.2023.02.001

Choi, Y., Han, S., & Lee, C. (2024). Exploring drivers of fintech adoption among elderly consumers. *Technology in Society, 78*, 102669. DOI: 10.1016/j.techsoc.2024.102669

Chowdhury, S., Budhwar, P., & Wood, G. (2024). Generative Artificial Intelligence in Business: Towards a Strategic Human Resource Management framework. *British Journal of Management, 35*(4), 1680–1691. DOI: 10.1111/1467-8551.12824

D, C., E, G., & E, J. (2021). *REGULATION OF ARTIFICIAL INTELLIGENCE IN BRICS AND THE EUROPEAN UNION.* КиберЛенинка. https://cyberleninka.ru/article/n/regulation-of-artificial-intelligence-in-brics-and-the-european-union

De Almeida, P. G. R., Santos, C. D. D., & Farias, J. S. (2021). Artificial Intelligence Regulation: A framework for governance. *Ethics and Information Technology, 23*(3), 505–525. DOI: 10.1007/s10676-021-09593-z

Dhongde, S., Kumar, S., Patra, S. K., & Mishra, S. K. (2025). Redefining Corporate Governance in Digital Era: Strategies for Mitigating Organizational risk. In *Approaches to global sustainability, markets, and governance* (pp. 427–447). DOI: 10.1007/978-981-96-6366-8_21

Efthymiou, I. (2025). Diversity, Inclusion, and Equity in Gig Economies. In Doon, R. (Ed.), *Sustainability and Adaptability of Gig Economies in Global Business* (pp. 231–260). IGI Global Scientific Publishing., DOI: 10.4018/979-8-3693-9385-7.ch009

Efthymiou, I., & Egleton, T. E. (2025). The Impact of Deep Fakes in Markets and Economies. In Gupta, G., Bohara, S., Kovid, R., & Pandla, K. (Eds.), *Deepfakes and Their Impact on Business* (pp. 19–50). IGI Global Scientific Publishing., DOI: 10.4018/979-8-3693-6890-9.ch002

Efthymiou, I. P. (2024). Exploring the frontier: New and future trends in research. In B. Orlando (Ed.), Innovation capabilities and entrepreneurial opportunities of smart working (pp. 48–68). IGI Global Scientific Publishing. DOI: 10.4018/978-1-7998-8797-3.ch003

Efthymiou, I. P. (2025). The role of e-government and e-governance in modern societies. In Wongmahesak, K., Ahmad, J., & Mustanir, A. (Eds.), *Public governance practices in the age of AI* (pp. 45–68). IGI Global Scientific Publishing., DOI: 10.4018/979-8-3693-9286-7.ch003

Eroğlu, M., & Kaya, M. K. (2022). Impact of artificial intelligence on corporate board diversity policies and Regulations. *European Business Organization Law Review, 23*(3), 541–572. DOI: 10.1007/s40804-022-00251-5

Giannini, A., & Kwik, J. (2023). Negligence failures and negligence fixes. A comparative analysis of criminal regulation of AI and autonomous vehicles. *Criminal Law Forum, 34*(1), 43–85. DOI: 10.1007/s10609-023-09451-1

Hasan, A., Aly, D., & Hussainey, K. (2022). Corporate governance and financial reporting quality: A comparative study. *Corporate Governance (Bradford), 22*(6), 1308–1326. DOI: 10.1108/CG-08-2021-0298

Horneber, D., & Laumer, S. (2023). Algorithmic accountability. *Business & Information Systems Engineering, 65*(6), 723–730. DOI: 10.1007/s12599-023-00817-8

Hossain, M. Z., Hasan, L., & Hasan, M. H. (2024). Corporate Governance as a global phenomenon: Evolution, theoretical foundations, and practical implications. *Journal of Financial Risk Management, 13*(02), 342–375. DOI: 10.4236/jfrm.2024.132017

Jain, V., Balakrishnan, A., Beeram, D., Najana, M., & Chintale, P. (2024). Leveraging artificial intelligence for enhancing regulatory compliance in the financial sector. *International Journal of Computer Trends and Technology, 72*(5), 124–140. DOI: 10.14445/22312803/IJCTT-V72I5P116

John, J., Smiju, I. S., Thampi, K., & Joseph, M. K. (2024). Environmental, Social, and Governance (ESG) sustainability through corporate social responsibility. In *Advances in logistics, operations, and management science book series* (pp. 31–52). DOI: 10.4018/979-8-3693-3880-3.ch002

K, N. K. (2025). Legal and financial approaches for ESG integration. In *IGI Global eBooks* (pp. 189–234). DOI: 10.4018/979-8-3373-0350-5.ch008

Lane, L. (2022). CLARIFYING HUMAN RIGHTS STANDARDS THROUGH ARTIFICIAL INTELLIGENCE INITIATIVES. *The International and Comparative Law Quarterly, 71*(4), 915–944. DOI: 10.1017/S0020589322000380

Meduri, K., Podicheti, S., Satish, S., & Whig, P. (2024). Accountability and transparency ensuring responsible AI development. In *Advances in human and social aspects of technology book series* (pp. 83–102). DOI: 10.4018/979-8-3693-4147-6.ch004

Nadella, G. S., Meduri, S. S., Maturi, M. H., & Whig, P. (2024). Societal impact and governance. In *Advances in human and social aspects of technology book series* (pp. 261–282). DOI: 10.4018/979-8-3693-4147-6.ch012

Okuno, M. J., & Okuno, H. G. (2025). Legal frameworks for AI service business participants: A comparative analysis of liability protection across jurisdictions. *AI & Society*, *40*(7), 5667–5683. Advance online publication. DOI: 10.1007/s00146-025-02288-9

Peng, Y., Ahmad, S. F., Ahmad, A. Y. B., Shaikh, M. S. A., Daoud, M. K., & Alhamdi, F. M. H. (2023). Riding the waves of artificial intelligence in advancing accounting and its implications for sustainable development goals. *Sustainability (Basel)*, *15*(19), 14165. DOI: 10.3390/su151914165

Petrin, M. (2024). The impact of AI and new technologies on corporate governance and regulation. Singapore Journal of Legal Studies, 90–106. DOI: 10.2139/ssrn.4891647

Radanliev, P. (2025). AI Ethics: Integrating transparency, fairness, and privacy in AI development. *Applied Artificial Intelligence*, *39*(1), 2463722. Advance online publication. DOI: 10.1080/08839514.2025.2463722

Radanliev, P. (2025). Governance of generative AI. *Policy and Society*, *43*(1), 42–54. DOI: 10.1093/polsoc/puaf001

Rajagopal, N. K., Qureshi, N. I., Durga, S., Asis, E. H. R., Soto, R. M. H., Gupta, S. K., & Deepak, S. (2022a). Future of Business Culture: An Artificial Intelligence-Driven Digital Framework for organization Decision-Making Process. *Complexity*, *2022*(1). DOI: 10.1155/2022/7796507

Ratnawat, C. P. (2025, June 25). *Revolutionizing Insurance Compliance: AI-Powered Automation for Regulatory excellence*. https://sarcouncil.com/2025/06/revolutionizing-insurance-compliance-ai-powered-automation-for-regulatory-excellence

Roundy, P. T. (2022). Artificial intelligence and entrepreneurial ecosystems: Understanding the implications of algorithmic decision-making for startup communities. *Journal of Ethics in Entrepreneurship and Technology*, *2*(1), 23–38. DOI: 10.1108/JEET-07-2022-0011

Saheb, T., & Saheb, T. (2023). Topical review of artificial intelligence national policies: A mixed method analysis. *Technology in Society*, *74*, 102316. DOI: 10.1016/j.techsoc.2023.102316

Salako, A. O., Fabuyi, J. A., Aideyan, N. T., Selesi-Aina, O., Dapo-Oyewole, D. L., & Olaniyi, O. O. (2024). Advancing information governance in AI-Driven cloud ecosystem: Strategies for enhancing data security and meeting regulatory compliance. *Asian Journal of Research in Computer Science*, *17*(12), 66–88. DOI: 10.9734/ajrcos/2024/v17i12530

Samuel, P. K, N. R. A., Rajesh, S., M, N. K., & A, N. K. R. (2023). AI-Based big data algorithms and machine learning techniques for managing data in E-Governance. In *Advances in electronic government, digital divide, and regional development book series* (pp. 19–35). DOI: 10.4018/978-1-6684-7697-0.ch002

Shaban, O. S., & Omoush, A. (2025). AI-driven financial transparency and corporate governance: Enhancing accounting practices with evidence from Jordan. *Sustainability (Basel)*, *17*(9), 3818. Advance online publication. DOI: 10.3390/su17093818

Shandilya, S. K., Datta, A., Kartik, Y., & Nagar, A. (2024). Navigating the regulatory landscape. In *EAI/Springer Innovations in Communication and Computing* (pp. 127–240). DOI: 10.1007/978-3-031-53290-0_3

Sharma, R., & Haralayya, B. (2025). Corporate Governance and AI Ethics: A Strategic Framework for Ethical Decision-Making in business. SSRN *Electronic Journal*. DOI: 10.2139/ssrn.5252708

Singhania, M., & Saini, N. (2021). Institutional framework of ESG disclosures: Comparative analysis of developed and developing countries. *Journal of Sustainable Finance & Investment*, *13*(1), 516–559. DOI: 10.1080/20430795.2021.1964810

Sklavos, G., Theodossiou, G., Papanikolaou, Z., Karelakis, C., & Ragazou, K. (2024). Environmental, Social, and Governance-Based Artificial Intelligence Governance: Digitalizing firms' leadership and human resources management. *Sustainability (Basel)*, *16*(16), 7154. DOI: 10.3390/su16167154

Ulnicane, I. (2024). When code isn't law: Rethinking regulation for artificial intelligence. *Policy and Society*, *43*(2), 194–206. DOI: 10.1093/polsoc/puae020

Vettriselvan, R., Velmurugan, P. R., Regins, J. C., Maheswari, S. U., & Joyce, R. (2025a). Best practices, ethical challenges, and regulatory frameworks for AI integration in banking. In *Advances in computational intelligence and robotics book series* (pp. 377–410). DOI: 10.4018/979-8-3693-9356-7.ch015

Walter, Y. (2024). Managing the race to the moon: Global policy and governance in Artificial Intelligence regulation—A contemporary overview and an analysis of socioeconomic consequences. *Discover Artificial Intelligence*, *4*(1), 14. Advance online publication. DOI: 10.1007/s44163-024-00109-4

Zhao, J., & Fariñas, B. G. (2022). Artificial intelligence and sustainable decisions. *European Business Organization Law Review*, *24*(1), 1–39. DOI: 10.1007/s40804-022-00262-2

Chapter 2
Beyond the Binary:
EU Copyright Law and the Hybrid Nature of AI-Assisted Works

Philippe Jougleux
https://orcid.org/0000-0003-3938-5449
European University, Cyprus

ABSTRACT

The rapid integration of generative artificial intelligence into creative processes has reignited complex debates in copyright law. In the European Union, some foundational issues are increasingly settled: the input stage is governed by text and data mining exceptions under the DSM Directive, while fully autonomous AI outputs remain outside copyright protection due to the requirement of human authorship. A more nuanced and unresolved issue concerns AI-assisted creation, where AI serves as a tool within a broader human-led creative process. This paper first outlines the legal framework applicable to AI training and the exclusion of AI-generated works from protection. It then explores the legal and conceptual space of AI-assisted creation, proposing a layered understanding of originality that reflects the cumulative nature of human creative input. Finally, it considers the risk of infringement when AI-generated content closely resembles protected works. The paper concludes that existing copyright principles can address these challenges and guide future judicial developments.

DOI: 10.4018/979-8-3373-5452-1.ch002

1. INTRODUCTION

The technology of Artificial Intelligence itself did not cause much of a stir in the field of intellectual property for decades, until the blossoming of synthetic content production models with the revolution of generative AI, mostly produced through Large Language Models (LLMs) or Multimodal models. These new kind of deep learning machines require, as part of their training, a large amount of data, and obviously, some of these data may be protected by Copyright law. Since then, the AI sector has been on collision course with a branch of law that has already undergone many changes since the beginning of the digital age.

Copyright law has traditionally focused its attention mainly on the art market. At the same time, from architectural works to jewellery or simple furniture, it did not from the outset limit its protection to artistic endeavours, and instead intended to cover any original intellectual work created. With this potentially broad reach, copyright law was destined to play an essential role in the digital age.

Nonetheless, the current revolution of AI systems outlines a new battle in a constant war between the interests of creators and those of users, in alliance with the Internet giants. Three separate fronts can be distinguished. Typically, the questions of the legal nature of input data (information used during the training of the AI) and output data (content generated by the AI) are raised in parallel. The first issue concerns the legality of the providers' use of protected works as feed material for AI training. In this context, the EU had adopted a proactive solution that promote innovation and development of the AI sector, but at the expense of creators. The second issue, on the contrary, analyses the outcome of AI production and in this context a dichotomy is necessary. It will analyse how the application of the general principles of intellectual property law leaves almost no room for protection. However, a distinction must be made between AI generated content, to which the door of protection is closed, and AI enabled content, where, on the contrary, copyright protection is possible.

The chapter will first present the issues that are more or less already settled, at least in EU: the issue of the data input, and the issue of AI generated content's protection (part 2). Then, it will focus on the huge challenge that subsist: the issue of AI assisted content (part 3). It will be argued that such a challenge can be solved by continuing to apply a certain definition of the concept of originality, as set by the Court of Justice of the European Union (CJEU).

2. THE (ALMOST) SETTLED LEGAL ISSUES RELATING TO AI-GENERATED WORKS

2.1. Feeding Protected Works Into the AI and the Data Mining Exception

The problematic issue of input data into the AI system crystallises worldwide tensions between the economic protagonists of the cultural industry and AI providers. Surprisingly, the EU adopted very early (in 2019) a legal solution that provides, compared to other countries, an increased stability and that gives a fairly large head start to innovation. This solution is, however, strongly contested as it is seen as not respecting the interests of creators.

2.1.1 The Legalisation of the Use of Protected Works as Input Data in Directive 2019/790

Due to the inherent cross-border nature of intellectual property, there were very early attempts at harmonisation at the international level. The Berne Convention, drafted in 1886, is still in force, which regulates at a global level the general principles of copyright law (Burger, 1988). At the same time, at EU level, there has been an ongoing effort at further harmonisation with the express intention of establishing a Union-wide intellectual property law (Hugenholtz, 2012). Consequently, an EU Copyright law has progressively emerged, that covers the main topics of the legal regime, with the exception of the author's moral rights, as the EU is considered to have no competence in this area (Phil Collins v Imtrat Handelsgesellschaft mbH, 1993). Most importantly, the summa divisio of copyright law between a right to control access to the work (the right of communication to the public) and a right to control copying of the work (the reproduction right) is adopted.

Article 2 of the Information Society Directive (Infosoc Directive) (Directive 2001/29/EC, 2001) defines the reproduction right as any direct or indirect, temporary or permanent reproduction, in whole or in part, by any means and in any form and recognises as rightsholders the author and holders of neighbouring rights (such as performers, as regards the recording on a physical medium of their performances; phonogram producers, as regards their phonograms; producers of the first fixation of films on a medium, as regards the original and copies of their films; broadcasters, as regards the fixation of their broadcasts, whether broadcast by wire or radio, including by cable or satellite).

The reproduction right is independent of the permanence of the reproduction (as the infosoc Directive mentions both "temporary or permanent" reproduction) and therefore even a technical reproduction without the purpose of transmitting the work to a new person falls within the scope of the right. Is exempted only the case of a temporary act of reproduction, which is transitory or incidental, which is an integral and essential part of a technological process, and, thirdly, which has the sole purpose of enabling transmission between third parties through an intermediary or the lawful use of the work (Directive 2001/29/EC, 2001, Article 5(1)). In light of the jurisprudential interpretation of this exception (Infopaq International A/S v Danske Dagblades Forening, 2009), it can be concluded that all the temporary and transitional acts of reproduction do not fall within the scope of the reproduction right.

To apply this exception to the AI training process, it should be first of all mentioned that, depending on the training technique, the data may be converted into another form and the original text may be destroyed in the process. Indeed, the AI's "feeding" process could then be considered to be a temporary and transitional operation. However, the processed data from the AI still exists, somewhere, internally in the AI's model. In this context, it is recalled that any copying is considered to be a reproduction of a work, regardless of the final form. Therefore, it must be accepted that the reproduction here is rather transitory, but not temporary, so that the exception does not apply.

In practice, the training of a generative AI requires a huge amount of data. The process of feeding the AI with data is qualified as 'data mining' in the EU, but technically the training encompasses a wide range of techniques that can be grouped under the name 'data scrapping' (OECD, 2025). What these techniques have in common, however, is the digital copying of data to an internal database of the AI systems.

Consequently, when a protected work is transferred to an AI for training purposes, it does not matter in the first place that the work is not transmitted to a human being. Once the work is stored in the AI model, it is legally an act of reproduction, which is subject to the control of the author. This specific issue has been taken into consideration by the EU legislator.

The harmonisation of EU copyright law is characterised by a gradual approach which roughly corresponds to three phases. In the first phase, specific issues, such as the law on the protection of software or databases, were regulated. This was followed in 2001 by a second phase in which harmonisation moved on to substantive and horizontal issues such as the definition of rights and exceptions, duration or enforcement. This harmonisation necessarily uses as model an high threshold of protection and it has led to an approach of protecting authors' interest at the expense of users' interests. The third phase of harmonisation therefore seeks to restore a delicate balance on this issue. In this context, the EU legislator has inserted into EU Copyright law some new exceptions, collective management control and a mechanism for protecting authors against producers.

Directive 2019/790 (Directive 2019/790, 2019) on Copyright in the Digital Single Market is an example of this trend, as the legislation, among other legal instruments, adds new exceptions to the authors' rights. In particular, Articles 3 and 4 introduce into EU law the exception of “data mining”. Data mining is understood here as any automated analytical technique aimed at analysing texts and data in digital form with a view to generating information, including, but not limited to, patterns, trends and correlations (Directive 2019/790, 2019, Article 2(1)).

In the light of this definition, it is quite difficult to dispute that feeding an AI system with input data constitutes an act of 'data mining'. Indeed, it is by nature an automated analytical technique. In practice, feeding the AI with data may be accompanied by additional actions before or after the analysis. There is a technique of feeding with supervision of a human who prepares the data before the analysis, but this fact does not transform the analysis into a non-automated one. Also, the fact of the existence or not of "trainers", i.e. people who subsequently judge the result of the analysis of the data by the AI and send feedback, is irrelevant. In any case, the essence of the process (the analysis of the data) is by nature automated and digital.

It should be noted that the definition targets 'data'. It is not limited to texts (literary, journalistic or scientific works), but also covers images, videos or even music. Of course, data can also mean simple information, raw data, such as numbers, or works that have fallen into the public domain, in which case the exception mechanism does not even need to be used.

Article 3 of the Directive first ensures absolute freedom in this area, for research purposes. In other words, it is impossible for the author to oppose the extraction of data negotiated in the context of research on AI systems. The possibility of a contrary contractual provision is expressly rejected and no compensation mechanism for authors is provided for. The criterion for the application of Article 3 is organic: mining for research is not sufficient, but data mining by research institutions is covered.

For example, in Germany, the Hamburg District Court (District Court of Hamburg, 2023) ruled on a dispute between LAION, a non-profit organisation, and Robert Kneschke, a photographer. The case revolved around LAION's creation of a dataset for training AI models through "web scraping" (extracting data from web jumps) of publicly available images, including one of Kneschke's images. Kneschke claimed that LAION infringed his copyright by reproducing one of his images without permission as part of the dataset creation process. The court dismissed the lawsuit, finding that LAION's activities were covered by the text and data mining exception for scientific research.

Article 4, by contrast, concerns the commercial exploitation of data. In this context, an exception for data mining is also established, but with more reservations. In particular, it is provided that the exception "shall apply provided that the use of works and other subject matter of protection referred to in this paragraph has not been expressly restricted by the rightholders of their rights in an appropriate manner, such as by machine readable means in the case of content made publicly available online" (Directive 2019/790, 2019, Article 4(3)).

In essence, an opt-out system is being introduced. In other words, the consent of the rightholders to data mining is presumed unless they expressly object. Obviously, the objection must be expressed in a way that is understandable to the machine, as the process is automatic. If the protected work is behind a paywall, such as for example some journalistic articles, this is considered an inherent restriction by the rightholders.

Where, on the contrary, the content is freely accessible on the internet, the simplest and most logical means of expressing intent is the classic "robots.txt" file that webmasters are accustomed to install. This file was originally intended for search engines to determine what is allowed to be recorded from the website. By the same token, new commands can be proposed to the AI companies. For example, it is possible to include the following lines in the file:

```
"User-agent: anthropic-ai Disallow: / User-agent:
GPTBot Disallow: /"
```

This command prohibits the famous general-purpose AI applications Claude and ChatGPT from mining the website data. For a general prohibition to all AI systems, it is possible to simply enter the command "*User-agent: * Disallow: /*". Note that this protection is not technical per se, but legal, in the sense that the inclusion of this command does not practically prevent mining if the AI's robot is programmed in such a way it ignores this command. It is just that the mining in such a context lacks legality.

Using the robots.txt file is not always feasible and therefore does not provide a totally efficient protection of the rightholder. It is typically only possible to use the file in the context where the website is owned by the beneficiary and it leaves the question, for example, of works that are uploaded to social networks or works that are uploaded by third parties to other websites. For this reason, the Commission has launched a process to establish a general digital database of works that have been opted out from the data mining regime (Commission, 2025). The purpose of this database is namely to record all refusals so that this information is accessible to AI providers.

Finally, the data mining exception requires “legal access”. Legal access is not the same as free access to online content (Directive 2019/790, 2019, recital 14). For example, many suspicions and accusations relate to whether the famous ChatGPT model was trained using partially protected works (books) that it found on “torrent” networks (which are commonly exploited for illegal circulation of works by pirate networks) (Pirate Monitor, 2023). In such a case, the mining exception cannot obviously be applied. Obviously, it is not feasible for an automated scanning and extraction tool to distinguish the legality or otherwise of a public release of a work, and this should not affect the liability of the provider (Griffiths et al., 2022). However, in light of the relevant CJEU case law (GS Media, 2016), it would not be unreasonable to expect providers to carry out reasonable checks on the authenticity of the sources, in general, that they target with their scanning robots.

In conclusion, the Article 4 mining exception provides a stable legal framework for the development of the AI industry in the EU. However, it does not provide an absolute freedom to the AI provider to train their AI as they wish, as the possibility of refusal (the opt-out mechanism) applies. When the new exception was adopted, it was observed by several commentators that this mechanism entails a risk of slowing down innovation and technology development of AI systems in the EU (Margoni & Kretschmer, 2022; Rosati, 2019; Strowel & Ducato, 2021), with the logic that, if widely applied, EU AI providers would be forced to use only legacy data (or data obtained through general licensing). However, the advantage of a clear solution must be taken into account accordingly. Compared to the US, for example, where the issue is referred to multiple courtrooms (Various class action lawsuits, 2023), it can be argued that the EU has a secure legal framework regarding input data that has the advantage of legal stability.

2.1.2. The Current Challenges to the Data Mining Exemption and the Imposition of a Transparency Obligation

The legal regime of the AI's training is therefore entirely based on the application of the data mining exception. This solution has led to many critics and challenges.

The main issue regarding the implementation of the data mining exemption to generative AI's training is chronological. As mentioned above, the exemption was adopted by the EU legislator in 2019. The democratisation of the use of generative AI occurred around 2022. The main argument then is that it is not feasible under a teleological interpretation to apply the data mining exception to this phenomenon. At the same time, the idea that the creative capabilities of AI now threatens creators is promoted in the media (Marr, 2023; Chayka, 2023). It is then called for the introduction of a new legislative mechanism to make it compulsory for rightholders to receive a fair remuneration when their works are used at the AI training stage (Senftleben, 2023).

However, although it is possible that the legislature may have miscalculated the expansion of the AI revolution, it is not disputed that AI was already part of the EU legislator's thinking when it enacted the mining exception (Rosati, 2024). In this context, the clarity of the text of the exception leaves no room for anything other than a grammatical interpretation and the argument of the teleological interpretation should be discarded.

Another issue concerns the application of the three-step test. Under this test, an exception to intellectual property rights is considered compatible with the Berne Convention only if it meets certain criteria (Berne Convention, Article 9(2)). Note that the test is also part of the acquis communautaire (Directive 2001/29/EC, 2001, Article 5(5)), and the CJEU uses it as a model for interpreting exceptions and even as a guarantor of the balance between conflicting interests in intellectual property (Funke Medien NRW, 2019). The three-step test consists of three separate analyses of the validity of an exception, which here specifically become three questions: (1) is the data mining exception a special case? (2) does it conflict with normal exploitation? and (3) does it cause "undue harm to legitimate interests"?

On the first issue, it is indeed not disputed that this is a fairly special case of exploitation of a work of mind. The second issue holds an inherent difficulty, as the market for licensing projects to AI providers had not really blossomed before the exception was established. It can be argued that AI training has so far not been part of the normal commercial exploitation of a work.

The third issue crystallises the criticisms against the exception. The production of works via AI may devalue human creativity by flooding markets with synthetic content without the actual creators receiving any compensation. However, it is noted that for this reason the commercial exception for mining was not designed to be absolute. Assuming that the opt-out regime works, the creator is guaranteed a fair remuneration through the drafting of licensing contracts.

Furthermore, the scope of the opt-out system is questioned. In intellectual property, each exception relates to a specific right and here the data mining exception neutralises the reproduction right. In this context, a fairly narrow interpretation can be argued: the exception does not apply in respect of post-training activities, i.e. acts that take place at a stage after the model has been developed. This means that, in this logic, the exemption does not cover the integration of a trained general purpose AI model into an AI system, its placing on the market, or its putting into service" in the EU (European Copyright Society, 2025).

However, the CJEU has previously warned against a strict and formal distinction of rights in determining the scope of an exception. The judges prefer to analyse, in the light of a teleological interpretation, which activities are ontologically covered by the exception. For example, in Ulmer (Technische Universität Darmstadt v. Eugen Ulmer KG, 2014), it was held that public libraries are allowed to digitise works (normally subject to the reproduction right) in their collections to make them available to users on special terminals, as permitted by the specific exception (the right of communication to the public) that gives them this freedom. In other words, the purpose of the exception matters to determine its effective range. It would be absurd in this context to allow training of an AI even for commercial purposes and then prohibit the AI from operating commercially without the permission of the rights holders. Consequently, this strict interpretation of the exception should be rejected.

In conclusion, the application of the data mining exception to general AI models is causing some tensions and pressures, as it is considered that the exception disproportionately harms the rights holders. However, it has also been argued that, on the contrary, the EU solution has the potential to increase the bargaining power of rights holders and lead to licensing agreements for AI providers (Keller, 2023). The key to success of this legislative initiative is the effectiveness of the opt-out nature of the system.

2.1.3. The EU AI Act and Copyright law

There is a clear drawback to the self-exclusion approach of Article 4: it relies on the public availability of training datasets. That is, the beneficiary must somehow be aware that his or her work has been or will be used in training (Quintais, 2023). Therefore, the whole scheme discussed above depends on whether the AI training is operated transparently.

The AI Act enacted in 2024 (Regulation 2024/1689, 2024) adds important clarifications in this context. First, and worth noting, the legislator takes it for granted in the Regulation that AI training with protected works infringes per se the reproduction right. It also confirms that the data mining exception applies generally to all AI training (Regulation 2024/1689, 2024, recital 105).

Furthermore, two provisions are introduced in the Regulation concerning general purpose AI models, which are directly aimed at complementing the data mining exception.

First, it is provided that the general purpose AI provider is required to "*put in place a policy to comply with Union law on copyright and related rights, and in particular to identify and comply with, including through state-of-the-art technologies, a reservation of rights expressed pursuant to Article 4(3) of Directive (EU) 2019/790*" (Regulation 2024/1689, 2024, Article 53(1)(c)). In other words, the explicit intention of the legislator is that the opt-out regime in the data mining exception should be considered as a material obligation of the provider.

The reference to state-of-the-art technologies confirms that the provider is burdened with a high level duty of care (Efthymiou, I. P., 2026). It is asked the AI provider to make every effort to confirm that the beneficiary has not made use of the opt-out option. The compliance of the AI provider (the obligation to adopt and implement a copyright policy) is also checked by the supervisory bodies. It is clarified that "*With regard to the obligations imposed on providers of general-purpose AI models to put in place a policy to comply with Union copyright law and make publicly available a summary of the content used for the training, the AI Office should monitor whether the provider has fulfilled those obligations without verifying or proceeding to a work-by-work assessment of the training data in terms of copyright compliance. This Regulation does not affect the enforcement of copyright rules as provided for under Union law.*" (Regulation 2024/1689, 2024, recital 108).

Also, and perhaps more importantly, it is provided that AI providers shall prepare and make publicly available a sufficiently detailed summary of the content used for training the general purpose AI model, in accordance with a template provided by the AI Service (Regulation 2024/1689, 2024, Article 53(1)(d)). The introduction of an obligation to produce a summary meets a basic need for transparency in this field. As highlighted above, the delicate balance of the opt-out and opt-in regime relies on the ability of beneficiaries to confirm that the work has indeed not been incorporated into the training dataset.

It is explained that "(...) While taking into due account the need to protect trade secrets and confidential business information, this summary should be generally comprehensive in its scope instead of technically detailed to facilitate parties with legitimate interests, including copyright holders, to exercise and enforce their rights under Union law, for example by listing the main data collections or sets that went into training the model, such as large private or public databases or data archives, and by providing a narrative explanation about other data sources used. (...)" (Regulation 2024/1689, 2024, recital 107).

In conclusion, the duty to provide a summary adds an additional element towards an effective operation of the mining exception as a reconciliation mechanism between the conflicting interests of AI providers and IPR holders. However, ensuring this balance in practice will depend on the subsequent policy of collecting societies regarding the opt-out and also on the success of regular checks on the authenticity of the summaries proposed by AI providers.

2.2. The Non Protection of AI-Generated Works From Copyright Law

2.2.1. Legal Framework on the Conditions for Protection of a Work and Their Application to AI Systems

The focus of copyright law's specialist did not limit to the issue of input data. In general, content production via AI never ceases to amaze and surprise. Even before the big boom in general-purpose AI, several experiments such as "the new Rembrandt" in 2016, which managed to create a new painting in the style of the famous painter (Baraniuk, 2016), shed light on the potential creative capabilities of AI. Today, only 61% of viewers can distinguish between two images which one is created by an AI and which one is not (Waterloo News, 2024) (ironically, AI itself is much better at identifying synthetic content) (Ghiurău & Popescu, 2025).

In this context, one might reasonably ask: who does this synthetic content belong to? This question brings up another, more fundamental question: is it possible to protect such works in the first place? Various principles underlie the classic question of determining the conditions for the protection of an intellectual work by copyright. However, applying these principles, not much room is left for the theory that output data (AI-generated work) is protected by intellectual property. As it will be explained below, the necessary human intervention is missing.

Copyright law mainly concerns the protection of the result of an intellectual effort. In other words, an originality of the work is required for it to be entitled to protection. Consequently, 'output data', works produced by the AI at the request of the user, constitute works protected by copyright provided that they are considered to be original.

While everyone agrees with this introductory statement, defining a comprehensive and clear content to the concept of originality has, however, come to constitute an extremely difficult task. The Berne Convention did not define the concept of originality, preferring instead to give the courts flexibility by letting the appreciation of originality to the discretionary analysis of the judges. Such an approach was not particularly helpful in defining the limits of protection, and practice has traditionally created various theories on the interpretation of the concept (Judge & Gervais, 2009). Two main theories can be distinguished. The subjective approach, based on the 'romantic inspiration' of copyright law, explains that an original work must be understood as any work where a 'stamp of personality' of the author is found. On the contrary, in the objective approach, various tests such as the test of "statistical uniqueness" or the theory of skills and labour consider that originality is understood as the quality of a work which is ontologically distinct from any similar intellectual effort.

This different understanding of the concept of originality has a direct consequence for AI content generation. Since, in the subjective approach, demonstration of an organic link between the work and the personality of the creator is required, the AI-generated content is automatically excluded from the protection. On the contrary, since the objective approach refers exclusively to the work, in such context, the question of the protection by copyright law of AI-generated content is still left opened.

The EU's position on this issue should therefore be analysed in detail. In other words, it must be clarified whether an objective or subjective definition of originality prevails at EU level. As the establishment of a uniform interpretation of originality in the EU is a matter of the utmost importance for an effective harmonisation of intellectual property law, the CJEU has intervened in this matter and has chosen to impose its own interpretation of the concept in a series of judgments which have generalised and applied accordingly a specific legislative definition originally, which was originally devised for software (Infopaq International A/S v Danske Dagblades Forening, 2009; Eva-Maria Painer v Standard VerlagsGmbH, 2011). It should be noted that the European legislator in turn endorsed this judicial initiative (Directive 2019/790, 2019, Article 14). The EU definition is therefore as follows: a work is considered to be original if it is the personal intellectual creation of the author.

The key issue, therefore, is to assess whether or not the definition at the EU level of originality as the personal intellectual creation of the author allows for the protection of AI-generated content. In this context, it is observed that the definition borrows elements from the objective approach (the concept of personal work), but also from the subjective one (the reference to intellectual advice, which must come from the author). As a result, the logic of exploring an organic connection between the work and the author remains partly in the definition adopted in EU Copyright law. The EU definition of originality, as a compromise between different legal traditions, proposes a much lower level of protection than the 'stamp of personality' criterion. However, at the same time, it unquestionably adopts the anthropocentric approach to intellectual property.

Consequently, it appears clear that the definition of originality excludes the protection of AI-generated work. It is worth noting in this context that even in countries that adopt an objective approach to originality (such as the US), courts have held that a derivative work of AI without human intervention is not protected (Stephen Thaler vs Shira Perlmutter, 2025).

2.2.2. The Idea/Form Distinction

Following on from this finding that the criterion of originality stands as an absolute barrier to the protection of AI-generated content, it could be argued that there is, however, an intellectual contribution by a human being through prompting. Indeed, it is the user who determines the limits and purposes of the creation by his/her command, while the machine merely executes. The flourishing of an 'art of prompting' is also being discussed (Parra Pennefather, 2023). According to this approach, then, originality can possibly be found in the prompting, and in this context the user is the real creator of the work (Fritz, 2025).

Alternatively, but with the same thinking, it could be argued that the machine does indeed execute some commands, but these commands originate initially from the machine's own programming, combined with training. In this approach, the creators are the programmers of the AI and, at the final stage, the company (the AI provider) that hires it (Aziz, 2023). In other words, originality may exist in the design of the AI itself.

These two approaches succeed in avoiding the obstacle of the definition of originality as implying human intervention. Indeed, in these two approaches, it is possible to detect an human intervention, either through prompting (by the user) or through programming (by the AI provider). However, these two approaches face an essential problem, which relates to the general principles of copyright law, or even to the nature of intellectual property itself: the classic dichotomy between idea and form.

Copyright was originally conceived as an exception to freedom of expression, and the balance between the conflicting interests of the author and the public was largely based on the idea that protection was only for a particular expression, while the ideas on which the work is based remained free (Samuels, 1988). The principle received some criticisms. It was criticized whether it is indeed possible to distinguish an idea from the expression of an idea in the first place (Jones, 1990). It was also considered that it is a vague and indefinite mechanism for excluding protection (Rosen, 1992). Nevertheless, the centrality of this dichotomy in copyright law is not generally disputed. The principle works in conjunction with the criterion of originality. In practice, it implies that not only is a personal intellectual work of the author sought, but that this activity must be established specifically at the stage of performance, i.e. the shaping of the work.

It is therefore irrelevant whether the user's instruction or the internal function of the AI is original. The prompting can be considered as original as a literary work itself, and the AI as software. But with regard to the content itself generated by the AI, both prompting and designing are a matter of preparatory operations independent of the generation of the work. By applying the general principles of copyright law, these preliminary actions fall within the domain of the idea, not within the field of "expression". Such a conclusion comes from the fact that the AI is fully autonomous during the process of content generation. Therefore, it is not possible to use prompting or design as evidence of the originality of the AI-generated content.

2.2.3. Human Intervention in Creation as a Criterion for Protection

As if the two fundamental obstacles discussed above of the EU definition of originality and the application of the idea/form dichotomy were not enough to conclude on the non-protection of AI-generated content, copyright protection for AI-generated content is also challenged for another reason. It has been argued over time that copyright law implicitly requires another criterion, parallelly of originality: human creative intervention.

The requirement of a human intervention has been established in intellectual property long before the emergence of AI (Ginsburg, 2002). Of course, there are traditionally no practical issues of exploring a human intervention in creation. The problem has been discussed until now only in somehow eccentric decisions. For example, in 1927 a psychic claimed that his writings came from a ghost who communicated with him by automatic writing. The English courts explained to him that only a human being can be a creator in the sense of intellectual property (Cummins v. Bond, 1927). Similarly, in America, the Urantia Foundation claimed copyright to the "Urantia Book", claiming that it was written by celestial beings through a human acting as a "contact personality" (Urantia Foundation v. Maaherra, 1995). In this case, too, the courts concluded that whoever human wrote the literary work is the author.

More recently, the "Naruto" case, also known as the "Monkey's selfie" case, has been especially well publicized (Naruto v. Slater, 2018). This case involved a macaque named Naruto who took selfies using a photographer's camera (which he had stolen). The court confirmed that non-human creators cannot hold copyright as copyright law requires human authorship.

Similarly, again in America, the possibility of protecting a flower bed in a park was discussed in the Kelley case (Kelley v. Chicago Park District, 2011). This case concerned Chapman Kelley, an artist who created a wildflower garden in Grant Park in Chicago. Kelley then accused the park management of modifying his garden without his consent. The court held that a garden like "Wildflower Works" could not be protected by copyright because it lacked the requisite stability and authorship. That is, gardens are highly variable and largely shaped by natural forces.

These various cases highlight an implicit issue in intellectual property: there can be no work without an author, and the author must be human. In the EU, the issue has been indirectly analysed in the Premier league case (Football Association Premier League and others V QC Leisure and Others, 2011), which concerned the protection of a football match by copyright law. Indeed, one might reasonably ask why a football match is not considered protected work: it possesses a distinct form, which is original in the sense that each match is different and depends on the personality and expertise of the players (and let's say, in part, their intellectual efforts). However, the CJEU considers that the matches cannot be classified as a "work", that is, the product of the creator's personal intellectual work, as "sporting events cannot be considered as intellectual creations capable of being created" (Football Association Premier League and others V QC Leisure and Others, 2011, para. 98). In particular, the CJEU considers that since the games are governed by the rules of the game, they leave no room for creative freedom.

What follows from the premier league, Kelley and Naruto cases, is the existence of an additional criterion of protection, along with originality: the prerequisite of a creative will as evidence of authorship. Creative will is presumed in ordinary circumstances by human intervention. In the history of art it has certainly been argued that it is possible to produce art 'by mistake' (Hilde, 2000). From a legal point of view, however, only where a particular form is the result of a creative will does protection apply. The application of this basic principle to the field of AI leads to a clear conclusion. By its very nature, creation through AI is an autonomous process. The user does not interfere with its execution. Therefore, it is not possible to prove creative intent.

In conclusion, the protection of an AI-generated content is confronted with three fundamental principles of copyright law. In the absence of any specific legislative intervention establishing a specific intellectual property regime (a sui generis protection), it means that such works are by nature in the public domain.

3. AI-ASSISTED CONTENT THROUGH THE LENS OF THE CRITERIA OF ORIGINALITY

3.1. Intellectual and Technical Intervention: Originality at the Heart of an Atomist Vision of the Work-of-Mind

The analyses held in the previous section could reasonably leave the impression that AI-generated content ('the output data') can never receive a protection by copyright law. Nonetheless, this analysis applies only to AI-generated content, and it is necessary to make a distinction between AI-generated content and AI-assisted content (Hugenholtz & Quintais, 2021). In the second case, the content is not anymore seen as the result of an autonomous process led by the AI, but on the contrary, it is the result of a joint contribution between the user and the AI.

The concept of intellectual contribution has been developed in the law of co-creation as a criterion for determining authorship between co-authors. That is, it distinguishes the simple technical contribution, which may take place before (preparations, arrangements), during (providing support, etc.) or after (corrections, minor changes, control) (Fylde Microsystems Ltd v Key Radio Systems Ltd, 1998) the creation, from the intellectual contribution which is recognised on the basis of the criterion of originality. Practically, while a simple prompting would not suffice to determine an intellectual contribution (as the user has not at this stage any control on the execution), creation through multiple alliterations may enter into the category of AI-assisted content, assuming that it is possible to determine an original intellectual contribution in the alliterations.

Indeed, in copyright law, in the regime of joint creation, it does not matter that the intellectual contribution does not coincide in time with the original contribution or that one intellectual contribution is less or more extensive than another (Brighton and Dubbeljoint v Jones, 2004). Two alternative analyses may apply: AI-assisted creation as derivative work, or AI-assisted creation as a new form of co-creation. In copyright law, when the second work is simply a continuation of an original effort that was not completed, logically, rather than imposing the status of a derivative work, it is simply assumed that the work falls under the status of co-creation. This is the conclusion reached by judges in Italy in a case where the work of a first author was used to create a promotional video (Riccardo Pagani v. Leo Burnett Company S.r.l., 2015).

In the case of AI, the distinction between a derivative work and a co-creation work is only academic. In both cases, in practice, the sole beneficiary of the rights is the user who added the original contributions to the work, since, as we have seen, no rights can be recognised to the AI itself.

Nonetheless, applying the classical approach of joint creation to AI-assisted work allows a direct analysis of each case through the concept of intellectual contribution, which relies at the end on the concept of originality.

In practice, there are a variety of situations where AI and humans work together towards an end result. For example, it may be a text in which the author makes changes. Simple technical changes, such as corrections of accidental errors, are not considered spiritual contributions in the first place. However, it is not necessarily required that the changes be substantial to be considered intellectual. It has been explained by the CJEU in Infopaq (Infopaq International A/S v Danske Dagblades Forening, 2009) that even 11 words can, depending on the circumstances, add the necessary degree of originality.

In substance, as clarified by the CJEU in Painer, whether there has been editing or free use depends on the creative effort expressed in the original. The greater the creative effort in the original, the less likely it is that there is free use (Eva-Maria Painer v Standard VerlagsGmbH, 2011, para. 108). That is, the actual scope of protection of the finished work will depend on the amount of intellectual contribution by the author. It can be advanced that the CJEU as adopted in Painer an "atomist" definition of originality, by opposition to a globalist approach. Originality is not to be found in the global result of the creation, but in various creative components. With this same logic, it is widely accepted that the universe of a work of fiction, or even the protagonists, are protected as original creations.

It is not excluded, in this context, that the intellectual contribution may result from the confluence of small creative decisions expressed as typically technical contributions. Although one individual user's prompting, as we have seen, cannot be used per se as an element of intellectual contribution, the confluence of prompts through alliteration or through cumulation of content may, depending on the circumstances, indicate a creative intention.

For example, in China, a trial court accepted the originality of the final result of such a process (Wang & Zhang, 2024). Through Stable Diffusion, an AI that specializes in image generation, the plaintiff selected over 150 prompts, arranged their order and set specific parameters. He continued to adjust and modify these prompts and parameters until the final image aligned with his conception. To the judges, these steps sufficiently demonstrate that the challenged image was created as a result of the plaintiff's intellectual inputs. Therefore, such "intellectual achievements" went beyond mere "engineering" that lacked originality, or, in other words, it was proven in this case that the AI was not the source of creation but a tool in the hands of the actual creator.

The same finding would be acceptable in case which the user cumulate together multiple AI-generated content into a final derivative work. For instance, using an AI to produce multiple video sequences, another AI to produce a scenario, an AI to produce the voices, and then conjugating all these contents together to build a short movie would result in an intellectual creation. Paradoxically, while all these contents would be excluded from protection independently, following the logic of the CJEU in Painer, it will be possible to determine a creative intent into the adoption and cumulation of these contents into a work of mind.

Consequently, the status of the AI-assisted content potentially greatly differs from the one of the AI-enabled content, even if the distinction is a matter of in concreto appreciation from the judge. As long as an intellectual contribution is established through the processing of the content generation, the user is considered to be the author of the work and the work is entitled to protection. In essence, a distinction is made between the case where the AI is used as a producer of the work and the case where the synthetic content is only a raw material for a genuine human creation.

3.2. General Principles of Copyright Law Applied to AI-Assisted Content

3.2.1. The Presumption of Authorship

Although in theory the protection of output data faces legal challenges (as explained above, it is specifically confronted to the thorny issue of distinguishing between AI-generated content and AI-assisted content), in practice the user will benefit from the help of a general mechanism of Copyright law related to the presumption of authorship inscribed in the Berne Convention. In particular, the Convention states that "In order that the author of a literary or artistic work protected by this Convention shall, in the absence of proof to the contrary, be regarded as such, and consequently be entitled to institute infringement proceedings in the countries of the Union, it shall be sufficient for his name to appear on the work in the usual manner. This paragraph shall be applicable even if this name is a pseudonym, where the pseudonym adopted by the author leaves no doubt as to his identity." (Berne Convention, Article 15(1)).

Accordingly, when a user first publishes a synthetic work created by an AI, the burden of proving that the work originates from an AI falls on the third party who wishes to challenge the origin of the protection. In practical terms, therefore, the theoretical absence of protection of an AI-generated content must be put into perspective, not only because the boundaries between an AI-generated work and an AI-assisted work are still difficult to apprehend, but also because the presumption of authorship partially protects the user/creator by reversing the burden of the proof.

Nonetheless, in this context, it should be reminded that there exists an obligation to identify a synthetic work, imposed on AI providers by the AI Act. Such an identification could potentially neutralize the advantage that the presumption of authorship, provided of course that the tampering with the identification mechanism (watermarking or labelling) is relatively technically difficult to realize.

It is also noted that most general-purpose AI models have incorporated various parameters such as "temperature" and "random seed" (Vadlapati, 2023). Many AI systems, particularly those that produce creative outputs such as images, music or text, use algorithms that incorporate a random seed. The seed controls the specific randomness applied to an AI model. Similarly, temperature affects the degree of randomness in the output of the model when generating text. A higher temperature (e.g., 1.0 or above) results in more varied and creative outputs but less predictable, while a lower temperature (e.g., 0.2) produces safer, more deterministic responses that remain closer to probabilistic or common patterns. Consequently, in most cases it is not feasible to produce a stable content, in the sense that the same exact prompt from the user would produce the same result. This, combined with the amazing improvements in AI performance in the modern era, makes it considerably more difficult to prove the synthetic origin of content and therefore to doubt the protection of a work by copyright law.

3.2.2. The Existence of Related Rights

A distinction is made in copyright law between author rights and neighbours rights. The first category of rights protects the original work of the author, while the second category, also called 'related rights', concerns the protection of interests directly related to the creation. Since in general intellectual property is, as an English judgment once observed, a 'creature of statute' (Rimmer, 2002), there is no question of jurisprudentially recognising new rights in copyright law. A closed list of authors and related rights are listed by the EU legislator. Generally speaking, neighbouring rights protect the contributions of performers, producers and broadcasters. It should be noted that no related right is recognised to the AI provider, although the idea to create a new related right on AI creation has sometimes been presented as a solution to the issue of protection of AI-generated work (Hardman & Housel, 2023).

However, this does not mean that the related rights regime does not apply at all in this matter (Kempas et al., 2023). On the contrary, since the originality criterion does not apply to related rights, one of the most important obstacles to protection is removed from the equation. Three specific related rights in particular deserve attention here. Exploitation rights are granted to the phonogram producer, the film producer, and the online news producer.

With regard to music, it is worth noting that the neighbouring rights of phonogram producers protect recordings, regardless of human authorship. A recording produced by an AI could qualify to protection by the relevant related right, if a producer invested in its realisation. The concept of phonogram producer is not clearly defined in EU law. It follows from Directive 2001/29 that should be considered as phonogram producer anyone who is responsible for the material embodiment of the music (Directive 2001/29/EC, 2001, Article 11(2)). In an online AI, such as the famous website 'suno', where music is generated on the basis of a user's prompting, the music itself is first stored on the company's servers. It remains a matter of interpretation whether the creation and storage of the generated music by the service amounts to fixing the AI-generated music in a tangible form. Such a finding could be accepted without much theoretical difficulties. However, it would mean practically that, although the music itself will not be protected by copyright, the company will retain an exclusive right to the commercial exploitation of the digital file where the music is embodied.

Similarly, the same issue arises in relation to video production. In EU copyright law, a "movie" means a cinematographic or audiovisual work or moving images whether or not accompanied by sound or not (Directive 2016/115, 2016, Article 2(1)(c)). At the same time, the producer of the first fixation of a film is granted related rights of exploitation (Directive 2016/115, 2016, Article 3). An online service of video creation such as Google Veo 3 would be entitled to claim related rights on the exploitation of the audiovisual work.

It should be mentioned that the philosophy of most of these related rights is related to the concept of the assumed economic risk and the idea that investment on creativity should be remunerated. In this context and applying a teleological approach, it can be accepted that there is a sound case for the application of the protection regimes for producers of phonograms and audiovisual works to AI-generated content.

The same logic could potentially apply to other related rights. For example, the publisher of a newspaper has been granted a neighbouring right to the online news it produces (Directive 2019/790, 2019, Article 15). In this context, an economic operator who launches an online newspaper that would operate automatically (with articles written by an AI) could indeed claim this related right.

However, this logic does not apply systematically to all related rights. The main issue is the application to the AI of the neighbouring right protecting the performer. This is how singers, musicians and actors are traditionally protected in intellectual property law. The technical possibility to create photorealistic characters, to digitally de-age actors or to digitally resurrect performances of actors who have passed away is already a reality (Pennington, 2019). Can an AI (and by extension the AI provider that puts it into operation) that sings, reads a book or brings a digital actor to life claim related rights as a performer? The difference here is that the neighbouring right is not based on an investment, but on a human creative element (performance). Therefore, in this case, the application of the protection regime must be excluded. Even in the case whereas the AI copies an existing person, it cannot be accepted that this is per se a performance and no right to publicity exists at EU level that allows for a protection of a face by intellectual property. Nonetheless, in this case, the person, as data subject, is entitled to protection based on the data privacy legislation (the GDPR).

3.3 The Question of the Potential Illegality of AI-Assisted and AI-Generated Content

3.3.1 AI-Assisted and AI-Generated Content as Illegal Derivative Work

The fact that AI providers benefit from the data mining exception does not mean that they are completely immune against copyright law infringement. The protection applies only to input data, and the question of liability remains when the output data ends up resembling a prior work. Of course, in this case, the behaviour and goal of the users come also to the fore.

Responding in a note to a remark by a colleague that the theme of his latest book was similar to his own, Lord Byron wrote: "*As to originality, all pretensions are ludicrous; there is nothing new under the sun.*" (Galt, 1830, chap. 28). So it was already quite doubtful whether human creation exists ab initio, but AI-mediated production obviously depends on the dataset used during training. In parallel, it should be noted that the concept of expression is recognized an expansive definition, as explained above. The definition of the right of reproduction encompasses any kind of reproduction, even though adaptation.

Therefore, there is a quite high possibility that some AI-generated content may be considered as infringing the rightholder's right to reproduction. Typically, if a user asks a general-purpose AI such as ChatGPT to produce a short story in the world of Harry Potter, the machine will prepare a text that borrows elements from the named literary work. Regardless of whether the style or the story follows the original, the mere action of copying original elements of the special fictional universe constitutes a reproduction in copyright law.

It is difficult, then, to give an in abstracto answer to the question of the legitimacy of the output data (Guadamuz, 2024). The above example poses no legal challenge, on the ground that the user consciously asked the machine to infringe copyright law. If the user decides to copy the content and market it as an e-book on an online platform, for instance, his liability is automatically raised. However, the user may also instead ignore in good faith that the generated content is in fact an illegal derivative work. AI models do not deliberately memorize and reproduce training data in the human sense but may produce unintended results that resemble or reproduce portions of copyrighted material. If an AI is trained on a large dataset that includes copyrighted works, there is a small chance that it will reproduce portions of the material verbatim or create a fairly similar derivative work.

In this context, it should be reminded that liability in EU copyright law was originally conceived as an objective liability (Bell & Parchomovsky, 2019), and not a fault-based legal regime. Although the fault of the user may affect the amount of the sanction (Thomas, 1990), it is not a per se requirement of liability. In other words, ignorance of the fact that one is copying a preexisting work is not a defense against a claim of copyright infringement.

The Like Company case (Like Company, 2025) takes on essential importance in this context, as it offers the CJEU the opportunity to rule for the first time on whether the operation of a general-purpose conversational artificial intelligence (LLM-based chatbot) may involve an infringement of related and/or intellectual property rights, in particular where the content of its responses copies or closely resembles news articles available online. It is recalled that, under Article 15 of Directive (EU) 2019/790, press publishers are granted a related right over their digital publications, which applies regardless of the originality of the content. The company therefore claims that the AI of the Google search engine infringes that right by automatically creating short summaries of the news.

As it has already been observed, the fact that the chatbot's response is the result of a probabilistic calculation based on linguistic patterns does not automatically remove the provider's potential liability. The legal characterization focuses on the result of the act - i.e., the making available to the public of a protected extract - and not on the method of generation or the mechanical nature of the algorithm.

However, it will be argued here that the CJEU's analysis of the application of the right of communication to the public in the digital age could be applied by analogy. In the landmark cases GS Media, the CJEU had held that a hyperlink (and by extension any techniques allowing access to a protected content) leading to illegal content (i.e. a protected work illegally posted on the internet) does not automatically constitute an infringement of the right of communication to the public (GS Media, 2016). The court used the concept of the average prudent user, who, if not engaged in a commercial activity, is entitled to disregard the illegality unless the illegal origin of the work was obvious (Stichting Brein, 2017). This modern approach departs from the traditional strict liability mechanism of copyright law and inserts elements of a fault-based regime, in order to preserve a balance between freedom of expression and protection of the rightholders' interest.

It is proposed to apply the same reasoning here: the user bears a duty of care with regard to the exploitation of the output data, which depends on their status and on the obvious or not similarity of the output data to a pre-existing work. In other words, it is argued that while a professional user should exercise a professional duty of care in the exploitation of AI generated content, a non-professional user should be held liable only in case whereas the AI generated content obviously infringes preexisting work.

3.3.2 The Question of the Liability of the AI Provider or the Economic Operator

In the case where a user infringes the copyright of a third party through the generation of AI content, the complex legal issue of the intersection between secondary liability (or third-party liability or even vicarious liability) and contributory liability arises. It should be noted from the outset that this is a famous topic of discussion especially in EU copyright law

(Leistner, 2014), as national traditions, based on general principles of civil law, differ considerably here.

In this context, an AI provider operating its own online platform can be considered by analogy as a content hosting provider. The status of the hosting provider has a special significance, as this is one of the recognized cases where a relative safe harbor is provided to the company working as an intermediary. Under the E-Commerce Directive (Directive 2000/31/EC, 2000, Article 14), intermediary service providers, such as hosting services, can benefit from immunities from liability for illegal content uploaded by users, provided that they have no actual knowledge of the illegal activity or information and, once they become aware of it, act swiftly to remove the content or disable access to it. The Digital Services Act (DSA) (Regulation 2022/2065, 2022) confirms what had already been observed in the case law of the CJEU, namely that an additional criterion for the safe harbor of online intermediaries exists: including AI developers, the implementation of an effective notification and reporting mechanism (Regulation 2022/2065, 2022, Article 16). In essence, an intermediary is shielded from liability for the existence of illegal user-generated content in its server, if it removes or disables access to such content immediately upon receiving a valid notification. Practically, it means that AI developers must establish a robust notification and complaint system from the outset to ensure that they are protected against liability for copyright law infringement. In practice, in the context of AI, the user of an online service should have a means of alerting the system that the content may infringe intellectual property rights. In the case where the result of a prompt is allowed to be "shared" with others via a hyperlink (OpenAI, 2024), this possibility should be available to every possible person allowed access to the AI-generated content.

In conclusion, in the face of the great legal ambiguity that characterises the issue of secondary liability for the production of copyright infringing content, AI providers and operators have at their disposal a powerful potential tool to protect their commercial activities. However, two main caveats accompany this regime. Firstly, the system relies entirely on the effective establishment and operation of a whistleblowing system (which in practice has not yet been established by the most prominent AI providers). Secondly, since the platform falls under the category of 'Very Large Online

Platforms and Very Large Online Search Engines' from the scope of the DSA, it is burdened with additional obligations, including risk mitigation (Regulation 2022/2065, 2022, Article 35). In the context of copyright law, it means that where it is known that a particular platform is being used to produce copyright infringing content, the operator must take specific protection or filtering measures to avoid such result.

3.3.3 User's Liability for Illegal AI Generation and the Private Copying Exception

The private copying exception plays an essential role in striking a balance between the conflicting interests of the rightholder and the user in copyright law, traditionally. Without an act of communication (in the broad sense), there is practically very little need of protection and very little efficiency of copyright law's enforcement mechanisms too. Essentially, it does not matter to the rightholder whether someone who has legally purchased a book reads it once or a thousand times, uses it for decoration or gives it as a gift to a friend. Copyright law traditionally stops where personal activity begins.

This logic applies too, with some adjustments and adaption, to the digital age. An user is permitted to reproduce the work in any medium carried out by a natural person for private use and for non-direct or indirect commercial purposes, provided that the rightholders receive fair compensation (Directive 2001/29/EC, 2001, Article 5(2)(a)). Fair compensation, through the special levy scheme for digital storage systems, ensures that the scheme is consistent with the requirements of the three-step test (mostly that the rightholders are not deprived of a substantial amount of their remuneration). For instance, the CJEU had the opportunity in Austro-Mechana (Austro-Mechana Gesellschaft zur Wahrnehmung mechanisch-musikalischer Urheberrechte Gesellschaft mbH v Strato AG, 2022) to clarify that the "private copying" exception applies to the storage in the cloud of a copy of a protected work for private purposes.

Applying this legal framework to AI-generated content, it should be accepted that personal interactions between the user and the AI system, even though an online platform, are covered by this exception. From the moment the AI-generated content, while illegal, is not communicated to the public or reproduced and sent to third parties, it can be argued that the user is shielded from liability because of the private copying exception. On the other hand, the CJEU has already stated in the landmark ACI Adam case that the private copying exception may only benefit the lawful user (ACI Adam BV and Others v Stichting de Thuiskopie, 2014). If this case law applies to the situation of the user of an AI-generated content, the user would lose the benefit of the exception at the moment that there is evidence without any doubt that the result of his prompting would infringe a copyright.

Alternatively, to avoid the conceptual trap of the application of the private copying exception, it could also be argued that the user does not infringe any copyright prerogative in the first place, by prompting, even if the result infringes copyright law. From the moment that the user does not communicate to the public or reproduce in another medium the content, it is not liable for the AI generation.

4. CONCLUSION

This chapter has examined the legal challenges posed by the application of copyright law to AI-generated content. The topic has attracted considerable attention from both legal scholars and the broader public. Yet, despite emerging consensus on some fronts, litigation remains not only inevitable given the technical and conceptual complexity of the issues. It is also a necessity, in order to clarify the multiple interpretative uncertainties surrounding the intersection of AI and copyright law.

One key issue has already been addressed by the EU legislator: the legality of using copyright-protected works to train AI models, analysed through the scope of the data mining exception. Likewise, there is growing doctrinal agreement on the general non-eligibility of purely AI-generated content for copyright protection, due to the absence of human authorship.

However, two particularly thorny questions remain open: first, whether and under what conditions AI-assisted content can qualify as a protected work; and second, whether AI-generated outputs may infringe the exclusive rights of copyright holders. Importantly, these are not novel problems requiring wholly new legal inventions. Rather, longstanding principles of copyright law, especially those concerning the nature of originality and the role of human intellectual contribution, can be mobilized to address them.

This chapter has shown how courts may apply these established doctrines, particularly a layered or atomistic conception of originality, to distinguish between AI-generated and AI-enabled works. Doing so may provide much-needed clarity regarding the legal status of hybrid creations and contribute to a coherent legal framework for derivative works in the AI era.

REFERENCES

ACI Adam BV and Others v Stichting de Thuiskopie and Stichting Onderhandelingen Thuiskopie vergoeding. (2014). Court of Justice of the European Union, C-435/12, 10 April 2014, ECLI:EU:C:2014:254.

(2022). Austro-Mechana Gesellschaft zur Wahrnehmung mechanisch-musikalischer Urheberrechte Gesellschaft mbH v Strato AG. (2022). Court of Justice of the European Union, C-433/20, 24 March 2022. *ECLI:EU, C*, 217.

Aziz, A. (2023). Artificial Intelligence Produced Original Work: A New Approach to Copyright Protection and Ownership. *European Journal of Artificial Intelligence and Machine Learning*, *2*(2), 9–16. DOI: 10.24018/ejai.2023.2.2.15

Baraniuk, C. (2016). *Computer paints 'new Rembrandt' after old works analysis*. BBC News.

Bell, A., & Parchomovsky, G. (2019). Restructuring copyright infringement. *Texas Law Review*, *98*, 679.

Brein, S. (2017). Court of Justice of the European Union, C-610/15, 14 June 2017. *ECLI:EU, C*, 456.

Brighton and Dubbeljoint v Jones. (2004). England and Wales High Court (Chancery Division), EWHC 1157 (Ch).

Burger, P. (1988). The Berne Convention: Its history and its key role in the future. *The Journal of Law and Technology*, *3*, 1.

Chayka, K. (2023). Is A.I. Art stealing from artists. *The New Yorker*.

Commission. (2025). Call for tenders for the preparation of a feasibility study on a central opt-out register based on text and data mining (TDM) exemption. https://digital-strategy.ec.europa.eu/en/funding/call-tenders-feasibility-study-central-registry-opt-outs-under-text-and-data-mining-tdm-exception

Cummins v. Bond. (1927). Chancery Division, 1 Ch. 167.

Directive 2000/31/EC of the European Parliament and of the Council of 8 June 2000 on certain legal aspects of information society services, in particular electronic commerce, in the Internal Market ('Directive on electronic commerce').

Directive 2001/29/EC of the European Parliament and of the Council of 22 May 2001 on the harmonisation of certain aspects of copyright and related rights in the information society. (2001). ELI: https://data.europa.eu/eli/dir/2001/29/oj

Directive 2016/115 of the European Parliament and of the Council of 19 April 2006 on rental right and lending right and on certain rights related to copyright in the field of intellectual property (codified version). (2016).

Directive 2019/790 of the European Parliament and of the Council of 17 April 2019 on copyright and related rights in the Digital Single Market and amending Directives 96/9/EC and 2001/29/EC. (2019). ELI: https://data.europa.eu/eli/dir/2019/790/oj

District Court of Hamburg. (2023). 310 O 227/23.

Efthymiou, I. P. (2026). Bridging the Divide: Addressing the Leadership Gap. In *Bridging the Leadership Gap: Policies and Workplace Equality* (pp. 103-138). IGI Global Scientific Publishing.

European Copyright Society. (2025). Copyright and Generative AI: Opinion of the European Copyright Society January 2025. https://europeancopyrightsociety.org/wp-content/uploads/2025/02/ecs_opinion_genai_january2025.pdf

Eva-Maria Painer v Standard VerlagsGmbH, Axel Springer AG, Süddeutsche Zeitung GmbH, Spiegel-Verlag Rudolf Augstein GmbH & Co KG, Verlag M. DuMont Schauberg Expedition der Kölnischen Zeitung GmbH & Co KG. (2011). Court of Justice of the European Union, C-145/10, 1 December 2011, ECLI:EU:C:2011:798.

(2011). Football Association Premier League and others V QC Leisure and Others and Karen Murphy V Media Protection Services Ltd. (2011). Court of Justice of the European Union, C-403/08 and C-429/08, 4 October 2011. *ECLI:EU*, *C*, 631.

Fritz, J. (2025). Understanding authorship in Artificial Intelligence-assisted works. *Journal of Intellectual Property Law & Practice*, jpae 119. DOI: 10.1093/jiplp/jpae119

Funke Medien, N. R. W. (2019). Court of Justice of the European Union, C-469/17, 29 July 2019. *ECLI:EU, C*, 623.

Fylde Microsystems Ltd v Key Radio Systems Ltd. (1998). England and Wales High Court (Patents Court), EWHC Patents 340.

Galt, J. (1830). *The Life of Lord Byron*. Henry Colburn and Richard Bentley.

Ghiurău, D., & Popescu, D. E. (2025). Distinguishing Reality from AI: Approaches for Detecting Synthetic Content. *Computers, 14*(1), 1. DOI: 10.3390/computers14010001

Ginsburg, J. C. (2002). The concept of authorship in comparative copyright law. *De Paul Law Review, 52*, 1063.

Griffiths, J., Synodinou, T., & Xalabarder, R. (2022). *Commentary by the European Copyright Society on selected aspects of the implementation of Articles 3 to 7 of Directive (EU) 2019/790 on copyright in the digital single market*. Study by the European Copyright Society.

Guadamuz, A. (2024). A scanner darkly: Copyright liability and exceptions in artificial intelligence inputs and outputs. *GRUR International, 73*(2), 111–127. DOI: 10.1093/grurint/ikad140

Hardman, B., & Housel, J. (2023). A Sui Generis Approach to the Protection of AI-Generated Works: Balancing Innovation and Authorship. Available at *SSRN* 4557004. DOI: 10.2139/ssrn.4557004

Hilde, T. C. (2000). Intelligence, accident, and art as a practice. *Transactions of the Charles S. Peirce Society, 36*(4), 549–561.

Hugenholtz, P. (2012). Harmonisation or unification of European union copyright law. *Monash University Law Review. Monash University. Faculty of Law, 38*(1), 4–16.

Hugenholtz, P. B., & Quintais, J. P. (2021). Copyright and artificial creation: does EU copyright law protect AI-assisted output? *IIC - International Review of Intellectual Property and Competition Law*, 52(9), 1190–1216. DOI: 10.1007/s40319-021-01115-0

Infopaq International A/S v Danske Dagblades Forening. (2009). Court of Justice of the European Union, C-5/08, 16 July 2009, ECLI: EU:C:2009:465.

Jones, R. H. (1990). The myth of the idea/expression dichotomy in copyright law. *Pace Law Review, 10*(3), 551. DOI: 10.58948/2331-3528.1475

Judge, E. F., & Gervais, D. J. (2009). Of silos and constellations: comparing notions of originality in copyright law. In *Intellectual property protection of fact-based works*. Edward Elgar Publishing. DOI: 10.4337/9781849801898.00011

Keller, P. (2023). Protecting creatives or impeding progress? Machine learning and the EU copyright framework. Kluwer Copyright Blog. https://copyrightblog.kluweriplaw.com/2023/02/20/protecting-creatives-or-impeding-progress-machine-learning-and-the-eu-copyright-framework/

Kelley v. Chicago Park District. (2011). United States Court of Appeals for the Seventh Circuit, 635 F.3d 290.

Kempas, T., Allgayer, U., Byer, D., Garhart, N., Genovese, L. A., Kliska, N., Lovrics, C., & Mansour, D. (2023). Copyrights and neighboring rights in outputs made by or made by means of AI systems. INTA Copyright Committee, AI and 3D Sub-Committee. https://www.inta.org/wp-content/uploads/public-files/advocacy/committee-reports/20230724_Copyrights-and-Neighboring-Rights-of-Outputs-by-AI-Systems.pdf

Leistner, M. (2014). Structural aspects of secondary (provider) liability in Europe. *Journal of Intellectual Property Law & Practice*, *9*(1), 75–90. DOI: 10.1093/jiplp/jpt213

Like Company. (2025). Court of Justice of the European Union, C-250/25, registered on 3 April 2025, pending.

Margoni, T., & Kretschmer, M. (2022). A deeper look into the EU text and data mining exceptions: Harmonisation, data ownership, and the future of technology. *GRUR International, 71*(8), 685–701. DOI: 10.1093/grurint/ikac054

Marr, B. (2023). Is Generative AI Stealing from Artists? *Forbes*.

Media, G. S. (2016). Court of Justice of the European Union, C-160/15, 8 September 2016. *ECLI:EU, C*, 644.

Monitor, P. (2023). *OpenAI trains its GPT model using pirated e-books, contends authors' lawsuit*. Pirate Monitor Website.

Naruto v. Slater. (2018). United States Court of Appeals for the Ninth Circuit, 888 F.3d 418.

OECD. (2025). Intellectual Property Issues in Artificial Intelligence Trained on Scraped Data. OECD Artificial Intelligence Papers, No. 33.

Open, A. I. (2024). ChatGPT Shared Links FAQ. OpenAI Website. https://help.openai.com/en/articles/7925741-chatgpt-shared-links-faq

Parra Pennefather, P. (2023). The Art of the Prompt. In Creative Prototyping with Generative AI: Augmenting Creative Workflows with Generative AI (pp. 197–246). Apress. DOI: 10.1007/978-1-4842-9579-3_8

Pennington, A. (2019, September 16). Andy Serkis rallies for digital performer rights. Screen Daily. https://www.screendaily.com/news/andy-serkis-rallies-for-digital-performer-rights/5142919.article

Phil Collins v Imtrat Handelsgesellschaft mbH and Patricia Im- und Export Verwaltungsgesellschaft mbH and Leif Emanuel Kraul v EMI Electrola GmbH. (1993). Court of Justice of the European Union, C-92/92 and C-326/92, 20 October 1993, ECLI:EU:C:1993:847.

Quintais, J. P. (2023). Generative AI, copyright and the AI Act. Kluwer Copyright Blog. https://copyrightblog.kluweriplaw.com/2023/05/09/generative-ai-copyright-and-the-ai-act/

Regulation (EU) 2022/2065 of the European Parliament and of the Council of 19 October 2022 on a Single Market For Digital Services and amending Directive 2000/31/EC (Digital Services Act). (2022). ELI: https://data.europa.eu/eli/reg/2022/2065/oj

Regulation (EU) 2024/1689 of the European Parliament and of the Council of 13 June 2024 laying down harmonised rules on artificial intelligence and amending Regulations (EC) No 300/2008, (EU) No 167/2013, (EU) No 168/2013, (EU) 2018/858, (EU) 2018/1139 and (EU) 2019/2144 and Directives 2014/90/EU, (EU) 2016/797 and (EU) 2020/1828 (Artificial Intelligence Act). (2024). ELI: https://data.europa.eu/eli/reg/2024/1689/oj

Riccardo Pagani v. Leo Burnett Company S.r.l. (2015). Ordinary Court of Turin, 32855/2014, 31 March 2015.

Rimmer, M. (2002). A creature of statute: Copyright law and legal formalism. *Entertainment Law Review*, *13*(2), 31–38.

Rosati, E. (2019). Copyright as an obstacle or an enabler? A European perspective on text and data mining and its role in the development of AI creativity. *Asia Pacific Law Review*, *27*(2), 198–217. DOI: 10.1080/10192557.2019.1705525

Rosati, E. (2024). Is text and data mining synonymous with AI training? *Journal of Intellectual Property Law & Practice*, *19*(12), 851–852. DOI: 10.1093/jiplp/jpae092

Rosen, A. (1992). Reconsidering the idea/expression dichotomy. *University of British Columbia Law Review*, *26*, 263.

Samuels, E. (1988). The idea-expression dichotomy in copyright law. *Tennessee Law Review*, *56*, 321.

Senftleben, M. (2023). Generative AI and Author Remuneration. IIC - International Review of Intellectual Property and Competition Law, 54, 1535–1560. DOI: 10.1007/s40319-023-01399-4

Stephen Thaler vs Shira Perlmutter. (2025). US Court of Appeals (District of Columbia Circuit), No. 23-5233, 18 March 2025.

Strowel, A., & Ducato, R. (2021). Artificial intelligence and text and data mining: a copyright carol. In *The Routledge handbook of EU copyright law* (pp. 299–316). Routledge.

Technische Universität Darmstadt v. Eugen Ulmer KG. (2014). Court of Justice of the European Union, C-117/13, 11 September 2014, ECLI:EU:C:2014:2196.

Thomas, J. M. (1990). Willful Copyright Infringement: In Search of a Standard. *Washington Law Review (Seattle, Wash.)*, *65*, 903.

Urantia Foundation v. Maaherra. (1995). United States District Court for the District of Arizona, 895 F. Supp. 1347.

Vadlapati, P. (2023). Does Seed Matter? Investigating the Effect of Random Seeds on LLM Accuracy. [IJSAT]. *International Journal on Science and Technology*, *14*(3).

Various class action lawsuits. (2023). [Multiple pending cases including Author Guild v. OpenAI; Getty Images v. Stability AI; Sarah Andersen et al. v. Stability AI et al.]

Wang, Y., & Zhang, J. (2024, February 2). Beijing Internet Court grants copyright to AI-generated image for the first time. Kluwer Copyright Blog. https://copyrightblog.kluweriplaw.com/2024/02/02/beijing-internet-court-grants-copyright-to-ai-generated-image-for-the-first-time

Waterloo News. (2024). *Can you tell AI-generated people from real ones?* Waterloo News.

Chapter 3
Moral Rights and AI Creations:
The Future of Attribution and Integrity in Copyright Law

Anuttama Ghose
https://orcid.org/0000-0002-7210-4074
School of Law, Dr. Vishwanath Karad MIT-World Peace University, Pune, India

SM Aamir Ali
https://orcid.org/0000-0002-8686-0217
Symbiosis Law School, Symbiosis International University, Pune, India

Pallav Pallav
https://orcid.org/0009-0005-1753-9891
The West Bengal National University of Juridical Sciences, India

ABSTRACT

This study examines the intricate implications of artificial intelligence (AI) on copyright law, focusing on moral rights and the future of authorship and attribution. As AI-driven technologies improve in producing high-quality art akin to human creations, conventional notions of ownership, authenticity, and creative intent are challenged. AI-generated art, such as

DOI: 10.4018/979-8-3373-5452-1.ch003

pieces emulating the style of Studio Ghibli, prompts significant enquiries on originality and perception. The legal frameworks in numerous nations remain insufficient to address the distinctive challenges posed by non-human creations, particularly with moral rights, which pertain to personal values that transcend financial gain. The study argues that AI disrupts traditional concepts of authorship, highlighting the need for sophisticated copyright laws and policies that preserve human values and protect the moral rights of creators. This study investigates the intersection of AI, creativity, and copyright, highlighting the urgent requirement for novel legal frameworks in light of AI's increasing influence.

1. INTRODUCTION

Artificial intelligence (AI) is frequently regarded as a disruptive technology. The implications of this technology are not limited to the industrial sector; they also extend to various artistic disciplines, such as the creation of music or works of art (Miernicki & Ng, 2021). The swift advancement of AI technology has resulted in substantial changes in various industries, including art and creative endeavours. At present, AI has the capacity to generate high-quality works that closely resemble those created by humans. Nevertheless, ownership rights remain ambiguous despite these advancements, as current copyright laws do not explicitly grant copyright protection to works that are not the product of human creators (Miernicki & Ng, 2021). With the advent of systems like ChatGPT, Bard, Mi journey, Stable Diffusion, MuseNet, and Make-A-Video, even those without a technical background may now create material in a wide variety of formats, from text and images to video and audio, computer code, and more, sometimes with only a few words as input (Choudhary & Ali, 2023; Ghose & Ali, 2023). Notably, the outputs are becoming more and more similar to human-created works (Gaffar & Albarashdi, 2025). These technologies are becoming more accessible, increasing the likelihood that computer-generated material will be widely used in society. These factors exacerbate the urgency of the discourse regarding subjects like intellectual property, authenticity, and authorship (Gaffar & Albarashdi, 2025).

Studio Ghibli, a renowned Japanese animation studio, is renowned for its emotional storylines, intricate and beautiful hand-drawn animation, and culturally grounded narratives. One of the most intriguing applications of AI today is creating visual art that resembles the studio's unique creative aesthetic (Mathur & Gupta, 2024). The technical accuracy and charming artistry of AI-generated Ghibli-style art have captivated the imaginations and interests of many individuals, resulting in its increasing popularity. Nevertheless, the use of AI-Ghibli art is also provoking significant debates about artistic intention, authenticity, and originality (Agarwal, 2024). With a particular emphasis on the nature of quality, emotion, and authenticity, this research will investigate audience satisfaction and perception in these activities. We are interested in determining the extent to which the comparison of human-generated Ghibli art and AI-Ghibli style art will influence the public's interest in AI-Ghibli art as a legitimate creative force. This apparently harmless internet trend exposed complex controversies and gaps in our legal systems, from copyright issues to privacy rights. This demonstrates that our modern world isn't ready to deal with the media deluge that Generative AI threatens to unleash (Pangotra, 2025). However, the copyright laws in most nations cannot safeguard creative works that incorporate AI technology or computer-generated content (Ali et al., 2024). They fail to deal with the complex problems associated with AI-generated works and include creative material solely produced by computer algorithms or programs (Kumar, 2025). Considering this subject, it is important to note that there has not been nearly as much discussion over the connection between AI and copyright liability for machine-generated works or moral rights. A moral right's justification starkly contrasts with an economic right's (Gaffar & Albarashdi, 2025). The former protects the creator's private interests, whereas the latter protects the profit.

In order to establish the context, this article delineates the overview of conflicting domestic and international copyright laws and the safeguarding of moral rights under these laws. Based on this premise, the paper explores specific concerns regarding AI-generated content and moral rights, specifically whether AI, its creators, or consumers should be considered the legitimate proprietors of moral rights. In addition, this article explores moral rights issues by analysing how Studio Ghibli's peaceful ethos is employed to generate imagery that conflicts with the author's original objective. This research concludes by exploring future remedies, such as related rights and other forms of attribution rights.

2. THE MORAL RIGHTS FRAMEWORK IN COPYRIGHT LAW: JURISPRUDENTIAL JUSTIFICATIONS AND GLOBAL NORMS

In copyright law, "moral rights" describe the author's non-financial claims to his work (Darby, 2021). The author retains ownership of any commercial rights, such as the right to adapt, translate, publish, etc., until he assigns or licenses them. However, until the copyright expires, even after the creator dies, his moral right remains inviolate, regardless of his pecuniary rights (Jain, 2020). The concept of moral rights was previously called "*Droit Moral*" in French law (Jain, 2020). Certain intellectual property rights, such as the freedom to reveal, the ability to edit or remove works that have been made public, the right to be acknowledged, and the right to respect the work, which is occasionally translated as the right to integrity, have been recognised by courts in Germany and France (Jain, 2020). The American moral rights legislation was founded on two schools of thought, instrumentalist and natural law. According to natural law theory, the author is the legitimate owner of his work, and no one else can misappropriate it and omit the author's name (Sundara Rajan, 2025). According to instrumentalists, the objective of knowledge transmission must be achieved because the state grants the author intellectual property rights. Therefore, the author cannot prevent others from exploiting his work by appropriating his ideas and information. The European intellectual property law system's idea of moral rights was also shaped by the philosophers Kant and Hegel, who said that someone should not be able to tell someone else how to use their work just because they own it (Priya, 2008). They proposed that an author's work exemplifies their expertise, achievements, knowledge, and attributes (Priya, 2008). This means that the author can only partially give up certain "inalienable rights," not all.

The legal basis for moral rights in copyright law is deeply rooted in the ideas that emphasise the inherent and unbreakable bond between the creator and their work (Priya, 2008). Understanding Hegel's personality theory in this context is essential, as it asserts that the work created reflects the individual's dignity, individualism, and personality. From this viewpoint, the author or creator amalgamates their unique intellect and spirit to transmute their creation into an extension of their identity (Priya, 2008). Tampering with the integrity of their work through distortion, replication, or misattribution can be construed as a harm to the interior life and personal autonomy of authors, in addition to an economic harm (Simon, 2025). The moral rights framework also emphasises the significance of human dignity, based on France and Germany's civil law traditions. It recognises the creator's inherent right to govern and maintain the integrity of their work, which is linked to their human essence, rather than merely emphasising commercial interests (Simon, 2025). This idea says that creative work should be protected by law, respected, and made better by culture. Article 6 bis of the Berne Convention and Section 57 of the Indian Copyright Act, 1957, both recognise this right and stress the importance of moral rights. The Berne Convention for the Protection of Literary and Artistic Works (Paris Text 1971), under Article 6bis (1) mentions as below:

> *"Independently of the author's economic rights, and even after the transfer of the said rights, the author shall have the right to claim authorship of the work and to object to any distortion, mutilation or other modification of, or other derogatory action in relation to, the said work, which would be prejudicial to his honor or reputation."*

The 1928 modification of the Berne Convention was the first definitive measure to acknowledge and embrace moral rights, mandating contracting governments to safeguard the author's rights of attribution and integrity (Yu, 2014). Article 6bis required all contracting parties to safeguard moral rights within their respective domestic legal systems, leaving the establishment of compliance methods to the state's discretion. Consequently, several governments provide these rights to owners not via copyright law, but via tort or contract law (Yu, 2014). Even though the TRIPS agreement later mandated that the WTO state parties to the Berne Convention for the Protection of Literary and Artistic Works adhere to its substantive provisions, it was amended to exclude Article 6bis from its scope (Agarwal & Ojha, 2017). Article 9.1 stipulates that members are not entitled to any rights or obligations under Article 6bis. Consequently, members are unable to enforce Moral Rights through the WTO dispute settlement mechanism. Even though the United States and the United Kingdom have protected moral rights in their domestic legal systems, the exclusion of Article 6bis is unexpected due to its limited commercial significance (Killan, 2003). This is because TRIPS is a much more persuasive instrument than the Berne Convention, providing an express dispute settlement mechanism under the World Trade Organisation (Agarwal & Ojha, 2017). Further cultural rights, including the right to participate in cultural life in general and the material and moral rights of writers with regard to their works, are proclaimed in Article 27 of the 1948 Universal Declaration of Human Rights (Charlesworth, 2008). It states that:

> *"Everyone has the right to participate freely in the cultural life of the community, enjoy the arts, and share in scientific advancement and its benefits. Everyone has the right to protect the moral and material interests resulting from any scientific, literary or artistic production of which he is the author."*

This implies that all individuals are entitled to participate in any cultural activities. This article exemplifies a fundamental aim and concept of the United Nations, as stated in Article 1(3) of the United Nations Charter (Fischman Afori, 2004). In the second paragraph's exegesis, there are two perspectives on IP. From a single perspective, this right is comparable to a human right.

Recent technological advancements have jeopardised the very existence of the copyright law in the information-oriented society. Nevertheless, copyright law has adapted to the technical innovation by extending copyright principles to protect computer software and other comparable technologies. This allows copyright principles to experience a resurrected prestige in the world of information technology. In contradiction, moral rights have been overlooked, primarily due to their inability to address the digital revolution's challenges effectively.

3. AI AND THE DISRUPTION OF TRADITIONAL AUTHORSHIP: CREATIVE IDENTITY AND ITS DILUTION IN SYNTHETIC OUTPUTS

Copyright law has assumed a distinctive function in balancing the relationship between technology and society in the digital era. Despite the copyright framework's limitations, this has transpired. It is not well-suited to this position and has reportedly fallen short in important respects, such as protecting fundamental societal ideals like social justice and human rights and striking a fair balance between the interests of writers, right holders, and the general public (Ali & Ghose, 2024). Also, it has not assisted creatives and innovators with good social work. Copyright law has evolved to meet the challenges posed by the interplay between technology and society in the modern digital era (Marrone et al., 2024). This has taken place despite the limitations imposed by the copyright structure (Li et al., 2025). It isn't cut out for this role. It has reportedly fallen short in important respects, such as standing up for basic societal principles like social justice and human rights and striking a fair balance between the needs of writers, right holders, and the general public (Ghose et al., 2025).

Furthermore, it has failed to encourage innovation and creativity in all forms of beneficial social activity. As a result, moral rights may be more crucial than before when discussing AI. Restoring credibility in this altered setting is possible via moral rights. Another important thing they can do is help us remember how valuable human creativity is when it's at its weakest (Ghose et al., 2024).

AI fundamentally challenges human comprehension of authorship. Artificial intelligence has primarily caused unease due to its ability to imitate human creativity, particularly in writing and picture production (Ghose et al., 2024). The worth of human creativity has been doubted in a world where artificial intelligence is rapidly expanding and may one day supersede humans in many fields. Also, remember that various facets of human endeavours include creativity; producing intellectual, artistic, or creative works is only one example of the pinnacle of human civilisation. This means that many human activities and ways of life could be in jeopardy due to the development of AI. Therefore, it is crucial to guarantee that our approach to regulating AI through copyright law and policy is consistent with the overarching objective of reinforcing human values in the AI environment. It may be argued that copyright is in a special position to spearhead this movement. At its core, copyright is concerned with the creative process (Doshi & Hauser, 2024). Its historical birth was in reaction to dangers, most notably censorship, that were, in their respective times, existential dangers to human welfare, similar to how AI may be now. The focus on authorship in copyright laws is a crucial component of the AI environment. Importantly, the foundation of effective regulation may be the writers' unalienable moral rights, commonly called authorship rights (Marrone et al., 2024). Moral rights offer an additional, fascinating possibility beyond the traditional constraints of copyright law; they might provide direction for regulating artificial intelligence.

AI is now more than just a tool; it's a way for people to work together creatively, develop new ideas, and be completely independent. Scholars assert that this technological transformation reconstitutes creativity from solitary to collaborative achievements (Ivcevic & Grandinetti, 2024). AI doesn't have feelings or goals but integrates and predicts things, so it often doesn't seem like a real person. This situation has led to the creation of the word "scriptor," which comes from the work of Roland Barthes (1977). Barthes (1977) asserts that the conventional concept of an author is replaced by a force that produces writings from pre-existing expressions. In an AI-driven scenario, the distinction between human and machine authorship often leads to the erosion of the distinctive creative contributions that were formerly only attributed to human artists.

Because of this, AI-generated art shows how creative outputs are becoming more identical and less diverse. The increasing usage of AI-generated ideas in storytelling, art, and innovations makes human expression and creativity less distinctive (Marrone et al., 2024). Many research investigations have shown this to be true (Militsyna, 2023). These activities create a cultural atmosphere where generic creative production takes the place of new and unique experiences. This loss of attribution creates questions concerning moral rights, especially regarding honesty and giving credit where credit is due. Because it's hard to take credit for synthetic creations, it's hard to say how important art and artists are morally and reputationally (Doshi & Hauser, 2024). These conditions undermine the personal relationship between writers and their creation and reduce its societal meaning. So, AI is changing the idea of authorship and making the creative process less personal and more plural.

4. THE CASE OF STUDIO GHIBLI: A STYLISED INFRINGEMENT?

4.1 Background of the Case

Since we were little, we have been enchanted by Studio Ghibli's elaborate backdrops. The hand-drawn animation and meticulously painted stills from their films transport us to fantastical realms and provide inspiration for animators and artists (Arora, 2025). Compared to the faster-paced anime that had ruled the Japanese animation industry from the start, the hand-drawn stills of beautiful landscapes were distinctive at the time. People using ChatGPT4o model to create Ghibli styled art of themselves, famous people, or historical events have been on the rise recently, which is intriguing. Using the AI chatbot, users from around the globe and all over social media have been applying the signature style of the renowned Japanese animator Hayao Miyazaki to their photographs. In addition to increasing the art form's popularity, this instalment is calling into question the ethical principles underlying creative expression, the degree to which it requires invention and copyright violation. At the heart of the ongoing debates surrounding this phenomenon is whether this technique of creating Ghibli-style art is a homage to its esteemed authors or a classic case of creative exploitation (Pangotra, 2025).

Microsoft, OpenAI (ChatGPT's manufacturer), and Anthropic are the many media and entertainment corporations that have sued generative AI software developers. Claims of copyright infringement are at the heart of several litigations. Typically, the complaints state that AI firms unlawfully use copyrighted media information to train different types of large language models (LLMs). One such lawsuit against ChatGPT has started in the New York Times (Reed, 2024). US authors George RR Martin and John Grisham have also sued OpenAI, the proprietor of ChatGPT, alleging that their copyright was used without permission during the system training (Jordan, 2023). In the instance of Ghibli Art, the AI technologies produce Ghibli aesthetics for users' photographs without explicitly replicating the inventions from Ghibli Studio used in their films. This raises pertinent questions regarding the originality of such works and whether they constitute unauthorised derivatives. While AI-generated art does not directly replicate specific scenes from Ghibli, it undeniably mirrors its unique visual essence.

4.2 Applicability of Fair Use Doctrine

Furthermore, the doctrine of fair use within copyright law permits the reproduction of protected works under specific conditions, including educational purposes, critical analysis, parody, and transformative use, which may be debatable in the present case (Stim 2013). A work is deemed "transformative" when it contributes novel elements to the original, serving an additional purpose or exhibiting a distinct character, rather than simply replacing the original work. There has to be a clear difference between the original and the freshly produced work in terms of substance (Obhan, 2025). The art created by AI in the style of Ghibli appears to lack a clear intent, primarily relying on replicating patterns derived from its training data. This produces almost identical images that invite issues regarding whether the process is transforming or only replicating already-existing works (Bonfiglio, 2025).

The concept of the Idea Expression dichotomy states that copyright protects the act of expressing an idea rather than the idea itself. This implies that the copyright protection only applies to the finished product, not the process or style that went into making it. Because copyright protection would stifle creativity and invention, courts worldwide have repeatedly determined that it does not apply to methods, procedures, or aesthetic approaches. However, copyright infringement may occur if an AI-generated work closely mimics original copyrighted features, including particular characters, melodies, or unique visual patterns (HT News Desk, 2024). In the absence of explicit copyright infringement, AI that mimics a particular style is not infringing. However, legal action may be taken, particularly in commercial contexts, against AI-generated works that significantly imitate copyrighted works by artists. In fact, the Copyright Act of Japan, specifically Article 30-4, allows for a wide variety of uses of copyrighted works in the training of artificial intelligence models in Japan (Copyright Research and Information Centre, 2023). The article "*General Understanding on AI and Copyright in Japan*" was released by the Japanese Agency for Cultural Affairs in 2024 (Japan Copyright Office, 2024). The paper laid forth the principles of when copyright rules are applicable and when data may be used for AI without regard to copyrights.

4.3 The Moral Right Dilemma Surrounding Ghibli Art

Attribution rights allow artists to assert authorship of their work, prevent others from using the artist's name on work they did not create, and petition to remove their name from a work. Typically, artists endeavour to preserve their reputation by removing their name. The issue is that these artworks' style and specific visual design elements are so iconic that the AI outputs were referred to as "Ghiblified" in online discourse, even though the names of Miyazaki or Studio Ghibli are not associated with them (Ahmed, 2025). However, copyright law does not consider generic styles as a form of attribution. Consequently, artists like Miyazaki cannot attempt to eliminate an iconic "style" from another artist's AI-generated image. Conversely, integrity rights enable creators to safeguard their work against deliberate manipulation that might damage their "honour" or reputation. There may be a right to prevent a work's deliberate or severely negligent destruction if it has "recognised stature." An acknowledged work of stature is one that "has been acknowledged as such by a relevant community" due to its high quality, prestige, or calibre (*Castillo v. G&M Realty L.P.*, 2020). Courts are inclined to recognise works of visual art with "recognised stature" if they have the same level of renown and esteem as Studio Ghibli films (Ahmed, 2025). There is still no clear answer to whether AI outputs constitute distortion, mutilation, or modification. The actual destruction of tangible works of art, such as the painting over of iconic murals, has usually been the focus of case law. The courts may find it challenging to draw parallels between the destruction of a physical work of art and the deconstruction and reformulation of fragments of a visual piece because AI produces synchronised patterns of information based on massive quantities of visual input.

To grasp the concept of moral rights in this setting, one must consider the argument over whether or not training a model on visual artwork by digitally destroying and reassembling its recognisable parts constitutes an alteration of the source material. Is it possible for AI to only serve as a "medium" for changes detrimental to the artist's honour and reputation, going against Miyazaki's beliefs of making beautiful and human work? Also, if an AI-generated product uses the famous images to promote bad or violent messages, would it be considered mutilation? The solutions to these problems are vague and desperately need further examination of existing laws. Central to copyright law is the idea of balancing author protection and the public's access to important works of art.

4.4 Concerns about Creative Freedom and Personal Privacy

Open, inclusive, and pluralistic societies mostly depend on creativity—that is, the capacity of one to produce fresh and original material by means of imagination or invention. Important moral conundrums surround the ability of artificial intelligence to replicate the works of great artists like Miyazaki, as well as the clear technical difficulties (Kumar & Kumar, 2025). Some members of the creative community claim that although AI-powered tools have certain advantages, these instruments sometimes include uncredited or unlicensed content. Artificial intelligence uses artists' painstaking efforts to develop their styles. One should also consider the privacy issues related to Ghibli art and artificial intelligence use. The spread of images via artificial intelligence usually results in a surrender of control over private images, which can lead to a range of major consequences, including harassment, slander, and the commodification of personal data. The implications for society and individuals are far-reaching, and the impact of providing intimate photos and data to AI companies like OpenAI is a significant concern. Users voluntarily disclose sensitive information that can be utilised to train AI models when they upload their photos and data to AI platforms. This encompasses facial data, which can be employed to identify individuals, as well as other personal information that can be used to develop comprehensive user profiles (Kumar & Kumar, 2025).

A further worry about sharing private images and data with AI businesses is the possibility of constant monitoring and spying (Behera & Singh, 2024). Unbeknownst to consumers, AI systems may build comprehensive profiles of their actions and habits from the data they provide. As a result, people may find themselves susceptible to more surveillance, including targeted advertising, which may erode their sense of privacy. Discrimination, profiling, and other types of social control are just a few of the undesirable outcomes that might result from using AI algorithms to examine user data. A major issue with AI training is the lack of transparency, making it hard for consumers to know what happens to their data and how it is utilised (Sætra, 2022). It might be challenging for consumers to comprehend the use of their data by AI businesses like OpenAI because of the complicated algorithms and machine learning models that are employed to analyse user data. Bias, prejudice, and other types of social control are among the many unforeseen outcomes that might result from using AI algorithms to evaluate user input. To lessen the impact of these dangers, AI firms like OpenAI must make data gathering and usage open and accountable. Among these measures is the implementation of strong protections to avoid data abuse and the provision of clear and comprehensive information on the usage of user data (Bjørlo, 2024). On top of that, AI businesses should put an emphasis on user autonomy and permission, giving consumers the power to decide how their data is shared and utilised. Establishing suitable laws controlling the developments in artificial intelligence is essential to prevent unethical uses that usually compromise artistic freedom and efforts, to preserve the basic character of artistry and creativity (Almahfali et al., 2024).

5. COMPARATIVE LEGAL APPROACHES TO AI AND MORAL RIGHTS: LIMITATIONS IN ADDRESSING AI-CREATED DERIVATIVES

The tensions and voids in the copyright laws of various countries across the globe have been exposed by the interference of AI in the production of creative work, particularly as we discussed in the case of Studio Ghibli. To conduct a more comprehensive analysis of the debate regarding AI's creativity and the moral rights associated with these synthetic outputs, we will first attempt to comprehend the legislative provisions, judicial pronouncements, and enforcement mechanisms that are currently in place in India, the EU, the United States, and Japan. Section 57 of the Indian Copyright Act, 1957, explicitly addresses moral rights, which enable human creators to assert authorship and prevent their work from being distorted. It states:

> *"Independently of the author's copyright and even after the assignment, either wholly or partially of the said copyright, the author of a work shall have the right (a)to claim authorship of the work; and (b) to restrain or claim damages in respect of any distortion, mutilation, modification or other act in relation to the said work if such distortion, mutilation, modification or other act would be prejudicial to his honour or reputation" (Section 57, Indian Copyright Act, 1957)*

This principle is derived from Article 6 bis of the Berne Convention, which posits that moral rights are profoundly personal and non-transferable, as evidenced in the case of *Amarnath Sehgal v. Union of India* (2005), where the court emphasised on highlighted the importance of an artist's moral rights, specifically the right to integrity of the work and the right to prevent distortion, mutilation, or modification of their artistic creations. As long as a natural person commits the infringing conduct, this Act safeguards original human authors from the use of their work in any derogatory or misattribution form (Hutson, 2024). Therefore, this Act does not address the infringement of the AI's conduct. In the context of Ghibli Art, asserting that moral rights have been violated or that creative integrity has been compromised when AI serves as the sole creator, without human input, is challenging.

In the same vein, the copyright framework of the European Union, as interpreted and directed by the Court of Justice of the European Union in the cases of *Cofemel v G-Star Raw* (2019) and *Football Dataco Ltd v. Yahoo UK Ltd.* (2012), has established that copyrightable work is a reflection of the author's intellectual creations. The jurisprudential focus of this concept of creativity is frequently linked to the expression of one's personality, which is indicative of the moral rights doctrine that has been woven into the Berne Convention standards (Gaffar & Albarashdi, 2025). The standard of originality must be met to assert copyright and moral rights through these pronouncements. Suppose the reputation or integrity of the original creators is harmed by AI-generated Ghibli-styled images that are a copy of their idea. In that case, it is challenging to establish liability, as the perpetrator is a non-human entity.

Conversely, the US Copyright Act's Title 17 Section 106 prioritises economic rights over moral rights, as evidenced by legislation such as the Visual Artist Rights Act of 1990. It is challenging to establish violations in the context of Ghibli works that have been unauthorisedly adapted or reproduced in the United States in the absence of a more comprehensive approach to moral rights. The Ghibli phenomenon has made people think about more than just the legal ramifications of copyright infringement; it has also made them consider the moral consequences of capitalising on artists' work even when it goes against their creative goals. Regrettably, there is no contemporary legal mechanism that allows us to tackle such moral concerns. Authors have some moral rights, which are non-economic rights, as outlined in the Visual Artists Rights Act (VARA). The international copyright convention, the Berne Convention, mandates that nations provide writers with the fundamental rights of attribution and integrity. VARA was enacted to comply with this treaty. However, American moral rights are much more restricted than those of their European counterparts. For example, American "visual works" writers are the only ones with basic attribution and integrity rights, which only exist as long as the creator does. Artworks intended for display were strictly restricted to one-of-a-kind or limited-edition paintings, drawings, prints, sculptures, and photos. The film industry successfully lobbied to have moral rights safeguards removed from films. Moral rights as they stand would likely not be enough to safeguard against the emerging boundaries of AI outputs, even if Miyazaki's artwork could be considered a "visual work" eligible for VARA safeguards.

Artists have the right to be recognised as the original creators of their work, to have their names removed from works that do not include their work, and to prohibit others from doing the same. Artists often try to keep their reputations intact by removing their identity. The problem is that people on the internet started calling the AI-generated artworks "Ghiblified" even though they didn't create them or were affiliated with Studio Ghibli or Miyazaki. This is because the style and certain aspects of the visual design are so iconic. According to the US Copyright Regime, artists such as Miyazaki are not allowed to try to take away another's famous "style" from their AI-generated picture since broad styles do not constitute credit under copyright law. However, integrity rights enable creators to safeguard their work against deliberate manipulation that might damage their "honour" or reputation. There may be a right to prevent a work's deliberate or severely negligent destruction if it has "recognised stature." An acknowledged work of stature is one that "has been acknowledged as such by a relevant community" due to its high quality, prestige, or calibre. U.S. courts are inclined to recognise works of visual art with "recognised stature" if they have the same level of renown and esteem as Studio Ghibli films (*Castillo v. G&M Realty* L.P., 2020). There is still no clear answer to whether AI outputs constitute "distortion, mutilation, or modification." The actual destruction of tangible works of art, such as the painting over of iconic murals, has usually been the focus of case law. The courts may find it challenging to draw parallels between the destruction of a physical work of art and the deconstruction and reformulation of fragments of a visual piece because AI produces synchronised patterns of information based on massive quantities of visual input (Pasetti et al., 2025).

The Copyright Act of Japan, 1970, however, is rather unique. The widespread use of copyrighted works for information analysis, which commercial companies use to train artificial intelligence models, is permitted under Article 30-4.

Article 30-4 does not apply if a use is "*for enjoyment of the thoughts or sentiments expressed in the copyrighted work*, including,

a) The collection of works for AI training to generate materials similar to copyrighted works within the collected works.

   b)The collection of works as input data to generative AI for implementation of retrieval augmented generation (RAG)" (Japan Copyright Office, 2024).

The notion that human beings are capable of possessing copyright and moral rights to the extent that they are subject to administrative standards and legal frameworks is upheld by Japanese legislation. As a result, the legislation makes it easier to legally use Ghibli graphics to train artificial intelligence and evaluate information accessible to the general public. A further point to consider is that under Japanese law, artificial intelligence outputs are not subject to copyright or moral rights unless human authorship is incorporated in the creative process.

6. POLICY IMPERATIVES FOR ETHICAL AI PLATFORM LIABILITY:

Whether ChatGPT and other AI platforms should be liable for copyright infringement is unsettled. General-purpose AI systems like ChatGPT must be transparent and comply with copyright requirements under the EU AI Act, the most famous AI regulation (Cordella & Gualdi, 2024). The Act's Article 53 states that to comply with EU copyright laws, model providers must disclose a thorough overview of the training data used and honour opt-outs from text and data mining exclusions. The conduct itself creates no framework for responsibility. Alternatively, the proposed AI Liability Directive might be utilised to prosecute copyright infringement claims, since it establishes a "rebuttable presumption of causality" for damage produced by AI systems. The development of generative AI has surpassed recommendation algorithms on the internet since 2022. There have been defamation cases using popular chatbots like ChatGPT that depend on user instructions to produce outputs. Irish DJ Dave Fanning was not the broadcaster on the issue. However, a news piece featuring him and the heading "Prominent Irish broadcaster faces trial over alleged sexual misconduct" appeared on Microsoft's MSN online page not long ago (Carswell, 2024). As it turned out, BNN Breaking, a news company, used an AI chatbot to promote a paraphrased version of an item from another news site on MSN (Hill & Hsu, 2024).

In the case of *Mark Walters v. OpenAI* (2024), a radio presenter sued OpenAI in 2023 in a U.S. lawsuit, claiming that ChatGPT had defamed him. In a further instance, in the case of *Jeffery Battle v. Microsoft Corporation* (2023), the plaintiff said that when he conducted a search using his name on Microsoft's Bing, the search engine produced an artificial intelligence

(AI) summary that combined information about him with details about a similar person who had previously admitted to seditious conspiracy. The allegations are comparable to those that have previously given rise to defences under Section 230 of the Communications Decency Act (CDA), 1934 of the USA, but that provision was not used. Courts will have to decide whether generative AI tool providers may be held responsible for material created by their systems in response to user input if the defence is used in future instances. Since their models are "transformative" and users are not directly exposed to copyrighted information during training, OpenAI has asserted its entitlement to protection under the fair use theory in the United States. Courts consider four elements when deciding whether usage is fair: the quantity utilised, the nature of the work, the purpose of use, and the market impact. In *Campbell v. Acuff-Rose Music* (1994), the court stressed that fair use hinges on transformation, defined as adding new language or meaning.

The advancement of AI-generated art, as evidenced by Ghibli-styled images, has revealed numerous legislative voids in technology, copyright, and moral rights. Core policy imperatives should be implemented to address this issue, as AI platforms operate by recombining extant creative essence. The liability of ethical AI platforms will be able to accomplish transparency in outputs and acknowledge the source used in training models. Additionally, a more robust licensing regime that delineates the mechanisms for disseminating art and metamorphosis through AI will create legal enforceability and fortify the copyright framework, emphasising protecting moral rights. These accountability structures will encompass a broader perspective that encompasses not only users, but also developers and platform proprietors, to facilitate the sharing of moral obligations and ethical standards among them. To prevent reputational damages or misattribution, policies that emphasise strict liability and fault-based policies must be implemented to ensure prompt redressal through takedowns, reparations, and redesigns. The artistic legacy of Studio Ghibli should be governed in a manner that requires the evaluation of training datasets and platform interference by an ethical commission and the obtaining of additional permission before any misappropriation. Therefore, it is imperative to establish ethical AI platform liability to guarantee that technology contributes to developing culture, creativity, and artistry, rather than diminishing them (Gaffar & Albarashdi, 2025).

7. CONCLUSION

Given the current laws and principles, AI-generated content should not be granted moral rights. Many people are talking about AI liability, which is separate from moral rights, even though there's much dispute about whether or not AI may have its legal personality and, by extension, moral rights. The moral rights that AI should or should not have are complex, even considering the arguments in favour of giving AI moral rights. It may be important to differentiate between many kinds of moral rights first: There are several possible explanations for the attribution right, but the right to integrity may have its origins in the author's private life. Although there are practical issues, such as determining if the work results from human creative efforts and related evidential concerns, there are also potential intermediate solutions, such as establishing contributorship rights. The idea that moral rights serve a greater public good is one school of thought that supports their recognition. After all, who better to protect than the original creators, who have a vested interest in seeing their work through to completion? By doing so, we can ensure that creative works remain intact and respected by society. If this kind of public service is necessary, then there may be a case for establishing legal safeguards to preserve AI-created works for the benefit of society. We prefer to save for this when we further investigate national laws that indefinitely guarantee moral rights.

Finally, the emphasis is again placed on Al's custody regarding copyright responsibility. If ownership of Al were to be transferred to the developer or business that developed it by the work-made-for-hire doctrine, the responsibility for any copyright infringement that may arise would be placed on the developer or company that created Al. This is because the employer has control over and a financial interest in Al. On the other hand, the customer is responsible for paying for copyright infringement if the code or product Al created becomes a consumer item and ownership of the product is transferred to the consumer. This is because the consumer has complete control over the constituents that Al employs in its output.

REFERENCES

Agarwal, D. (2024). Artificial intelligence and artistic imitation: A legal analysis of the Ghibli-style image debate. *IIPRD Blog*. https://www.iiprd.com/artificial-intelligence-and-artistic-imitation-a-legal-analysis-of-the-ghibli-style-image-debate/

Agarwal, N., & Ojha, V. (2017). Moral rights: International framework and Indian approach. *Christ University Law Journal*, *6*(1), 1–20. DOI: 10.12728/culj.10.1

Ahmed, K. (2025, April 4). The studio ghibli ai art backlash: How panic over generative ai misses the big picture. *Frontline*. https://frontline.thehindu.com/science-and-technology/ghibli-ai-art-generated-images-moral-panic-copyright/article69411983.ece

Ahmed, S. (2025, March 29). The Ghibli-fication dilemma: When AI meets artistic legacy. *Medium*. https://medium.com/@sahin.samia/the-ghibli-fication-dilemma-when-ai-meets-artistic-legacy-bfeb716bfc54

Ali, S. M., Ghose, A., Saurav, S., & Deshmukh, S. (2024). Creativity and innovation in the age of artificial intelligence: A copyright dilemma. [Journal of Law]. *Padjadjaran Jurnal Ilmu Hukum*, *11*(2), 164–184. DOI: 10.22304/pjih.v11n2.a1

Ali, S. M. A., & Ghose, A. (2024). Navigating copyright law in the age of AI: The complex relationship between generative AI and artistic expression. In Saka, E. (Ed.), *Understanding Generative AI in a Cultural Context: Artificial Myths and Human Realities* (pp. 359–382). IGI Global., DOI: 10.4018/979-8-3693-7235-7.ch014

Almahfali, M., Hewidy, N., & Von Der Hülst, M. (2024). Capitalising on freedom of expression for creativity: A case study of Dawit Isaak Library, malmö, Sweden. *Nordic Journal of Human Rights*, *42*(2), 177–194. DOI: 10.1080/18918131.2024.2301715

Arora, S. (2025, March 29). *What is Ghibli? A journey through art and storytelling*. Adda247. https://currentaffairs.adda247.com/what-is-ghibli-a-journey-through-art-and-storytelling/

Barthes, R. (1977). The death of the author. In *Image-Music-Text* (Heath, S., Trans.; pp. 142–148). Hill and Wang. (Original work published 1967)

Behera, A., & Singh, B. P. (2024). Safeguarding privacy in the digital era: Balancing rights, security, and innovation. *Chanakya Law Review, 5*(2), 57–71. https://cnlu.ac.in/storage/2025/05/Safeguarding-Privacy-In-The-Digital-Era-Balancing-Rights-Security-And-Innovation-by-Ms.-Adyasha-Behera-Mr.-Bhanu-Pratap-Singh.pdf

Bjørlo, L. V. (2024). Freedom from interference: Decisional privacy as a dimension of consumer privacy online. *AMS Review*, *14*(1–2), 12–36. DOI: 10.1007/s13162-024-00273-x

Bonfiglio, J. (2025, May 8). Ghibli, ghiblification, copyright and style. *Authors Alliance*. https://www.authorsalliance.org/2025/05/08/ghibli-ghiblification-copyright-and-style/

Carswell, S. (2024, January 15). RTÉ's Dave Fanning initiates defamation case after his photo appeared in article about sexual misconduct trial of different broadcaster. *The Irish Times*. https://www.irishtimes.com/crime-law/courts/2024/01/15/rtes-dave-fanning-initiates-defamation-case-after-his-photo-appeared-in-article-about-sexual-misconduct-trial-of-different-broadcaster/

Charlesworth, H. (2008). Universal Declaration of Human Rights (1948). *Oxford Public International Law*. https://opil.ouplaw.com/display/10.1093/law:epil/9780199231690/law-9780199231690-e887

Choudhary, V. & Ali, Aamir S. M. (2023). ChatGPT and Copyright Concerns. *Economic and Political Weekly*, *58*(16), 4–5.

Copyright Research and Information Center. (2023). *Copyright Act of Japan*. https://www.cric.or.jp/english/clj/cl2.html

Cordella, A., & Gualdi, F. (2024). Regulating generative AI: The limits of technology-neutral regulatory frameworks. Insights from Italy's intervention on ChatGPT. *Government Information Quarterly*, *41*(4), 101982. DOI: 10.1016/j.giq.2024.101982

Darby, H. C. (2021, November 23). AI-created art and the moral rights of authors. *Columbia Journal of Law & the Arts Bulletin Blog*. https://www.jtl.columbia.edu/bulletin-blog/ai-created-art-and-the-moral-rights-of-authors

Doshi, A. R., & Hauser, O. P. (2024). Generative AI enhances individual creativity but reduces the collective diversity of novel content. *Science Advances*, *10*(28), 1–9. DOI: 10.1126/sciadv.adn5290

Fischman Afori, O. (2004). Human rights and copyright: The introduction of natural law considerations into American copyright law. *Fordham Intellectual Property. Media & Entertainment Law Journal*, *14*(2), 497–565.

Gaffar, H., & Albarashdi, S. (2025). Copyright protection for AI-generated works: Exploring originality and ownership in a digital landscape. *Asian Journal of International Law*, *15*(1), 23–46. DOI: 10.1017/S2044251323000735

Ghose, A. & Ali, Aamir S. M. (2023). Amplifying Music with Artificial Intelligence. *Economic and Political Weekly*, *58*(17), 4–6.

Ghose, A., Ali, S. M. A., & Deshmukh, S. (2024). Navigating the legal and ethical framework for generative AI: Fostering responsible global governance. In Ara, A., & Ara, A. (Eds.), *Exploring the Ethical Implications of Generative AI* (pp. 168–184). IGI Global., DOI: 10.4018/979-8-3693-1565-1.ch010

Ghose, A., Ali, S. M. A., & Deshmukh, S. B. (2025). Creative paradigms, generative AI, and copyright law: Investigating the intersection of AI and artistry. In Bajraktari, H. (Ed.), (pp. 103–122). Advances in Electronic Government, Digital Divide, and Regional Development. IGI Global., DOI: 10.4018/979-8-3693-7205-0.ch006

Ghose, A., Ali, S. M. A., & Mishra, A. M. (2024). Artistic expressions, generative AI, and legal tapestry: Exploring the dynamics of copyright laws in the confluence of AI and artistic creation. In Hai-Jew, S. (Ed.), *Making Art With Generative AI Tools* (pp. 198–214). IGI Global., DOI: 10.4018/979-8-3693-1950-5.ch011

Hill, K., & Hsu, T. (2024, June 6). The rise and fall of BNN Breaking, an A.I.-generated news outlet. *The New York Times*. https://www.nytimes.com/2024/06/06/technology/bnn-breaking-ai-generated-news.html

HT News Desk. (2024, March 29). *Using ChatGPT's Ghibli-style photos violates copyright laws, experts explain*. Hindustan Times. https://www.hindustantimes.com/world-news/using-chatgpts-ghibli-style-photos-violates-copyright-laws-experts-explain-101743257416332.html

Hutson, J. (2024). The evolving role of copyright law in the age of AI-generated works. *Journal of Digital Technologies and Law*, *2*(4), 886–914. DOI: 10.21202/jdtl.2024.43

Ivcevic, Z., & Grandinetti, M. (2024). Artificial intelligence as a tool for creativity. *Journal of Creativity*, *34*(2), 100079. DOI: 10.1016/j.yjoc.2024.100079

Jain, S. (2020). Moral rights of author under copyright laws. SSRN *Electronic Journal*. https://doi.org/DOI: 10.2139/ssrn.3902409

Japan Copyright Office. (2024). *General understanding on AI and copyright in Japan*. Legal Subcommittee, Copyright Subdivision, Cultural Council. https://www.bunka.go.jp/english/policy/copyright/pdf/94055801_01.pdf

Jordan, J. (2023, September 20). George RR Martin and John Grisham among group of authors suing OpenAI. *The Guardian*. https://www.theguardian.com/books/2023/sep/20/authors-lawsuit-openai-george-rr-martin-john-grisham

Killan, M. (2003). A hollow victory for the common law? TRIPS and the moral rights exclusion. *John Marshall Review of Intellectual Property Law*, *2*(2), 321–366. https://repository.law.uic.edu/cgi/viewcontent.cgi?article=1034&context=ripl

Kumar, A. (2025). Satisfaction of AI for Ghibli-style art: A study on perception, acceptance, and ethical concerns. *International Journal for Research in Applied Science and Engineering Technology*, *13*(5), 6487–6491. DOI: 10.22214/ijraset.2025.71350

Kumar, A., & Kumar, N. (2025). Satisfaction of AI for Ghibli-style art: A study on perception, acceptance, and ethical concerns. *International Journal for Research in Applied Science and Engineering Technology*, *13*(5), 6487–6491. DOI: 10.22214/ijraset.2025.71350

Li, W., Song, R., Zhang, B., & Yu, K. (2025). AI creativity and legal protection for AI-generated works in posthuman societal scenarios. *Sustainable Futures : An Applied Journal of Technology, Environment and Society*, *9*, 100749. DOI: 10.1016/j.sftr.2025.100749

Marrone, R., Cropley, D., & Medeiros, K. (2024). How does narrow AI impact human creativity? *Creativity Research Journal*, •••, 1–11. DOI: 10.1080/10400419.2024.2378264

Mathur, A., & Gupta, V. (2024). Animating the line: Studio Ghibli, AI-generated art, and the crosscurrents of copyright and AI law. *Indian Journal of Law and Legal Research*, *7*(2), 8534–8542.

Miernicki, M., & Ng, I. (2021). Artificial intelligence and moral rights. *AI & Society*, *36*(1), 319–329. DOI: 10.1007/s00146-020-01027-6

Militsyna, K. (2023). Human creative contribution to AI-based output – one just can't get enough. *GRUR International*, *72*(10), 939–949. DOI: 10.1093/grurint/ikad075

Obhan, E. (2025, April 1). The ghibli effect: Blurring the lines between creativity and copyright. *Obhan & Associates*. https://www.obhanandassociates.com/blog/the-ghibli-effect-blurring-the-lines-between-creativity-and-copyright/

Pangotra, A. (2025, April 10). Ghibli trend: Another ethical conundrum caused by AI? *CyberPeace*. https://www.cyberpeace.org/resources/blogs/ghibli-trend-another-ethical-conundrum-caused-by-ai

Pasetti, M., Santos, J. W., Corrêa, N. K., De Oliveira, N., & Barbosa, C. P. (2025). Technical, legal, and ethical challenges of generative artificial intelligence: An analysis of the governance of training data and copyrights. *Discover Artificial Intelligence*, *5*(1), 193. DOI: 10.1007/s44163-025-00379-6

Priya, K. (2008). Intellectual Property and Hegelian justification. *NUJS Law Review*, *1*(1), 359–366.

Reed, R. (2024, March 22). Does ChatGPT violate New York Times' copyrights? *Harvard Law Today*. https://hls.harvard.edu/today/does-chatgpt-violate-new-york-times-copyrights/

Sætra, H. S. (2022). The ethics of trading privacy for security: The multifaceted effects of privacy on liberty and security. *Technology in Society*, *68*, 101854. DOI: 10.1016/j.techsoc.2021.101854

Simon, D. A. (2025). Copyright's missing personality. *Houston Law Review*, *62*(5), 993–1054. https://houstonlawreview.org/article/138618-copyright-s-missing-personality

Stim, R. (2013, April 4). Measuring fair use: The four factors. *Stanford Copyright and Fair Use Center*. https://fairuse.stanford.edu/overview/fair-use/four-factors/

Sundara Rajan, M. T. (2025). *The moral rights of authors and artists: From the birth of copyright to the age of artificial intelligence* (2nd ed.). Oxford University Press. DOI: 10.1093/law/9780198791850.001.0001

Yu, P. K. (2014). Moral Rights 2.0. *Texas A&M. Law Review*, *1*(4), 873–900. DOI: 10.37419/LR.V1.I4.3

KEY TERMS AND DEFINITIONS

Artificial Intelligence: The theory and development of computer systems that can execute human activities, including visual perception, voice recognition, decision-making, and language translation.

ChatGPT: ChatGPT is an AI-powered natural language processing tool that lets you conduct human-like chatbot chats and more. Language models can answer inquiries and help with email, essays, and code writing.

Copyright: Copyright is a kind of intellectual property that protects original works of authorship as soon as an author records the work in a tangible medium. Copyright law encompasses several forms of creative works, including as paintings, pictures, graphics, musical compositions, sound recordings, computer programs, novels, poetry, blog entries, movies, architectural works, plays, and more.

Creativity: Creativity is a fundamental need for the safeguarding of copyright. In order to satisfy this requirement, a piece of work must include an element that surpasses the original. While directly quoting someone else's work is not deemed original, referring to the original work in order to express a new notion is considered original.

Ethical AI: The ethical principles of ethical AI include individual rights, privacy, non-discrimination, and non-manipulation. Ethical AI prioritises ethics in deciding AI usage.

Generative AI: Generative AI is an artificial intelligence that can generate text, pictures, audio, and synthetic data.

Moral Rights: Moral rights pertain to specific entitlements of writers, conferred by copyright law, that safeguard the personal connection between a creator and their work, regardless of the creator's ownership of the work or copyright.

Studio Ghibli: Studio Ghibli is a renowned Japanese animation film studio established in 1985 by animators and filmmakers Hayao Miyazaki and Isao Takahata, along with producer Toshio Suzuki. Studio Ghibli is renowned for its exceptional filming quality and artistry.

Chapter 4

Regulating AI in Healthcare:

Legal Accountability, Data Protection, and the EU AI Act in Practice

Muhammad Usman Tariq
https://orcid.org/0000-0002-7605-3040
Abu Dhabi University, UAE & University College Cork, Ireland

ABSTRACT

Artificial intelligence (AI) is changing healthcare quickly by improving how doctors diagnose illnesses, plan treatments, and offer personalized care. But as AI becomes more common, it also brings up important legal and ethical questions, especially about who is responsible when things go wrong, how to protect patient data, and how to properly regulate AI use. This paper examines the challenges and possible solutions for controlling AI in healthcare, with a special focus on the legal changes happening in the European Union. It discusses how the EU AI Act, the General Data Protection Regulation (GDPR), and the Medical Device Regulation (MDR) work together to manage high-risk AI systems in hospitals and clinics. The paper also looks at key issues like who is to blame when AI

DOI: 10.4018/979-8-3373-5452-1.ch004

makes decisions, how to safely handle private health information, and the difficulties developers face in meeting these rules. The study suggests a transparent, open, and fair way to regulate AI that supports new ideas.

INTRODUCTION

Artificial intelligence (AI) is rapidly changing healthcare, making significant changes in how doctors diagnose, treat, and care for patients. These tools can identify patterns in data that are not visible to humans, assisting doctors in detecting diseases earlier and more accurately, particularly in areas such as radiology, cancer, and heart conditions. Although AI has the potential to improve healthcare outcomes, increase efficiency, and make medical care more accessible, some serious risks must be considered. The use of AI in healthcare raises essential issues such as patient safety, consent, data protection, and decision-making processes. AI systems can sometimes show bias if the data on which they are trained are not diverse or if the algorithms have flawed assumptions (Olimid et al., 2024). For example, a tool that is trained mostly on data from one group may not work as well for other groups. Is it the developer, the doctor who used it, or the hospital that brought it in? Keeping patient data safe is another major issue. AI systems require a lot of personal health information, which is often private and must be kept secure. Collecting and using this data raises concerns about whether people give proper consent, how securely the data is stored, and whether it could be used in harmful ways. This requires that data be used lawfully, clearly explained, and only for necessary reasons. This can be difficult to achieve given the complex and sometimes unclear nature of AI algorithms. GDPR also grants people the right to understand how their data are used and the right to opt out of automated decisions, which can be difficult to manage in medical settings.

Transparency is essential for building trust and ensuring that AI is used properly. Many AI applications in healthcare are like black boxes, where the results are not clearly explained (Van Kolfschooten & Van Oirschot, 2024). Such ambiguity complicates the explanation of decisions to patients, the assessment of the reliability of AI, and intervention when necessary. Legally, this complicates the process of establishing who is at fault and adhering to medical practices. To use AI safely and ethically in healthcare, the technology must be explainable, transparent, and supervised by individuals. This chapter discusses the intersection of AI and healthcare with legal regulations, particularly in the European Union and international regulations. The GDPR has established stringent requirements for data protection in AI applications in the EU (Palaniappan et al., 2024). Nevertheless, as AI continues to transform, additional precise rules are required. Applications in health would be classified as high risk; that is, they would have to undergo rigorous checks, maintain detailed records, be overseen by individuals, and be of high quality in terms of accuracy and security. The act further emphasizes the need for strong and clear AI systems to reduce the threat of AI in medicine.

The world is working towards developing uniform regulations on AI, although there are still vast disparities across locations. The ethical guidelines provided by the World Health Organization (WHO) on AI in health include factors such as inclusivity, safety, transparency, and accountability. These are not laws, but rather suggestions. The United States is more lenient, on the other hand, making the process of self-regulation and surveillance the priority after the AI is employed instead of defining the strict rules in advance. These legal models influence the development, testing, and use of AI, as well as its safety and efficacy in patients, especially regarding cross-border information exchange. Determining liability when AI causes harm is one of the most difficult legal problems to solve. Conventional rules for treating injuries are not appropriate when the injury is caused by the decision or recommendation of an AI system. Concerns have been raised regarding whether AI tools are subject to the laws of product liability or the rules of professional negligence, depending on whether they are treated as products or services. Another area of legal challenge is informed consent. Informed consent typically refers to the situation in which a physician discusses the risks and benefits of a treatment with the patient to allow him to make an informed choice. However, with AI, particularly in tools that are not easily discernible or usable independently, it may prove difficult to discuss with patients how decisions are made. Is it possible to have a patient who provides valid consent, but neither the patient nor the doctor knows how an AI tool reached its conclusion? This implies that AI systems should be made more transparent and new regulations should be established to share information in healthcare facilities. As the utilization of AI grows, it becomes increasingly essential that government agencies and healthcare organizations create strong regulations and standards that will help make AI usage fair and responsible. This would ensure that AI tools are biased, regularly updated, and tested, and that they are monitored by groups of people in different fields, such as law, technology, and medicine. Such systems may assist in ensuring that AI does not contribute to the further aggravation of inequitable treatment within medical care or cause additional issues. An additional larger ethical responsibility also exists to ensure that AI benefits the entire population, and not only those who live in resource-abundant regions.

AI has significant potential in healthcare, but it also poses significant risks. Laws must change along with technology to protect patients, hold professionals accountable, and build public confidence (Konnoth, 2024). As this chapter will explain, having strong rules based on clear values such as openness, safety, and fairness is essential to ensure that AI helps improve, rather than harm, the quality and fairness of healthcare (Palaniappan et al., 2024). The European Union's detailed approach, primarily through laws such as the GDPR and the proposed AI Act, is a good example of how to balance new technology with protection. Working together across countries, updating laws as things change, and keeping a close eye on ethics will be key to dealing with the challenges of AI in healthcare. By examining the rules in different places and comparing them, we can better learn how to use AI responsibly in the future of medicine.

LEGAL FRAMEWORKS GOVERNING AI IN HEALTHCARE

The management of AI in healthcare is evolving rapidly, particularly because it is necessary to strike a balance between emerging trends and safety, ethical principles, and trust in the system. The proposed AI Act is an important step in this direction for the European Union. This is a significant new law that will likely introduce explicit and uniform rules regarding AI technology applications (Konnoth, 2024). The classification of AI according to possible risks is one of the main components of the AI

Act. Healthcare applications are regarded as high-risk because of their ability to have a direct impact on the lives of people. This implies that safety, reliability, and responsibility must be ensured when using these tools. Risky AI systems will be required to follow strict norms, including a full check-up, periodic control, and powerful human control. The aim is to ensure that AI applied in diagnosis, treatment planning, patient care, or decision support does not cause harm or reduce the quality of medical care to the patient.

The AI Act also requires transparency and proper record keeping. Builders should monitor the development of AI systems, their data, and their functionality. This also enables regulators and medical professionals to see how AI makes important medical decisions (Olimid et al., 2024). The developers are also held liable by law to install sensible quality control and monitoring AI systems once they are put in use. Such steps are also fundamental in healthcare, as the decisions taken must be accurate and reproducible, particularly when dealing with matters that concern the lives of people.

At the heart of AI in healthcare is the use of personal data, which can be sensitive and must be protected from misuse. The EU's GDPR is very important for data handling. GDPR sets rules, including ensuring that data is used legally, fairly, and transparently, and that it is not kept longer than necessary (Palaniappan et al., 2024). These rules create a safe way to handle health data but also limit the development and use of AI. Often, using health data for training AI requires people to give consent or fall under certain legal exceptions, such as public health benefits. There is a challenge between the GDPR's right to explanation, especially from Article 22, which limits automated decisions that affect people, and the use of AI models that are hard to explain, such as "black box" systems. While the GDPR supports transparency, some modern AI models use complex networks that are difficult to explain. This makes it difficult for doctors to explain AI decisions to patients. Regulators and experts are still discussing whether a full breakdown of how decisions are made is needed or whether a general understanding of outcomes is sufficient in medical settings. Regardless, the GDPR pushes developers and medical institutions to clearly explain AI's role clearly and protect patients' rights in digital health.

Another important law is the Medical Device Regulation (MDR), which regulates the use of medical devices in the EU. Most AI systems applicable in the healthcare industry, particularly diagnostic or treatment systems, are considered medical devices. The MDR, which will be implemented in 2021, will require more testing and monitoring than its predecessor. AI systems are medical devices that require the fulfillment of safety and performance standards and must pass approval procedures prior to sale. AI tools must be safe and effective in medicine, which is why the relationship between the AI act and the MDR is needed. Although these laws work together, they are not the same (Van Kolfschooten & Van Oirschot, 2024). The AI Act builds on the MDR without repeating its checks and adds extra rules for AI-specific risks. This helps prevent placing too much burden on developers while maintaining strong oversight. This shows that the EU is trying to create a unified legal system in which both medical device standards and AI-specific rules cover medical AI. This guarantees the technical safety and effectiveness of AI systems, as well as ethical, fair, and accountable standards.

However, these other regions did not follow the same pattern. The FDA is also an important part of medical AI regulation in the United States (Konnoth, 2024). The FDA has an informal and evolving approach to AI because it is aware that software may evolve over time. They developed an SaMD framework that assists in considering AI-based medical products, such as machine learning tools. The FDA also launched a so-called Predetermined Change Control Plan that enables certain AI-based systems to be updated once approved, without full re-assessment, provided those updates fall within the scope of previously agreed limits. This makes the news of AI real and relevant but raises the problem of control and security when updates become a source of new threats (Palaniappan et al., 2024) or prejudices. In this regard, the FDA emphasizes transparency, auditability, and real-world performance monitoring. The FDA method lacks the holism of the EU AI Act; however, it is risk-based and thus serves to facilitate novelty without deteriorating safety.

In 2023, the MHRA announced that it had a plan to revise its medical device regulations, and that AI and machine learning were given special priority. This strategy will involve data transparency, enhanced surveillance once the devices are released to the market, and enhanced security.

Similar to the EU, the UK is considering ways to ensure that AI systems are responsible and transparent and address the special issues that arise with AI systems that can learn and modify themselves. The MHRA also collaborates with other societies, such as companies, researchers, and patient groups, to build a regulatory system that keeps people safe and builds confidence without halting advancement. The World Health Organization (WHO) has been at the forefront of providing ethical standards for the use of AI in health at the global level. Although the WHO cannot issue laws, it has a considerable impact on standardization and the pursuit of standardization across national borders. In 2021, the WHO proposed six principles to govern AI usage in health in a report entitled Ethics and Governance of Artificial Intelligence, which includes: protect individual freedom, help people, be clear, take responsibility, include everyone, and ensure sustainability. These values are purported to help governments, developers, and healthcare professionals behave responsibly in their use of AI (Konnoth, 2024). The WHO also reports that it is crucial to ensure that digital health tools are available across all countries because unfair access to them can aggravate health conditions. New WHO projects are to develop digital health certificates, enhance system sharing, and assist countries in developing their own rules that best suit their needs and are compatible with those around the globe. As summarised in Figure 1, GDPR obligations form the legal substrate for all medical-AI deployments, with device and AI-specific controls layered above; this interlock explains why compliance burdens compound for high-risk use cases.

Figure 1. Regulatory architecture for medical AI.

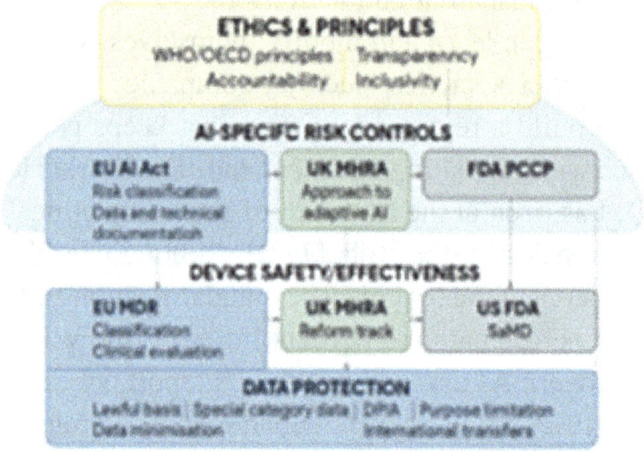

Looking at these various frameworks, we find some similarities and differences. Patient safety, transparency, and accountability are core values shared by the EU, US, UK, and WHO. However, the methods by which they achieve this are very different. The EU is utterly demanding and thorough, and laws such as the AI Act and MDR establish very clear rules (Olimid et al., 2024). The US takes a more versatile path, as it is more concerned with monitoring the product once it has been used, and it can be changed very quickly to adapt to new ideas. The UK desires to strike the golden mean and embed a few of the EU standards but still maintains a more sovereign approach to adapting to emerging changes in the global order. Meanwhile, the WHO's mission is to establish ethical norms and assist low- and middle-income countries in establishing their own regulations based on international concepts. In practice, these frameworks must respond to rapid changes in AI technology, unequal information quality, and different levels of readiness in different institutions. One must always practice a fine line so that the rules do not appear to be a huge burden but, at the same time, do not expose people to too much danger (Konnoth, 2024). Ensuring the ability to integrate systems and secure endorsements between nations will be even more critical as AI devices are applied in various healthcare environments. These rules are important for people working with healthcare AI (developers, doctors, patients, and lawmakers) because they need to know them to ensure compliance with the law and design systems that are safe, effective, and fair. The regulation of AI in healthcare is still evolving, influenced by the current discourse and changing in response to new information. Laws and policies, such as the EU AI Act, GDPR, MDR, and others in the US, UK, and other regions of the world, are part of a larger attempt to position AI in a way that positively impacts society. Such a law must keep pace with technology without undermining the most important principles of human dignity, trust, and justice (Ebenibo et al., 2024). With the power of AI growing, regulations and rules that will guide its use will also need to grow to ensure that the future of medicine is not only promising but also responsible.

KEY LEGAL CHALLENGES IN AI-ENABLED MEDICAL SYSTEMS

AI systems, especially those used for diagnosis and treatment, raise questions about who is responsible, whether decisions are fair, and how much control patients have over their care, among others. One major issue is who should be held accountable when something goes wrong (Van Kolfschooten & Van Oirschot, 2024). If an AI system causes a mistake, such as a wrong diagnosis or an evil treatment plan, it is not clear who is to blame. Traditionally, legal responsibility in medical cases has focused on human doctors' actions. However, if a doctor uses an AI tool and something bad happens, it is not so simple to decide whether the doctor, the hospital, the software maker, or the company that approved the AI should be held responsible. Currently, legal rules for areas such as tort law have not yet fully caught up with the way AI interacts with human decisions.

Some legal frameworks, such as product liability laws, may help with this, especially if AI systems are treated as medical devices. For example, the EU's Product Liability Directive could apply if a flaw in the AI system is proven to have caused harm. However, defining a "defect" in software, especially when the AI can behave in unpredictable or unclear ways, is not always easy (Ebenibo et al., 2024). In addition, some AI systems change over time as they learn from new data. This makes it difficult to determine whether the original creator should be held responsible for the actions of the AI after it was first released. The EU is updating its product liability rules to better handle these situations. However, there are still significant gaps, especially when harm arises from an unexpected mix of AI and the complex nature of medical care. Another major legal issue is the transparency and explainability of AI decisions, particularly in serious medical situations. Many of the most powerful AI systems in healthcare, such as those using deep learning, work as "black boxes." They can make accurate predictions or recommendations, but their inner workings are complex. This lack of transparency causes legal and ethical issues (Pantanowitz et al., 2024). Doctors are legally required to explain the reasoning behind medical decisions to patients, especially when obtaining informed consent. However, if the AI's logic cannot be explained, it is difficult for doctors to meet that obligation.

From a legal standpoint, the lack of transparency also makes it difficult to assess whether a healthcare provider acted negligently or followed proper procedures (Chau, 2024). If something goes wrong, courts want to know if the provider made a reasonable decision based on the information available. However, if the AI recommendation does not come with a clear explanation, how can the provider verify its accuracy? This forces doctors to either completely trust the AI or ignore it, both of which are risky. Some rules, such as the EU's proposed AI Act, aim to fix this by requiring high-risk AI systems to be explainable and auditable. However, making AI fully explainable often means sacrificing some of its performance, which creates a conflict between legal requirements and technical limits. Another crucial legal concern is algorithmic bias and discrimination in AI systems used in healthcare settings. AI tools are only as good as the data on which they are trained (Naidoo, 2024). Many medical datasets do not represent all groups equally and often include more data from white males, leading to poorer performance for women, ethnic minorities, and older patients. This can result in issues such as underdiagnosing heart disease in women, misidentifying skin conditions in people with darker skin, or making inaccurate mental health assessments across cultures. When these biased outcomes occur, they are not just medical mistakes; they can also be illegal discrimination under human rights or anti-discrimination laws.

Legal systems are starting to address these problems, but it is not easy within the framework of existing laws. Anti-discrimination laws usually require clear proof of bias or unequal impact, which is difficult to demonstrate when AI systems work behind the scenes in complex healthcare settings (Olimid et al., 2024). In addition, many legal systems do not yet recognize algorithmic discrimination as a specific type of harm, leaving victims with few options for legal help. Some places, such as the EU, are trying to address this by requiring AI developers to check and reduce bias throughout the product's life. This includes using diverse data, conducting regular audits, and building technical protections to ensure fairness across different groups. However, enforcing these rules is challenging, and many legal and ethical questions regarding fairness in AI are still being addressed.

In addition to problems with liability, transparency, and bias, informed consent has become a significant concern in AI-assisted healthcare. Usually, this includes details about the diagnosis, treatment plan, risks and benefits, and other available options (Ebenibo et al., 2024). However, with AI in healthcare, it is more difficult to provide truly informed consent. Patients might not know the role of AI in their diagnosis or treatment, especially if the technology is part of medical software and its use is not clearly explained.

Even when patients know that AI is being used, it is still difficult to explain how the system works in a way that makes sense. AI models, especially those that use machine learning, are so complicated that it is not easy to break them down into simple terms. Simply informing a patient that an algorithm analyzed their medical information and suggested a treatment is insufficient for obtaining proper consent if they do not understand what that means or how the decision was made (Van Kolfschooten & Van Oirschot, 2024). This becomes even harder in urgent or high-pressure medical situations, where decisions need to be made quickly and there is little time for detailed explanations. In these cases, doctors have a big responsibility to ensure that AI support, rather than weakens, patients' ability to make their own choices. To address this, some legal experts and policymakers have suggested a new way of thinking about informed consent when it comes to AI (Konnoth, 2024). This could mean new ways of communicating with patients to help them understand the general idea of how AI makes decisions, even if they cannot understand the technical parts. This might also mean creating standard forms or statements that clearly explain the role of AI in medical decisions, the level of human input required, and any known limits or problems with the system. Simultaneously, in the same breath, there is an emerging conception that informed consent should be accompanied by algorithmic responsibility. This includes ensuring that artificial intelligence systems are equitable, accurate, and dependable to ensure that patients do not assume full responsibility for safeguarding themselves.

These overlapping questions, such as whose responsibility it is, the clarity of things, whether the system is biased, and whether the patient is sufficiently informed, demonstrate that it is such a significant issue that the law should keep pace with new technologies. Even though AI can be implemented in such a way that it may positively contribute to the improvement of healthcare, it must be implemented so that it does not infringe on patient rights and does not contradict their expectations. Legal changes are needed to understand the specifics of AI, including its unpredictability, complexity, and harmfulness (Olimid et al., 2024). This could include revising old legal principles, such as strict liability or duty of care, to new contexts or new legal principles to be applied to algorithmic tools altogether. Ultimately, the goal is to apply AI in healthcare in a manner that inspires trust, protects the most vulnerable, and holds people accountable if anything goes wrong. This will require not only legal reforms but also collaboration between lawyers, technologists, doctors, and ethicists. It also implies being more transparent and honest with patients and engaging the general population in determining how AI is applied in medicine. With a broad, universal approach, we can only manage the legal issues surrounding AI in healthcare and maximize the technology's potential to improve human health.

DATA PROTECTION AND PATIENT PRIVACY

The use of artificial intelligence in healthcare has changed the way patient information is gathered, stored, analyzed, and used. One important issue that comes with this change is ensuring that patient data remain private and secure, mainly because large sets of data, often containing private health details, are needed to train and improve AI tools. The GDPR follows key ideas, such as collecting only the minimum necessary data, using data only for the intended purpose, and ensuring that data is processed lawfully. These rules are essential for using AI in medical settings because they help protect people's privacy, keep data safe, and prevent its misuse. One of the main ideas of the GDPR is data minimization. This means that only the data necessary for a specific purpose should be collected. However, the law requires that data collection must be conducted carefully. This becomes tricky when it is unclear how valid specific data might be until after analysis (Konnoth, 2024). Developers must find a way to collect sufficient data for AI to work while still following the law. This often requires working with data protection officers and ethics boards to ensure that the data collected are necessary and used correctly.

Another essential idea is the limitation of purpose. In healthcare, this becomes a significant issue when data from routine care are later used for training AI or research (Chau, 2024). While using data for other purposes can be helpful, such as developing tools to detect rare diseases, it is not always allowed without clear reasons. When data are used for other purposes, there must be proper consent, a good reason, or strict protections in place to keep it safe. If these are not met, it could violate GDPR rules and lead to legal problems. Lawful processing is also a significant part of the GDPR. This means that using health data, which is a special category, requires specific reasons (Konnoth, 2024). For example, explicit consent from patients may be required, or there may be a legal duty or a need to protect someone's health. In practice, this means that every AI project in healthcare must have a clear legal justification for using data from the start. Although consent sounds simple, it has its tricky parts. Under the GDPR, consent must be explicit, specific, and freely given. However, in healthcare settings, patients may not fully understand data usage due to power imbalances, time pressures, or the complexity of AI tools. This makes it difficult to ensure that they truly agree on how their data are used.

The use of sensitive health data to train AI models is one of the biggest challenges in medical AI. Training accurate and general AI tools often requires data on various health issues, different groups, and long-term health records. This implies the collection of a large amount of private data, often over long periods and from many sources. Health data are among the most protected types of personal information because of the potential harm if they are misused or if security measures are inadequate (Van Kolfschooten & Van Oirschot, 2024). If health data are misused, it could lead to discrimination, social stigma, or a loss of trust in healthcare systems. To prevent this, developers and healthcare providers must use strong data governance practices, such as using fake names, encrypting data, controlling who can access it, and conducting regular checks. In addition, developing AI models often involves using data from many hospitals, regions, or even countries. This raises issues regarding moving data across borders and using cloud services for storage and processing (Chau, 2024). While this can help create better and more general AI tools, it also raises serious data protection concerns. Under the GDPR, data can only be moved outside the EU if the country meets a certain level of protection, as determined by the European Commission. The Privacy Shield has made it more difficult for healthcare providers and AI companies to comply with these rules when moving data internationally.

Cloud computing is often used in AI projects, which adds more privacy risks to the data. Storing and processing health data in third-party clouds can be risky because it raises questions about who controls the data, who is responsible if there is a problem, and how secure the data are. Healthcare organizations must ensure that their cloud providers follow GDPR rules, including policies on where the data are stored, who can access it, and how they handle breaches (Olimid et al., 2024). Contracts with cloud companies must clearly define who is responsible for data protection and what happens in the event of a data breach or system failure. An area that is receiving more discussion is data anonymization and the ethics of using data in different ways. People often think that anonymizing data helps reuse it without hurting privacy because truly anonymized data are not covered by the GDPR. However, in reality, it is difficult to make data completely and permanently anonymous, especially with health data (Fessenko & Jasperse, 2024). This type of data has many clues that could help identify someone, and there are complex connections between the different pieces of information. Methods such as differential privacy, data masking, or grouping data can reduce the risk of re-identification. However, none of these methods are entirely safe, especially now that there are powerful tools for computing and matching data from different sources. Therefore, data that are called "anonymized" might still pose privacy risks, especially when mixed with other datasets.

The ethical side of anonymization also raises the issue of consent. If data are stripped of personal details and used for purposes that were not shared initially, should people still have a say in how they are used? Some believe that once data are anonymized, they no longer belong to individuals. However, others argue that people should still have some control over how their health data are used, even if it is not identifiable. Broad consent, where people agree beforehand to future uses without specific details, remains a topic of debate. Critics argue that it does not provide informed consent (Olimid et al., 2024). There is also concern that certain groups, such as those who are already vulnerable, might be overrepresented in datasets used for research, leading to exploitation and trust issues. Ethical problems also arise when data are used for profit. Although health data are often collected for public benefit or medical care, they can later be used by private companies to create AI tools. Even when data are anonymized, using them for commercial purposes raises questions about fairness and transparency. Patients may not be comfortable with their data being used in products that do not directly benefit them. Institutions need to consider not only whether it is allowed by law, but also whether it is fair and how it affects public trust in healthcare.

Being open and accountable for how data is used is key to addressing these issues. Healthcare providers and AI companies must clearly explain to patients and the public how data is gathered, processed, and shared, including future uses. Data management systems should have checks and balances, such as ethics committees or data oversight groups, to ensure that the secondary use of data follows public values and laws. Involving patients in decisions through public meetings or shared decision-making models can help build trust and support (Konnoth, 2024).

REGULATORY GAPS AND COMPLIANCE OBSTACLES

As artificial intelligence continues to change healthcare, the current rules and laws are not keeping pace. One major problem is that the laws and standards for digital health and AI are not all connected. Although some places have started making or using laws for AI, these laws often work separately, leading to different rules and confusion for those involved. In the European Union, several overlapping rules exist, such as the GDPR, Medical Device Regulation (MDR), and proposed AI Act (Fessenko & Jasperse, 2024). Each of these rules has a different purpose: data protection, safety of medical devices, and general AI rules; however, they do not fit together smoothly. An AI tool used for diagnosis may have to follow all three rules simultaneously. This layered system makes it difficult to follow the rules, especially when different rules have conflicting requirements or no clear advice on how to follow them.

This problem is not limited to the EU. Globally, there are significant differences in the regulation of digital health and AI. In the United States, there are many different rules between federal and state governments and between different agencies, such as the FDA, FTC, and HHS. The FDA's rules for software as a medical device (SaMD) are progressive, but they do not always match up with privacy rules such as HIPAA or with state laws that can be stricter. In the UK, the MHRA is working on new rules for AI in healthcare after Brexit; however, the overall legal situation is still changing. Meanwhile, many countries in the Global South lack robust digital health laws and often use imported technologies that are not well-adapted to their local laws, culture, or healthcare needs. This mixed system of rules hinders cross-border collaboration, causes uncertainty for companies that operate internationally, and hinders the safe use of AI in healthcare.

Startups and small-to medium-sized companies (SMEs) are especially affected by these rule problems. These companies are often leaders in developing new AI tools for applications such as disease detection, patient tracking, and personalized treatment. However, their limited resources make it very difficult to deal with all the legal rules from different systems (Van Kolfschooten & Van Oirschot, 2024). Unlike large companies that can have their own legal teams and compliance departments, SMEs often need to hire outside consultants, which costs more and slows down their product development. Following the GDPR alone is a significant challenge, requiring detailed data protection plans, legal frameworks for data use, and systems to handle people's data rights. When combined with the rules for medical devices and AI under the EU AI Act, the burden is even greater. Many SMEs also struggle to determine the proof needed to show that they are following the rules. For example, clinical validation under the MDR can be costly and time-consuming for small developers, particularly when AI tools must be tested on diverse populations or for rare diseases (Olimid et al., 2024). The AI Act's proposed compliance checks add more confusion because the exact standards for high-risk AI systems are still being decided. This uncertainty discourages investment in healthcare AI because it is difficult to determine the cost and chances of bringing a product to market. In some cases, it may even hinder the development of promising innovations because of concerns about legal risks or the cost of compliance.

Another problem is that the current rules and checks are insufficient for AI systems. Traditional rules assume that products are fixed and predictable and can be tested using standard methods (Konnoth, 2024). AI systems, on the other hand, are dynamic and depend on data. They can change over time with new information or be used in different healthcare settings. This makes it difficult to track their performance once they are in use. Regulatory bodies do not have enough personnel or resources to keep checking these tools, especially when they are part of larger healthcare computer systems or online platforms. There is also no agreement on how to properly check AI systems in healthcare. Some regulators have suggested using algorithmic impact checks or independent audits to ensure that AI is fair, accurate, and safe (Fessenko & Jasperse, 2024). However, there is no general agreement on how to conduct these audits, who should conduct them, or what standards to use. For example, how do you measure bias in an AI tool used for emergency care, and what level of difference is acceptable, legally or ethically? In addition, how do you balance making AI more understandable while maintaining its accuracy? Without clear answers, oversight is inconsistent and typically occurs only after problems arise, rather than before. This gap in the rules hurts public trust and leaves developers without clear ways to be held responsible.

To address these problems, there is growing interest in using regulatory sandboxes, which are special environments where AI can be tested and improved under the supervision of regulators (Zahra, 2025). Sandboxes help balance innovation and oversight by allowing developers to experiment with new technologies while staying within legal limits. In healthcare, sandboxes can help test AI tools in pilot programs or limited settings, allowing real-world use without putting patients at risk of harm. These environments also help regulators learn about the technology, identify possible risks, and create better guidelines based on real experience instead of mere guesses. Several countries are now trying out special programs called regulatory sandboxes for AI and digital health applications. In the UK, the Information Commissioner's Office (ICO) has established a sandbox that focuses on data protection and AI. In Singapore, the Health Sciences Authority has set up a sandbox that allows AI developers to work closely with health officials to test their systems before they are widely used. These efforts exemplify how different groups can collaborate to create better regulations. They also showed that being flexible with rules does not mean removing rules altogether. Instead, it can help make regulations more adaptable and better suited to specific situations in the future.

Although these sandboxes are promising, they have some limitations. They often require a lot of resources and only help a few participants. Companies that are already supported by institutions or the government may benefit more. There is also a risk that what is learned in these sandboxes will not lead to broader regulatory changes. Instead, they may remain isolated experiments (Olimid et al., 2024). For sandboxes to make a real difference, they must be part of a broader regulatory update plan. To handle the challenges AI faces in healthcare, a variety of approaches are necessary, including changing old laws to fit new realities in medicine, providing more support for regulatory experts, and creating ways for innovators and regulators to continue to share feedback. Making rules stricter or adding new standards is not enough. The entire system of rules must be more organized, open, and easy to understand. This means making digital health laws consistent across different areas, explaining how data protection, medical device rules, and AI management work together, and offering practical help for small and medium-sized companies (Konnoth, 2024). This also implies a change in the way we monitor AI systems to match their unique and changing nature. Ensuring strong and flexible ways to hold people accountable is key. As the healthcare industry becomes increasingly dependent on AI to improve diagnosis, streamline processes, and provide personalized care, getting regulations right is more important than ever. Poorly designed or inconsistent rules can either halt innovation or put patients at risk. The way forward requires ongoing discussions, experiments, and changes. Regulatory sandboxes, focused reforms, and efforts to build capacity can all help in this process, connecting innovation with regulation in the rapidly changing world of digital health.

CASE STUDIES AND JURISPRUDENCE

The use of artificial intelligence in healthcare is causing more legal problems and regulatory changes, highlighting the challenges in controlling these new technologies. Examining real-life cases and court rulings helps to demonstrate how laws are being used to deal with the new dangers that AI brings. These cases highlight the difficulty of ensuring that AI systems are responsible, protect patients, and follow rules. One significant legal issue involves diagnostic errors made by AI tools, particularly in radiology. In a well-known case in Europe, a hospital was sued after an AI tool used in radiology missed early signs of lung cancer in a patient's scan, leading to late treatment and worse outcomes. The patient's family claimed that the hospital was negligent in relying on the AI tool. The hospital argued that the tool was approved under medical device rules and had been well tested. However, the court looked at how much human supervision was involved and raised important questions about what doctors should do when using AI to make decisions. The court found the hospital partially responsible because it failed to document the radiologist's review properly and lacked clear plans for handling the differences between human and machine results. The court stated that even if an AI tool is approved, doctors and hospitals are still responsible for checking the results and keeping patients safe. The ruling did not state that AI use was illegal, but it stressed the need for teamwork between people and AI and better ways to manage risks (Pesapane & Summers, 2024). This decision led many hospitals in the EU to update their rules for using AI in diagnosis, including better records, human checks, and clearer roles.

A user complained that the company used personal health data without sufficient transparency or proper permission. A data protection authority examined the company's practices, checking how consent was given, whether they used only necessary data, and how they explained AI's role (Pham, 2025). The authority found that the company broke GDPR rules, including not telling users how the AI made decisions, not obtaining full permission for using sensitive data, and not having enough human control over automated advice. The company was fined and had to change its data handling. They must explain how the AI works, what data it uses, and how decisions are made in a clearer and more accessible manner. They also need to create a better consent system, allowing users to choose which data they share and for what purpose. This case study highlights the importance of following the GDPR when using AI in healthcare, not just to meet the rules but also to build trust with users. It also showed that GDPR's rules about automated decisions, especially Article 22, are very relevant even when AI is merely providing suggestions and not making decisions. This case had wide effects on digital health, making telemedicine providers and AI developers rethink how they handle data and incorporate privacy into their systems from the beginning.

The third case focuses on the approval of an AI medical tool for diabetic retinopathy detection. A European startup developed an AI tool that uses retinal scans to identify early signs of the condition, helping doctors refer patients for treatment. The tool was considered a high-risk medical device under EU rules; therefore, the company had to undergo a detailed approval process. They worked with a government-approved body to check the tool's safety and effectiveness (Fessenko & Jasperse, 2024). The tool also fell under the draft AI Act because it was used for medical purposes and could affect the health outcomes. This meant more rules about risk management, data control, human oversight, and ensuring AI decision-making is clear. The company had to handle both sets of rules, which made the process more complicated. The MDR required detailed proof of the tool's safety and plans for checking it after use. The AI Act added rules about ethical and social risks, making the paperwork and oversight even more detailed. The company also had to follow GDPR because it used patient images and data for both development and real-time use. All these rules were needed to make sure the AI tool was safe and fair for patients.

Despite the complexity, the device got approval from regulators under the MDR, making it one of the first AI-based diagnostic tools to be authorized through the new, stricter review process. At the time of approval, the AI Act was still being written, but the company chose to follow many of its expected rules, treating them as good practices. This forward-thinking action was welcomed by the regulators and helped in assessing the device as having more benefits than risks (Goktas & Grzybowski, 2025). The success of this case showed that it's possible to follow different regulatory standards if companies invest in good records, teamwork across different areas, and start talking with regulators early. It also showed that developers of high-risk AI medical tools need to go beyond just showing the tool works well and must also show they are fair, accountable, and transparent. This case also provides practical lessons for future applicants. One important lesson was the value of planning early and having someone inside the company who knows about regulations (Dramburg, 2025). The startup hired a compliance officer who managed the paperwork, testing, and data privacy checks. This person ensured all the documents met the needs of MDR, GDPR, and the AI Act, saving time and keeping everything consistent. Another lesson was the benefit of working with outside groups, like patient advocates and independent experts, to build trust and make sure the tool met real medical needs without causing new problems. Regulators noticed that this approach helped the tool gain trust and acceptance in society, and it set a good example for others in the field.

Taken together, these case studies show the many challenges of bringing AI into regulated healthcare. They show how current laws are being used and changed in real situations, and how legal ideas are evolving to meet the specific challenges of AI in medicine. In the case of diagnostic mistakes, courts reminded everyone that human supervision is still necessary, even with innovative technology. In the data privacy case against a telemedicine service, regulators emphasized the need for openness, permission, and explicit protections against hidden algorithm decisions (Lund et al., 2025). In the approval for the AI diagnostic tool, regulators showed they are willing to help innovators who approach compliance in a thoughtful, all-around way. Still, they also made it clear that ethics and society are becoming as important as demonstrating the tool's effectiveness.

These legal decisions also show broader trends in how AI is being regulated in healthcare. There is a growing understanding that old, one-size-fits-all rules are not working for the fast-changing and different nature of AI. Instead, regulators are moving toward more flexible and team-based approaches that focus on ongoing checks, working with different people, and making sure AI aligns with ethics (Aboy et al., 2024). However, to get there, regulators need more skills, more precise guidance for developers, and rules that are the same around the world to reduce confusion and help new ideas. As more AI tools come to market and are tested in real-world settings, more legal cases and government decisions will continue to shape how we deal with responsibility, fairness, and safety in the age of smart medicine.

TOWARDS AN ETHICAL AND LEGALLY COHERENT MODEL

As artificial intelligence becomes more deeply involved in medical care, it's becoming clearer that we need a strong, clear ethical and legal system to manage it. Old rules for medical law and ethics were made for situations where humans made decisions, with clear roles, responsibilities, and ways to get consent (Pecchia et al., 2024). AI changes this by using complex systems that make or affect medical choices through hidden algorithms, probability, and patterns that even the people who made them might not fully understand. Because of this, healthcare systems need to think differently about how to maintain ethical standards and legal accountability as intelligent machines become more common.

A key part of this change is ensuring that humans remain in control when AI is involved in medical decisions. Even though AI can process information faster and more accurately than humans, the doctor should always be the final decision-maker (Schmidt et al., 2024). This means doctors must be able to understand what AI suggests, make judgments based on their knowledge, and override AI recommendations when needed.

Good human oversight isn't just about having a person monitor AI. It also means building structures, processes, and training that help healthcare workers understand and use AI responsibly. This includes teaching doctors how well or poorly specific AI tools work, ensuring they understand their level of control, and ensuring AI results are transparent and explainable. AI systems should be built with interfaces that show recommendations clearly and highlight areas where there might be uncertainty or danger (Cantero Gamito & Marsden, 2024). Laws should require these human-centered design features as a standard for using AI in medicine. This could include shared decision-making plans, records that track how AI and doctors work together, or ways to assign responsibility when things go wrong fairly by putting human oversight into both how AI systems are built (Rosic, 2024). The rules that govern them can help healthcare systems maintain their integrity and public trust as they use AI more.

Beyond individual AI systems, a bigger change is needed in how we manage AI in healthcare. Rather than blaming government rules alone, we should have them that clearly show governments and business firms collaborating to establish standards. This implies that as governments establish broad guidelines on safety, transparency, and responsibility, firms and other entities may establish more precise guidelines, tools, and techniques to help define and remedy risks. Lastly, even less rigorous and responsive rules can be changed to follow the emerging technologies and very real concerns with such a kind of partnership (Ijaiya and Odumuwagun, 2024). For example, an AI tool used to treat cancer may be more sensitive to potential risks than an AI tool used for mental health, and co-regulation can address these differences without sacrificing the laws.

Along with regulatory frameworks, digital health charters and ethical impact assessments should also be developed to depict the bigger global scope of the influence of AI in society (Vujicic, 2024). These recommendations go further than statutory provisions and cover values such as fairness, transparency, and inclusiveness in creating and using AI in healthcare provision. Institutions, regions or even entire countries can create digital health charters and use them to establish standards regarding the use of patient data, clarify how AI can be made accessible and how it can be used to make care available to all. These charters may assist trust, internal controls and engagement on all sides, and may aid in the way healthcare is financed, in the manner projects are sanctioned, and in the manner new tools are embraced. Ethical impact assessments are a more detailed way to check the possible effects of specific AI tools. They start early in development and continue as the system is used, looking at how it might affect individual rights, differences between groups, the roles of doctors, and social standards. These assessments can find hidden biases, unexpected problems, or unfair impacts on vulnerable people. Importantly, they should include a variety of people, not just developers and doctors, but also patients, ethicists, and community members (Palaniappan et al., 2024). These insights can help shape how the AI is built, how it's managed, and what actions are taken to prevent harm. Even though these assessments are not required everywhere yet, more places are starting to consider them, especially for big AI projects. Some areas, like Canada and parts of the EU, are already trying these models, and their experiences can help others follow suit.

Finally, as medical AI becomes a global tool, working together across countries is key to making sure we have laws and ethics that are consistent and fair. AI systems often work across borders, use data from many places, are used in different countries' health systems, and are supported by cloud platforms in different countries. However, laws about AI are still very different from one place to another, with each country having its own rules for safety, data, and approval (De Micco et al., 2024). We need models of government working with private companies on setting standards instead of only government rules. It implies that where governments establish general principles regarding safety, transparency, and responsibility, companies and other organizations may develop their own more detailed rules, tools, and approaches to spotting and reducing risks. With this type of partnership, the rules may be more flexible, responsive, and adaptable to new technologies and real challenges (Ijaiya and Odumuwagun, 2024). An example is as follows: AI tool used to cThis causes problems among developers, makes it harder to comply with regulations, and can jeopardize the quality and equity of care. International cooperation is not based on equality of rules in all countries, but on establishing common values, mechanisms to understand the others rules, and mechanisms to keep an eye on the other countries AI practices.

Organizations such as the World Health Organization (WHO), the Organisation of Economic Co-operation and Development (OECD), and the International Medical Device Regulators Forum (IMDRF) are developing strategies to assist countries in collaborating on digital health and AI regulations. To illustrate, the WHO has developed a set of guidelines on the ethics and management of AI in health care. These regulations are based on such basic values as respect of the freedom of people, openness and transparency, inclusion and accountability (Mennella et al., 2024). More than 40 countries include in the list of the varieties of AI systems discussed in the OECD AI Principles and state that they are trustworthy, strong, and respect human rights and democratic values. These plans provide countries with a starting point to match their laws and to help them communicate with one another across the borders. The negotiation of countries or companies, including the agreement between the EU and the US on the exchange of information and managing electronic objects can help to make the rules more fixed and to avoid misunderstanding of the legislation.

There are also issues that require international cooperation, particularly those which touch on many countries such as the unfairness of AI in treating health data, spreading unproven or malicious technologies to other countries and using AI in the ways that harm individuals or that individuals are unfairly controlled (Cancela-Outeda, 2024). ancer treatment will not carry similar risks compared to one in mental health, and co-regulation will help mitigate these differences without reducing the uniformity of laws. This model involves co-regulation through dynamic risk assessments. Such tests will allow regulators and developers monitor how the risks of AI systems keep varying as they evolve and are deployed. Regulation does not require a single check at the beginning but is an ongoing process of checking, refining, and adjusting. This might involve monitoring the quality of AI systems at any point in time, needing to check in with AI systems occasionally, or reviewing rules over time depending on the application of AI. The EU AI Act is one of them, and cooperation and technical assistance are needed to implement these rules. The possibilities are assisted by getting partners, both publicly and privately, to finance spaces where AI systems can be tested, provide uniformity in terms of risk, and develop risk-free methods of sharing information between businesses, physicians, and governmental bodies. Co-regulation is also beneficial for innovation, but it allows the rules to be less complex and more accessible, especially for small businesses that might otherwise be discouraged by the complexity of regulations.

Besides legal regulations, digital health charters and ethical impact measures must also be created so that the larger picture of the role AI plays on society could be demonstrated (Vujicic, 2024). These recommendations extend beyond legal stipulations and incorporate other values such as fairness, transparency, and inclusivity in the design and use of AI in healthcare. Institutions, regions, or entire countries can create digital health charters that can assist in establishing standards surrounding the use of patient data, the clarity of AI, and ways to make care accessible to all. These charters may favor confidence, internal scrutiny and participation by every stakeholder, and may assist in the financing of healthcare, the reception of endeavors or plans, and the reception of novel instruments. A united international effort can help set clear rules, such as banning social scoring or AI tools that ignore people's consent. It can also help spread good practices and learning between countries. Supporting countries with fewer resources to build up their ability to regulate is also essential, so they can participate and benefit from ethical AI development (Solaiman & Malik, 2025).

CONCLUSION AND POLICY RECOMMENDATIONS

As artificial intelligence keeps changing how healthcare is delivered, the rules and laws that govern it must also change to make sure that new technology works with the key values of safety, responsibility, and respect for people (Tang et al., 2025). The legal and ethical issues brought up by AI are no longer just ideas; they are honest and urgent. From tools that help doctors diagnose diseases and robots used in surgeries to online health services and systems that predict health outcomes, AI is already playing a role in making medical decisions and affecting patient outcomes. In this situation, it's clear that rules shouldn't just respond to problems after they happen or be scattered across different areas. Instead, a planned, unified approach is needed to support innovation while ensuring patient safety. This is where legal responsibility, strong data protection, and the use of frameworks like the EU AI Act become very important.

Deciding who is to blame when an AI system helps cause a mistake, whether it's the maker of the system, the doctor using it, or the hospital, is a fundamental question that current laws haven't fully worked out. Courts and lawmakers need to create new rules that recognize how AI shares decision-making with humans in medical care (Butt, 2024). This includes updating what is considered good medical practice, clearly stating the role of doctors in monitoring AI, and creating systems for holding people responsible in a way that encourages safety and openness. Clear rules for checking work, keeping records, and having human checks in place should be required any time AI is used for diagnosing or treating patients. These steps will help doctors stay in control and make it easier to assign responsibility when problems happen. Just as important is making sure that data protection rules are followed when developing and using AI systems. However, putting these rules into practice isn't the same everywhere, mainly when AI uses data in new ways, trains models, or moves data across borders (Kilian et al., 2025). Government agencies need to give more precise instructions and help build the ability of both public and private groups, especially smaller companies, to follow these rules. Being open with patients about how their information is used, how AI affects decisions, and what rights they have is not only a legal requirement but also essential for keeping people's trust in digital health tools.

The EU AI Act, once it's entirely in effect, aims to fix several gaps by labeling AI used in healthcare as high-risk and requiring specific rules about managing risks, handling data, keeping humans in charge, and being open about how AI works. However, its success will depend a lot on how well it's enforced, how it works with other rules like the Medical Device Regulation and GDPR, and the guidance given to developers who have to follow these different rules (Palaniappan et al., 2024). Policymakers should make sure the AI Act isn't just a list of things to check off but instead promotes a culture of responsible development. They should also look into using controlled testing areas, partnerships between government and private groups, and assessing the ethical impact of new technologies to ensure alignment with legal standards and societal values. In short, making rules for AI in healthcare needs a balanced and future-focused strategy that is clear legally, committed to ethical values, and works together across countries. With strong systems for holding people accountable, strict data protection, and thoughtful use of new rules, AI can be directed toward improving, not harming, healthcare quality, fairness, and trust.

REFERENCES

Aboy, M., Minssen, T., & Vayena, E. (2024). Navigating the EU AI Act: Implications for regulated digital medical products. *NPJ Digital Medicine*, *7*(1), 237. DOI: 10.1038/s41746-024-01232-3 PMID: 39242831

Butt, J. (2024). Analytical study of the world's first EU Artificial Intelligence (AI) Act. *International Journal of Research Publication and Reviews*, *5*(3), 7343–7364. DOI: 10.55248/gengpi.5.0324.0914

Cancela-Outeda, C. (2024). The EU's AI Act: A framework for collaborative governance. *Internet of Things : Engineering Cyber Physical Human Systems*, *27*, 101291. DOI: 10.1016/j.iot.2024.101291

Cantero Gamito, M., & Marsden, C. T. (2024). Artificial intelligence co-regulation? The role of standards in the EU AI Act. *International Journal of Law and Information Technology*, *32*, eaae011. DOI: 10.1093/ijlit/eaae011

Chau, M. (2024). Ethical, legal, and regulatory landscape of artificial intelligence in Australian healthcare and ethical integration in radiography: A narrative review. *Journal of Medical Imaging and Radiation Sciences*, *55*(4), 101733. DOI: 10.1016/j.jmir.2024.101733 PMID: 39111223

De Micco, F., Grassi, S., Tomassini, L., Di Palma, G., Ricchezze, G., & Scendoni, R. (2024). Robotics and AI into healthcare from the perspective of European regulation: Who is responsible for medical malpractice? *Frontiers in Medicine*, *11*, 1428504. DOI: 10.3389/fmed.2024.1428504 PMID: 39309674

Dramburg, S. (2025). Legal and regulatory challenges for digital health technologies with a focus on the European legal situation. In *Digital Allergology: From Theory to Practice* (pp. 39–47). Springer Nature Switzerland. DOI: 10.1007/978-3-031-71021-6_3

Ebenibo, L., Enyejo, J. O., Addo, G., & Olola, T. M. (2024). Evaluating the sufficiency of the Data Protection Act 2023 in the age of artificial intelligence (AI): A comparative case study of Nigeria and the USA. *International Journal of Scholarly Research and Reviews*, *5*(01), 88–107. DOI: 10.56781/ijsrr.2024.5.1.0044

Fessenko, D. S., & Jasperse, A. (2024). Ethics at the heart of AI regulation. *AI and Ethics*, *5*(3), 3387–3398. DOI: 10.1007/s43681-024-00562-y

Goktas, P., & Grzybowski, A. (2025). Shaping the future of healthcare: Ethical clinical challenges and pathways to trustworthy AI. *Journal of Clinical Medicine*, *14*(5), 1605. DOI: 10.3390/jcm14051605 PMID: 40095575

Ijaiya, H., & Odumuwagun, O. O. (2024). Advancing artificial intelligence and safeguarding data privacy: A comparative study of EU and US regulatory frameworks amid emerging cyber threats. *International Journal of Research Publication and Reviews*, *5*(12), 3357–3375. DOI: 10.55248/gengpi.5.1224.250110

Kilian, R., Jäck, L., & Ebel, D. (2025). European AI standards: Technical standardisation and implementation challenges under the EU AI Act. *European Journal of Risk Regulation*, *16*(3), 1–25. DOI: 10.1017/err.2025.10032

Konnoth, C. (2024). AI and data protection law in health. In *Research Handbook on Health, AI and the Law* (pp. 111–129). Edward Elgar Publishing.

Lund, B., Orhan, Z., Mannuru, N. R., Bevara, R. V. K., Porter, B., Vinaih, M. K., & Bhaskara, P. (2025). Standards, frameworks, and legislation for artificial intelligence (AI) transparency. *AI and Ethics*, *5*(4), 3639–3655. Advance online publication. DOI: 10.1007/s43681-025-00661-4

Mennella, C., Maniscalco, U., De Pietro, G., & Esposito, M. (2024). Ethical and regulatory challenges of AI technologies in healthcare: A narrative review. *Heliyon*, *10*(4), e26297. DOI: 10.1016/j.heliyon.2024.e26297 PMID: 38384518

Naidoo, T. (2024). Overview of AI regulation in healthcare: A comparative study of the EU and South Africa. *South African Journal of Bioethics and Law*, *17*(3), 121–126. DOI: 10.7196/SAJBL.2024.v17i3.2294

Olimid, A. P., Georgescu, C. M., & Olimid, D. A. (2024). Legal analysis of EU Artificial Intelligence Act (2024): Insights from personal data governance and health policy. *Access to Justice in Eastern Europe*, *7*(4), 120–142. DOI: 10.33327/AJEE-18-7.4-a000103

Palaniappan, K., Lin, E. Y. T., & Vogel, S. (2024). Global regulatory frameworks for the use of artificial intelligence (AI) in the healthcare services sector. *Health Care*, *12*(5), 562. PMID: 38470673

Palaniappan, K., Lin, E. Y. T., Vogel, S., & Lim, J. C. (2024). Gaps in the global regulatory frameworks for the use of artificial intelligence (AI) in the healthcare services sector and key recommendations. *Health Care*, *12*(17), 1730. PMID: 39273754

Pantanowitz, L., Hanna, M., Pantanowitz, J., Lennerz, J., Henricks, W. H., Shen, P., Quinn, B., Bennet, S., & Rashidi, H. H. (2024). Regulatory aspects of artificial intelligence and machine learning. *Modern Pathology*, *37*(12), 100609. DOI: 10.1016/j.modpat.2024.100609 PMID: 39260776

Pecchia, L., Maccaro, A., Matarrese, M. A., Folkvord, F., & Fico, G. (2024). Artificial intelligence, data protection and medical device regulations: Squaring the circle with a historical perspective in Europe. *Health and Technology*, *14*(4), 663–670. DOI: 10.1007/s12553-024-00878-z

Pesapane, F., & Summers, P. (2024). Ethics and regulations for AI in radiology. In *Artificial Intelligence for Medicine* (pp. 179–192). Academic Press. DOI: 10.1016/B978-0-443-13671-9.00001-6

Pham, T. (2025). Ethical and legal considerations in healthcare AI: Innovation and policy for safe and fair use. *Royal Society Open Science*, *12*(5), 241873. DOI: 10.1098/rsos.241873 PMID: 40370601

Rosic, A. (2024). Legal implications of artificial intelligence in health care. *Clinics in Dermatology*, *42*(5), 451–459. DOI: 10.1016/j.clindermatol.2024.06.014 PMID: 38936641

Schmidt, J., Schutte, N. M., Buttigieg, S., Novillo-Ortiz, D., Sutherland, E., Anderson, M., de Witte, B., Peolsson, M., Unim, B., Pavlova, M., Stern, A. D., Mossialos, E., & Van Kessel, R. (2024). Mapping the regulatory landscape for artificial intelligence in health within the European Union. *NPJ Digital Medicine*, *7*(1), 229. DOI: 10.1038/s41746-024-01221-6 PMID: 39191937

Solaiman, B., & Malik, A. (2025). Regulating algorithmic care in the European Union: Evolving doctor–patient models through the Artificial Intelligence Act (AI Act) and the liability directives. *Medical Law Review*, *33*(1), fwae033. DOI: 10.1093/medlaw/fwae033 PMID: 39257157

Tang, D., Xi, X., Li, Y., & Hu, M. (2025). Regulatory approaches towards AI medical devices: A comparative study of the United States, the European Union and China. *Health Policy (Amsterdam)*, *153*, 105260. DOI: 10.1016/j.healthpol.2025.105260 PMID: 39951854

Van Kolfschooten, H., & Van Oirschot, J. (2024). The EU Artificial Intelligence Act (2024): Implications for healthcare. *Health Policy (Amsterdam)*, *149*, 105152. DOI: 10.1016/j.healthpol.2024.105152 PMID: 39244818

Vujicic, J. (2024). Algorithmic accountability and ethical oversight: Legal challenges in transatlantic AI regulation. *International Journal of Scientific Research Archives*, *13*(2).

Zahra, Y. (2025). Regulating AI in legal practice: Challenges and opportunities. [JOSAPEN]. *Journal of Computer Science Application and Engineering*, *3*(1), 10–15. DOI: 10.70356/josapen.v3i1.47

KEY TERMS AND DEFINITIONS

Legal Accountability: Responsibility for AI-related medical results.

Data Minimization: Gather only vital patient health data.

High-Risk AI Systems: AI tools with substantial patient impact.

Chapter 5
Relational Technologies: Human-AI Interaction and the Ethics of Care in Long-Term Social Work Practice

Stavros Parlalis
https://orcid.org/0000-0003-3572-7122
Frederick University, Cyprus

ABSTRACT

As AI technologies become increasingly integrated into long-term care settings, they are not only transforming service delivery but also influencing the quality of human relationships within these environments. This chapter delves into the evolving dynamics of human-AI interaction from a Social Work perspective, emphasizing ethical considerations, relational aspects, and person-centered care in long-term care contexts. Grounded in core Social Work values – dignity and worth of the individual, the importance of human relationships, and social justice – this chapter critically examines how AI technologies (e.g., robotic companions, predictive analytics, and ambient monitoring systems) intersect with the daily lives of older adults, care workers, and social workers. This chapter presents a compelling case for a Social Work-driven framework to guide the development and implementation of AI in long-term care. It underscores the importance of ensuring that technology serves as a tool to enhance, rather than replace, human connection, while upholding individuals' dignity and rights.

DOI: 10.4018/979-8-3373-5452-1.ch005

1. INTRODUCTION

Long-term care has witnessed the increase of Artificial Intelligence (AI). The impression of care and the delivery methods used in the past have correspondingly changed. AI-driven companions and predictive health analytics with ambient monitoring systems are some of the innovations used by care support workers, social workers and older adults. These innovations enhance social interaction by improving safety and efficiency; however, they leave concerning questions on the care environments and technology's connection on the quality of human relationships.

This chapter seeks to understand the changing relationships through a Social Work angle. AI's benefits are on the increased dignity, autonomy and social belonging of older persons. These benefits also come with risks, therefore the chapter seeks to show how technology-supported care and AI affect the relationships, professional boundaries, and daily lives of care support workers, residents, and therapeutic relationships.

The role of social work in the intersection of AI technology and long-term care still needs to be explored more, which revolves around the ethical and relational aspects and the nuances of personhood. To strategize AI in social work interventions framework, while balancing the overlapping AI social work care outcome and identity concerns outcome, social work's core tenets of social justice, the dignity of the person, and the procedural elements of the human connection need to be prioritized.

The chapter also has AI augmenting care through robotic companions, predicting analytics, and ambient monitoring systems, and their interfaces with elders, care workers, and social workers. By balancing the advantages and limitations of AI in care, the chapter provides a basis for ethically and relationally sensitive interventions.

To honor persons and our communal nature as human companions, the chapter highlights central social work values, urging a relational responsive AI integration. It aims to offer social workers as well as care practitioners and those who work in policy a cautious and considered way forward to steer how AI technology gets integrated in the interest of furthering – and not undermining – human relationship and care.

2. RELEVANCE TO SOCIAL WORK — LINKING AI INTEGRATION TO CORE SOCIAL WORK VALUES

The incorporation of AI technologies within long-term care facilities is pertinent to Social Work practice with both opportunities and difficulties. Social Work rests on deriving values that recognize the dignity and self-worth of the individual and the significance of human relations and the advocacy for social justice (Harden and Turnage 2025). This framework is crucial for addressing the ethical and relational aspects of AI use in caregiving.

Professional Social Work upholds the respect for the individual and the right to self-determine (Borowski 2025). AI technologies are designed to enable personalized care plans, illness and preventive care detection systems, and individuals' intervention preferences; they can honor this principle. Conversely, AI without guiding principles to value the recipients of care, to enhance human engagement, or to maximize control over individual dignity, would have negative ramifications (Oladokun 2025). It is social workers who have the greatest opportunity to ensure that the dignity and care of recipients are AI values. Empathy and social relationships are fundamental in social work practice. The introduction of AI in the form of robotic companions and monitoring systems may significantly change the quality and type of human interactions during care. For example, AI technology might promote social interaction, provide companionship, and relieve staff burdens, thereby increasing the potential of the staff to spend time with clients (Ojo and Afolaranmi 2024). Conversely, the overdependence on technology may remove the genuine human interaction needed in care, which is why social workers are needed to defend connectedness in care practices (Rahman et al. 2025). Furthermore, social work as a profession works toward the promotion of social justice in the face of persistent social structures. The introduction of AI has social justice implications, which primarily revolve around issues of access, inclusivity, and biases that the technology may carry with it. Social workers are crucial in the promotion of responsible AI in social work practice to ensure equity in care (Ho & Ng, 2025). Protecting the community and the people`s rights is a paramount concern. Social Work is fundamental in giving social care practitioners a set of elements that define the core principles of responsible social work practice. The idea that social work is in a good position to offer care through AI integration ethics and policy is based on the values mentioned above. Instead of considering technology as a value-neutral or efficiency-driven innovation, this framework emphasizes the significance of using it as a tool to promote ethical behavior and human connection.

3. OVERVIEW OF AI TECHNOLOGIES IN CARE SETTINGS

AI is rapidly changing the long-term care landscape, bringing new possibilities as well as intricate problems. Within the settings of older adults, AI comes in three general categories: robots, predictive analytics, and ambient monitoring. Each possesses its characteristics, pros and cons, and ethical implications. Robotic companions, from humanoid social robots to more animals, are developed to engage with residents (e.g. for quality interaction, social stimulation, and mental activity) (Chita-Tegmark and Scheutz (2021)). Social robots are able to talk, play games or simply remind the user of certain tasks, while pet robots are able to simulate the companionship of real pets without the operators having to take care of them. It has been suggested that there is evidence these robots can reduce loneliness, improve mood and stimulate cognitive engagement (Riches et al. 2022). But it is questionable of how much can be faked, how much should be subbed out to machines for comfort, and how much can be depleting of human contact. Similarly, predictive analytics leverage artificial intelligence in the analysis of health-based information to anticipate risks (Kosaraju 2024). This technology can identify falls, non-adherence to medication schedules and disease, or hospital admissions in the long-term care space. Early warning and predictive analytics refer to all of these, meaning more proactive and evidence-based patient care and clinical decision making and also serve to support predictive analytics, which serve prevention, pro-active and data informed use interventions (Edoh et al. 2024). Yet issues of ethics include the accuracy of algorithms, the risk for bias, and the degree to which autonomy and informed consent are vested in the care workers and elderly people themselves (Tilala et al. 2024). Finally, ambient monitoring systems enable real-time monitoring of the occupants' activity, behavior and their environment, which are detected by sensors, cameras, etc. These systems are meant to provide safety by identifying quickly and precautionary falls, unpredictable behavior or changes in health status (Fritz and Cook 2025). Regardless of the attempts to develop their responsiveness and efficiency, they do not come without serious implications regarding privacy, surveillance and consent (Martinez-Martin et al. 2021), one of constant and ongoing surveillance and seeming violations of personal freedom. These advances in AI technology, while seemingly promising transformation across long-term care spaces, and efficient care delivery, safety, care and social connection, these technologies should be used relationally, ethically and person-centered to ensure the technologies supplement (not replace the human) of care.

4. CURRENT TRENDS AND ADOPTION OF AI IN LONG-TERM CARE FACILITIES

The rise in demand for eldercare services and a scarcity of workers are driving AI to be adopted in long-term care facilities. It is stated in the literature that AI emerges as the most eagerly anticipated innovation slated for adoption offered by senior living communities, with the potential to transform the delivery of care (Wong et al. 2024). Intelligent types of eldercare in global regions, such as the UK, USA and Japan are advanced in applying AI technologies (Zhu et al. 2023). However, for all the promise that it holds, the application of AI in long-term care is not without its challenges. A prominent issue relates to the abandonment of technology post-adoption; studies have indicated that there is technology abandonment, where some nursing homes have stopped using approved technologies (Berridge and Grigorovich 2022).

4.1. Potential Benefits of AI Integration in Long-Term Care

The use of AI in long-term care has the potential to offer many benefits that may have a meaningful impact on care quality and resident quality of life. One of the biggest benefits of that is better tracking of health. Technologies that empower AI, such as ambient sensors, wearables and predictive analytics platforms allow care professionals to track residents' health in real time (Etli et al. 2024). Such technologies can capture minute alterations in mobility, the rhythm of sleep or vital signs that might otherwise escape attention, permitting early intervention and minimizing risks, such as fall hazards, infections or medication mistakes. Another advantage is the greater efficiency of care provision. Artificial intelligence systems can deal with everyday jobs, including reminders of medicine, appointments and monitoring of health Stand levels, etc., and as a result, healthcare workers can direct their attention to direct contact between patient and worker and complex ones (Maleki Varnosfaderani and Forouzanfar 2024). Through automation of administrative and operational processes, AI can improve team efficiency, which may lead to a reduction in staff burnout and improved service quality (Nguyen and Malik 2022). AI also supports early recognition of health problems through predictive analytics. If an AI application examines both historical and contemporary data along with understanding social workers, nurses, and physicians practices as patterns emerge in a client's health journey, indicating their health deteriorating, AI will help connect the dots and utilize predictive analytics so that trained professionals can implement proactive interventions (Kumar and Suthar 2024). Not only can this lead to better clinical outcomes, but it can also support individual care plans in ways that align with the Social Work values of dignity, autonomy, and empowerment through person-centred care. Additional approaches related to social robots, AI-mediated virtual communication as well as group work are also methods through which AI can strengthen social engagement opportunities to provide companionship and emotional supports to the people who reside in long-term care homes (LTC) that may be experiencing social isolation, feeling lonely, or experiencing cognitive decline (Oh et al., 2025). When and where the use of these tools are intentional, they can only be a support to social interaction and provide an opportunity to keep potential connections and relationships with others, and to enhance emotional and social well-being for older adults. There are clearly described benefits of how AI can support responsive, efficient, and person-centred approaches to care in long-term care, when reasonable ethical, relational, cultural competency best practices have been seriously considered and put in place.

4.2. Possible Dangers of AI in Long-Term Care

Although AI technologies may improve long-term care monitoring or even safety, there are substantial obstacles to their application that must be managed in an acceptable way. These include issues related to depersonalization, diminished human contact, privacy violations and the potential to entrench existing societal inequities - any of which may have long-lasting consequences for health and care outcomes for older adults (Dailah et al. 2024).

The introduction of AI-enhanced care technologies such as robotic care or automated monitoring may inadvertently diminish the human aspect of care (Nasir et al. 2024). As tasks that have historically been performed and provided by caregivers – including emotional support, social interaction, wellness check-ins, etc. – are taken over by machines or robots, the elderly might consider these interactions to be mechanical as opposed to relational. This may paraphrase dignity and individuality, which is an established value in Social Work, and represents a possibility of loss of any form of human connection (Turkkan Zencirli and Altin, 2025).

While AI improves the effectiveness and security of monitoring and using predictive analytics to enhance care, there is a potential downside of over-exploiting this technology; there will be diminishing opportunities for human-to-human contact for residents and caregivers (de Ruiter et al., 2023). For some older adults, loneliness, social isolation, and declining mental health have become health risks in their own right, so the reduction in human physical contact in residential care is concerning.

Moreover, AI systems generally obtain data continuously, not only the behavior, health measures, but also all movements that take place in the caregiving environment. This raises ethical questions regarding data security, consent, and personal data ownership (Nandy 2023). If there are no good policies in place that are enforced, monitoring systems can intrude upon the residents' privacy, reduce their autonomy, and/or create overwhelming feelings of vulnerability or distrust (Doe 2025).

In addition, applying new technologies like AI in long-term care can actually amplify social, economic, and digital inequalities. For example, wealthier people will likely have access to advanced technologies, which may not be the case for poorer people who will receive less care since their technology may be inferior; therefore, the quality of care can be of average level. Furthermore, intentional or unintentional bias in the form of exclusive and non-representative data or other flawed design work (Panarese 2025) can also have adverse effects on people with health problems more often and to a greater extent against more marginalized populations, which also goes against the social justice values of Social Work.

To minimize the risks, there needs to be a relationship aware approach that reduces the risk that long-term care practice influenced by AI will strip or remove human dignity, autonomy and equity. Social Workers can advocate for equitable and ethical use of AI, protections around residents'/patients' privacy, and center the relationships, nurturance, and emotional needs of all people in long term care.

5. A SOCIAL WORK APPROACH TO HUMAN-AI INTERACTION

When considering the incorporation of AI into long-term care environments, it should not be assessed only on the technical level, but also through fundamental Social Work values. Three core values – the dignity and worth of a person, the importance of human relationships, and the principle of social justice and equity – provide an essential lens for discussing the way technologies impact the lives of older adults, caregivers, and communities (Xu et al., 2024). Social work holds potential because it's based on the foundation that all human beings are of inherent worth. Where AI solutions in long-term care are either robotic companions or predictive analytics to improve services, they must be designed and applied so that they respect the individuality of older adults and do not reduce them to data points or passive recipients of services (Mhlanga 2024). Respect for informed consent, privacy, and avoiding leaving room for cultural, linguistic, or personal preferences are some of the means to uphold dignity (Adeniyi et al., 2024). For instance, ambient assistive systems that help promote independence, should be implemented collaboratively, allowing each individual to establish the level of monitoring they deem respectful and appropriate (Solanki, Grundy and Hussain 2023). Moreover, the relationships between people is at the core of achieving and maintaining well-being in a person, which is a fundamental importance in Social Work. AI technologies can be used to enhance and hence strengthen those relationships, or they can have the opposite effect. If robotic companions can bring some measure of comfort, they cannot replace the emotional connection of humans interacting with one another (Mitchell and Jeon 2025). Social workers will play a crucial role in making sure technology is improving therapeutic relationships and caregiving rather than taking the place of them (Harris and Stout 2022). Creating contexts in which AI allows to reduce administrative burden (i.e., documentation), so that caregivers can spend more time interacting with residents, and encourages human interaction (Smriti 2024).

Furthermore, while the rapid uptake of AI has the potential to accentuate inequalities, this is due in part to the possibility that access will be determined by the available resources, available to wealthier institutions or simply because AI will consider institutional biases when developing their algorithms. This means that if maintaining power by manipulating care is one of the consequences of new technologies; it is incumbent on the care profession, grounded in social justice, to offer appropriate vigilant supervision to ensure that the benefits of AI should be considered a public good first and foremost and to identify, evaluate and eliminate discriminatory practices as much as possible (Hamblin 2022). As an example, predictive systems should receive thorough review to eliminate harmful bias against the welfare of vulnerable groups (Hall et al. 2024). All staff (regardless of if they are social workers or have a different professional background) must available training to utilize the AI, ethically aimed towards obtaining good social outcomes. Finally, social workers are best placed to contest power inequities in digital care contexts and influence and advocate for policies to protect the rights of those who are disadvantages and neglected (Sanders and Scanlon 2021). Importantly, combined values derived from long-term care have to be grounded in an ethic of care aimed at protecting dignity, building human relationships and achieving justice.

6. IMPACT ON CARE RELATIONSHIPS WITH OLDER ADULTS AND

The term 'therapeutic relationship' is one that underpins long-term care and the work of social workers to achieve empathy and trust in a reciprocal, respectful manner (Ferguson et al. 2022). The disruptiveness of AI has its challenges and opportunities for the workplace. For instance, AI applications, such as predictive analytics and robotic companions, could enable carers to explore and tailor interventions through compressed engagement in relational ways (Thomas et al. 2025). For instance, an alarm system that monitors and notifies of early signs of distress enables staff to manage such signals with reassurance and role model before they become more prominent. When the staff is able to prove they are tuned in to the client's needs and responds relationally it supports the therapeutic relationship. Without care, an overreliance on the abilities of technology runs the risk of allowing all the individuals to be objectified into a data point (Ferdman 2024), leaving staff that provide care reflecting judgments based on what data tells them. With technology predicting and replacing meaningful conversations by chatting with staff, there is a risk that the individual feels they are no longer being "heard" and respected as a person and the fragility of therapeutic relationships is undermined (Chouliara at al. 2024).

Older adults appear to be ambivalent regarding AI technologies. While robotic companions or digital tools can help reduce feelings of loneliness, facilitate leisure-based contacts, or encourage individuals to engage in physical activity, there is also a risk of the digital relationships creating more loneliness when they are used to supplant the more work of multiple human interactions (Candiotto 2022). The elderly user may receive solace from the robot or digital tool, but it may provide less overall emotional support than feelings of human interaction with those practices (Meng and Dai 2021), if the experience involves grief, existential awe, or emotional need. Variations in cultural attitudes, differences in digital literacy and other factors of the lives of elderly shape perceptions of AI, and interaction with AI technologies. There needs to be an emphasis on personalized and contextual designs to enable these differences and differences in importance to be considered.

On the other hand, professionals such as social workers and nurses are in a process in which they have to reimagine care work, since AI is being integrated into their practices (Wassal et al. 2024; Mehmood 2024). In some cases, automated monitoring and task delegation to robots result in a reduction of their work (Gustafsson, Kazlou and Wihlborg 2024), thus allowing them to concentrate more on relational aspects of care. In other scenarios, new problems emerge which range from learning unfamiliar technologies to resolving more ethical issues or even adjusting to increased scrutiny of their work (Dhirani et al. 2023). This also brings in a possibility of blurring professional boundaries; for instance, when algorithms recommend interventions, care workers might be conflicted between their clinical judgment and technical recommendations (Montomoli et al. 2024). These challenges underscore the immediate necessity for training and guidance on ethics besides support at the institutional level toward making a change effective.

7. INSERTING AI IN AN INDIVIDUAL-CENTERED, SOCIAL WORK-INFORMED WAY

Even though the integration of AI into the long-term care creates new opportunities, on the same time it creates make challenges for the field of social work practice. The ethical concern for social workers is the extent to which AI will enhance the human elements of quality care (Diez 2023), which they have no choice but to consider as these technologies become more dominant. It needs to be approached in a balanced and principled manner that centers on the person as the primary focus of all AI deployments, and the profession's commitment to human dignity, human relationship, and social justice is not abandoned (Becker 2021). A list of guiding principles are presented and discussed below.

7.1 Enhancing Human Connection, Not Replacing It

The primary focus of social work centered integration of AI is to ensure that technology is used to deepen, not replace, human contact (Fahad 2024). AI technologies have to be designed and deployed to promote intersectional caregiving among care receivers, family, and care providers (Milella and Bandini 2024). In practical terms, this means that AI tools have to be viewed as promoters of human contact, not as instruments of autonomous action. Predictive analytics systems, for example, can be used to relieve social workers of monotonous and repetitive transactional systems (Abdalla, Al-Maamari and Al-Azki 2024), thus enabling them to spend the bulk of their time in therapeutic conversations and relationship building. Robotic companions for example, should be used to promote interactions, assist caregivers in memory prompting and recall, and other supports to complement the work of caregivers (Robinson and Nejat 2022). This principle requires careful assessment of the quantity and quality of human contact provided by AI. New technology must be evaluated in terms of how it encourages real human contact (Magliocca et al. 2024). Tools that promote isolation or face-to-face disengagement should be nixed, while ones that support interpersonal communication and connection should be prioritized. Overall, social workers have to make sure that AI systems and tools values individuals' human value, which include empathy, intuition, and the capacity for emotional connection rather than focus only on data collection, data analysis and patterns design.

7.2 Ensuring Informed Consent and Preserving Agency

There also must be respect for autonomy and self-determination through strong informed consent protocols more extensive than standard models employed in medical or care environments (Wiertz and Boldt 2022). As complex and as opaque as AI systems are, social workers will need to ensure that individuals are fully informed not only of the technology utilized but also how they function, what data they are collecting, and for what purposes information is being collected (Mishna et al. 2021).

Informed consent to utilize AI must address a number of levels of decision-making. Service users must be informed about how the tools of AI operate (e.g., tools to track falls or prompt patients to take medication), the means of gathering and analyzing underlying data, and the potential implications for privacy and quality of care (Williamson and Prybutok 2024). Transparency in decision-making pathways that are generated by algorithms that influence care advice or resource allocation is key.

Agency is a way of working, not just a one-off decision; it is more than the "decision-at-point-of-decision" and is a commitment to ongoing choice and control. People must have the power to be able to change the way they receive AI, power to be able to switch certain features off, and power to opt for human alternatives whenever they want (Birhane et al. 2022). That is, designing AI systems to be adaptable, so that technology turn-off does not lead to lower quality care.

Social workers also should advocate for the rights of people with cognitive disability or other impairments that may limit their capacity for traditional informed consent. It may involve strategies to 'think outside the box', patterns of consent, approaches to contact with family or familiar supporters, or the use of technological solutions that are respectful of the individual's values and preferences.

7.3 Fostering Cultural Competence and Inclusion

It is anticipated that AI will be developed and implemented in ways that the long-term care population's cultural, linguistic, and socioeconomic diversity is considered (Neves et al., 2023). This requires moving away from a one-size-fits-all solution to an understanding that the use and success of technology adoption rests more on culture and individual preferences. When it comes to deploying AI, cultural competence means understanding how each culture sees tech, privacy, families being part of care decisions, and communication. For instance, some cultures are more family-oriented, where decisions are made by family members, while others are more individualistic (Knight et al. 2024). AI strategy and its technologies and deployment methodologies should have the flexibility to do so. Inclusion is transcending several possible barriers for AI adoption, such as language, tech illiteracy, physical disability, and scarcity of resources (Almufareh et al. 2024). This includes making AI interfaces accessible, delivering education and support in multiple languages (Mageira et al. 2022), and attempting to identify how technology solutions don't through design exclude or negatively impact certain types of people. Social workers need to encourage diverse AI development teams and test procedures that examine how technologies interact with various demographic groups (Pham et al. 2024). This entails tracking for algorithmic bias that has the potential to cause disparate treatment or outcomes by race, ethnicity, sex, socioeconomic status, or other rationales.

7.4 Training and Education for Staff

Effective implementation of AI requires comprehensive education programmes within both the technical and ethical domains (Schiff, 2022). Staff training should not just remain at the functional level but include awareness of the relational and ethical aspects of using AI in care settings. It is necessary for all staff to be trained on how to use AI systems and how to solve possible technical issues they might face. Just as important, or maybe more important, is teaching staff the social and ethical use of AI. Staff must be taught to provide person-focused care in spite of technology assistance, to recognize and neutralize probable negative effects on human relationships (McCall et al. 2023), and to respect the rights and wishes of residents. Training must include scenario practice under which staff can rehearse management of complex situations in which technology meets human care (Aicken et al. 2021). Such as when AI suggestions contradict professional judgment, residents are resistant to the use of surveillance technology, or there are complaints from families about privacy and data use. Overall, ongoing education is necessary, as AI technologies change. Periodic refreshing, refresher training, and experiences in which employees can exchange perspectives and concerns guarantee integration of AI into social work values intact (Wassal et al. 2024). Support and supervision systems must be compulsory in professionals' training, in order to assist them in working their way through the emotional and ethical issues in utilizing new AI systems (Bankins and Formosa 2023).

7.5 Participatory Design with Residents and Families

Active participation of care recipients and their families in planning and designing AI technologies is imperative so that the latter are actually planned and designed to address their needs and satisfaction. This participation goes beyond the stages of consultation and must also include active decision-making about technology adoption, functionality, and assimilation into care practices (Mulvale et al. 2024). Participatory design strategies have to be introduced early on in the designing process in order to engage elderly people and their families in the identification of care issues that could be supported by technological solutions. Their input is crucial, aiming at providing the correct method of choosing AI technologies, while considering how they could be integrated into the care context. This even includes choices of information sharing, alerting systems, user interfaces, and the decisions that need to be made around the balance of automated and mediated care. Ongoing feedback processes are necessary during the implementation phase to tap into resident and family perceptions. These can be official processes of assessment, or informal mechanisms for giving feedback to register concern, propose or ask for change (Wu et al. 2021). Social workers have a vital role to play in encouraging these discussions and ensuring that all voices are heard, even those of individuals resistant to sharing their voice or who cannot communicate at all. Engagement of the family must be weighed against privacy and autonomy concerns. While families may be engaged in planning care, their role in decision-making about AI matters must respect the right of the resident to self-determination and privacy (Annoni 2025). Social workers can make this possible through the establishment of an open discussion balancing family interest against person desire and rights.

7.6 Monitoring Outcomes and Refining Practice Based on Feedback

Ongoing oversight and assessment are needed to ensure integration of AI meets its function of maximizing care without compromising person-centered practice (Alshammari et al. 2024). Activities must shift from functional purposes, such as efficiency or reducing cost, to the relational and quality-of-life purposes. Monitoring should be for quantitative and qualitative indicators. Quantitative data can be performance indicators like quality of care, safety outcomes, and service efficiency. No less vital are qualitative indicators in residents', family members', and staff members' experience, e.g., quality of relationships, satisfaction with the care received, perception of autonomy and dignity, and quality of life (Gilbert et al. 2021).

Collecting feedback needs to be an integral part of everyday practice and not set aside in the interest of formal evaluation time. This type of evaluation may include quick check-ins during the care interaction, regular focus groups, and continued observance of the impact AI technologies may have on daily living in the care setting. Given workers' relationships and working knowledge of the individual's unique experience, social workers are in the best position to conduct this type of evaluation. The monitoring and feedback system should highlight negative and positive impacts. It will involve the establishment of indicators that would suggest AI is making individuals less talkative or reinforcing a sense of surveillance or privacy invasion or leading to isolation (Puplampu 2024). There would need to be established mechanisms for mitigation of potential harm like changing or stopping the technology intervention anytime. This will need flexibility in the installation and care processes to adapt to user feedback. The flexibility will entail some of the adjustments as tuning AI system settings, adjusting training programs, adjusting implementation strategies, or abandoning specific technology (Kovalevskyi 2024). Such flexibility translates to devotion to patient care because AI solutions are tailored to suit people's needs rather than technology or organizational needs.

As illustrated above, as valuable as AI technologies can be in social work in long-term care, it is vital that such practice leads with value sensitivity, relational thinking and notions of individuality. To enhance optimal human engagement, autonomy and consent, diversity and cultural competence-oriented principles with effective and ethical approaches (Alanazi et al. 2024). Each of engaging staff with multi-dimensional training, participatory design, and ongoing monitoring and tuning is an essential technique they close the practice-principles gap. The success of this venture hinges on an unwavering commitment to people-centric decisions when considering technology, and ensuring the requisite human elements remain in supporting quality care. Well-considered study of and intent engagement in AI adoption and potential in social work can provide assurance that emerging technologies enhance, rather than diminish, dignity, relationships, and quality of life prominent in social work.

8. FUTURE DIRECTIONS AND POLICY IMPLICATIONS

The application of AI technologies within long-term care facilities raises both deeply troubling questions to be tackled from a social work standpoint (Neves et al. 2023) and possibly exhilarating opportunities as they continue to evolve. Strong advocacy, deeply informed policymaking, and ongoing questions regarding ethical practice and the role of human relationships will be necessary in shaping the future of AI-based health care. This section explores the use of AI as a supportive mechanism while also identifying significant gaps in what we presently know about long-term impacts.

8.1 Future Directions

Opportunities for Innovation, AI as an Augmentative Tool for Care Delivery

AI has enormous potential for enhancing collective, not replaceable, human interaction in care (Alrassi et al. 2021) as well as to support care teams and social workers by providing person and culturally appropriate care. We can make the uptake consistent with the values of social work by attempting to develop AI innovation in a human-centered process that prioritizes human dignity and real relationships (Ystgaard and de Moor 2023).

Enhanced Assessment and Care Planning

Next-generation AI systems have the potential to alter social work assessments in a whole-person manner, as these systems may compile information from multiple sources while considering the importance of individual stories and individual autonomy (Reamer 2023). Through predictive analytics, social workers can anticipate emerging needs and emerging risks and therefore facilitate preventative approaches to crisis management, rather than simply crisis response (Nuwasiima, Ahonon and Kadiri 2024). These systems should supplement social workers' clinical judgement, as well as, critical thinking rather than supplant either. This keeps social workers at the centre of understanding complex human situations.

Individualized Intervention Plans

AI can compile highly customized intervention plans for social workers by identifying successful patterns with similar groups or individuals grounded in their own unique traits and behavior (Fahad 2024). This approach is deemed to be very effective in addressing the diverse cultural, linguistic, and social requirements of residents in long-term care facilities. AI systems could figure out what the best engagement patterns are for the person who has a memory problem for elders, or the activities that are culturally right for them, and communication strategies that work for some, also based on some types or background.

Augmented Communication and Connection

Despite being a shorthand for the processes and machinery involved with machine learning and decision-making algorithms, AI could have a better chance to make humans better by eliminating communication barriers rather than increasing them (Goldenthal et al. 2021). For residents and social workers who are not using the same language, voice recognition software could even translate speech in real time. By enabling daily video calls, updating on care progress, and enabling virtual visits to care plan meetings, AI-based apps can also help families keep in contact with carers (Milella, Russo and Bandini (2023).

Administrative Effectiveness in Relationship Building

One of the most useful uses of AI is its ability to free social workers from bureaucratic tasks (Meilvang 2023). This provides additional time spent on building relationships and therapeutic contact. AI can handle mundane paperwork tasks, preliminary assessment reports can be generated for social workers to utilize as a template (Netto 2024), and care-related communications can be managed. This increased efficiency benefits all involved staff in the sector: balancing paperwork with meaningful client contact.

Ongoing Learning and Adaptation

AI systems of the future need to incorporate feedback loops to learn from the results of interventions in social work and increasingly improve their recommendations (Nuwasiima, Ahonon and Kadiri 2024). The systems must incorporate quantitative (e.g., better health status and decreased occurrences) as well as qualitative (e.g., relational satisfaction, dignity, and cultural responsiveness) measures, which are essential for successful social work practice.

8.2 Policy and Advocacy Roles for Social Workers — Protecting Rights, Justice, and Ethical Deployment

Social workers have the responsibility to advance policies that protect vulnerable populations and promote social justice in the design and implementation of AI technology (Ahn et al. 2025). This is extremely important in long-term care facilities, where there are power imbalances. AI can exacerbate or reduce existing inequalities.

Informed Consent and Digital Rights

Social workers must establish strong informed consent procedures that go beyond simply consenting to the use of technology. Policies must require residents and families to be made aware of what information is being gathered, how it is used, and how the AI systems make decisions regarding their care (Panahi 2025). This includes protecting the right to have someone review AI-recommended actions and the right for individuals to decline certain uses of AI without penalty or a decrease in quality of care.

Privacy and Surveillance Oversight

The growth in surveillance networks and predictive analytics raises concerns about privacy and dignity within the care system. Social workers need to advocate for policies that place strict controls on surveillance technologies (Byrne, Kirwan and McGuckin 2019), require regular audits of data-harvesting practices, and promote monitoring for therapeutic purposes and not institutional ones. That means being a supporter of legislation that gives rights to residents over their data and being an opponent of abusing AI technology as a tool of punishment or discrimination.

Equity in Access and Design

Social workers ought to encourage AI development processes that aim to reduce existing inequalities. Promoting diverse representation in AI development teams, mandating testing for bias across a range of demographic groups, and guaranteeing accessibility for individuals with disabilities and from diverse cultural backgrounds are all part of this. Before AI systems are employed in care settings, policies should allow for equity impact assessments (Berdahl et al. 2023).

Professional Standards and Training

Standards for practice must be developed and shared by social work organizations based on AI. This involves competency guidelines development for social workers working with AI systems, developing ethical decision-making guidelines taking into account AI, and educational programs in social work that make people ready to work in technology-saturated settings (James et al. 2024).

Regulatory Accountability and Oversight

Social workers should advocate for regulatory settings that ensure AI systems utilized in care settings come with extremely high levels of effectiveness, safety, and ethics. For example, AI providers need to show how their systems affect care relationships as opposed to just care outcomes and ensure transparency in the algorithms' decision-making process.

Labor and Professional Autonomy Protections

As AI technology evolves, social workers should assert their professional independence and protect themselves against the deskilling of their profession (Howe 2023). This means ensuring that AI supports and strengthens social work decision-making, rather than determining it. Social workers must fight to establish workforce protections against the employment of AI to minimize staffing levels or undermine their status in care groups (Maota and Maota 2025).

8.3 Research Gaps — Areas Needing Further Research

There has been an increase in interest regarding AI applications within a care context; there remains an understanding of the relationship component of care, which is fundamental to social work practice. Further addressing these areas will be paramount to developing evidence-based ways of integrating AI that are consistent with social work values and ethics.

Long-term Relational Effects

One of the key areas of research is the long-term effect of exposure to AI systems on care givers and care receivers. Longitudinal research needs to be conducted in order to determine whether the widespread use of AI companions or AI-enabled care benefits or harms residents' ability to develop meaningful relational bonds. Research also needs to examine whether the long-term use of AI tools erodes social workers' empathy, clinical reasoning, and skill building for building relationships (Fahad 2024).

Cultural Competence and AI

Research is also limited regarding how AI systems function when cultural variations present themselves, and whether they are tools supporting culturally attuned social work practice. Research should assess how well AI systems comprehend communication patterns, help-seeking behavior, and cultural manifestations of distress. There should also be studies to examine whether AI tools can meaningfully assist social work with diverse client populations (Lehtiniemi 2024) or contribute to cultural homogenization, which goes against individualized care.

Impact on Care Relationships Across Populations

There is a need for research on how AI affects relationships in care across populations such as individuals with variable cognitive impairment, mental health needs, and disabilities, and an array of cultural backgrounds. It is important to identify if specific groups of people are at risk of experiencing negative relational impacts through the use of AI (Abdulai 2025) and if there are protective factors that could inform the development of targeted implementation plans.

Ethical Decision-Making in AI-Assisted Practice

After analyzing implications of relationships and bias on care delivery, there is also a need for research into how social workers are managing ethical challenges that arise from a reliance on AI (Segal 2025) as opinions provided through AI conflict with professional judgment. Research must explore how the AI suggestions were negotiated against clinical judgment, presumably on client confidentiality, self-determination, and well-being (Nordesjö, Scaramuzzino and Ulmestig 2022). Identifying best practices for ethical social work practice in relation to AI possibilities is important to the profession and practice.

Efficacy of Different Implementation Models

In an effort to continue practice in incorporating AI into care, there must be research on the care models for incorporating AI into care. We must consider examining which models enhance the quality of care outcome and relationships. This encompasses assessing a participatory design approach mode of development between families and residents that were engaged in AI development (Birhane et al. 2022), implementation and evaluation processes, or phased roll out over time compared to a complete roll out, or even how the caregivers were trained and supported in training whether the nature of training and support affected the implementation of AI care.

Economic and Equity Developmental Research

There is a need to understand the economic effect of AI in care from an equity standpoint. To the same purpose, there should be an estimation of how much the uptake of AI contributed towards decreased or increased inequities in the quality of care provided to service users in long-term care. Also, the cost effectiveness of AI tools from a relational and quality of life viewpoint has to be assessed (Jacob et al. 2025).

Unintended Consequences and Systems Impacts

Research will have to consider the broader systems impacts of A.I. implementation. That is, it will have to examine the impact of AI on family engagement in care, community connections, and the social fabric of care settings. Working on developing the unexpected unplanned consequences of AI needs to be an emphasis, especially since they might only appear when there is extensive reliance on AI.

Relational Outcome Measure Development

Finally, we must create and pilot test measures of outcome that are sensitive to relational dimensions of care that are important to social work. A good health outcome measure would measure dignity, autonomy, cultural sensitivity, and relationship satisfaction - we require a means to be able to measure the impact on the most underrated aspects of care.

CONCLUSION

Research priorities, policy, and plans for implementation today shape the course to the future of AI in long-term care. Social workers have a unique ethical responsibility to construct towards a future modality in which we are deepening the profession's fundamental values of human dignity, social justice, and relationships in care (Henrickson 2022). Social workers, by way of innovation, advocacy, and research, can drive the AI technologies to become instruments that amplify human elements of care so that all of our endeavors count.

The future presents a challenge in which social workers will need to get ahead as advocates, ethical guardians, and relationship facilitators in AI-mediated care settings. By centering human relationship, being serious about informed consent and cultural competency, and keeping an eye out for equity and privacy issues, social workers can take an active part in shaping AI to enhance well-being among older adults.

Thus, the final success of AI in long-term care is not measurable in terms of functioning but in the richness of human relationships that it can deliver to and restore to the dignity that is the over-riding theme of authentic care. With careful, value-laden integration, AI can be an ally in being a good collaborator in enriching the relational foundations that turn care truly transformative.

REFERENCES

Abdalla, S., Al-Maamari, W., & Al-Azki, J. (2024). Data analytics-driven innovation: UTAUT model perspectives for advancing healthcare social work. *Journal of Open Innovation, 10*(4), 100411. DOI: 10.1016/j.joitmc.2024.100411

Abdulai, A. F. (2025). Is Generative AI Increasing the Risk for Technology-Mediated Trauma Among Vulnerable Populations? *Nursing Inquiry, 32*(1), e12686. DOI: 10.1111/nin.12686

Adeniyi, A. O., Arowoogun, J. O., Okolo, C. A., Chidi, R., & Babawarun, O. (2024). Ethical considerations in healthcare IT: A review of data privacy and patient consent issues. *World Journal of Advanced Research and Reviews, 21*(2), 1660–1668. DOI: 10.30574/wjarr.2024.21.2.0593

Ahn, E., Choi, M., Fowler, P., & Song, I. H. (2025). Artificial intelligence (AI) literacy for social work: Implications for core competencies. *Journal of the Society for Social Work and Research, 16*(1), 9–26. DOI: 10.1086/735187

Aicken, C., Hodgson, L., De Vries, K., Wilkinson, I., Aldridge, Z., & Galvin, K. (2021). 'This Adds Another Perspective': Qualitative Descriptive Study Evaluating Simulation-Based Training for Health Care Assistants, to Enhance the Quality of Care in Nursing Homes. *International Journal of Environmental Research and Public Health, 18*(8), 3995. DOI: 10.3390/ijerph18083995

Alanazi, M. A., Shaban, M. M., Ramadan, O. M. E., Zaky, M. E., Mohammed, H. H., Amer, F. G. M., & Shaban, M. (2024). Navigating end-of-life decision-making in nursing: A systematic review of ethical challenges and palliative care practices. *BMC Nursing, 23*(1), 467. DOI: 10.1186/s12912-024-02087-5

Almufareh, M. F., Kausar, S., Humayun, M., & Tehsin, S. (2024). A conceptual model for inclusive technology: Advancing disability inclusion through artificial intelligence. *Journal of Disability Research, 3*(1), 20230060. DOI: 10.57197/JDR-2023-0060

Alrassi, J., Katsufrakis, P. J., & Chandran, L. (2021). Technology can augment, but not replace, critical human skills needed for patient care. *Academic Medicine, 96*(1), 37–43. DOI: 10.1097/ACM.0000000000003733

Alshammari, E. O. M., Alshammari, M. B. S., Al Anazy, A. K. M., Al-Anzi, M. A. H. A., Alfiras, K. S. A., Alshamry, M. A. S., & Asiri, A. A. M. (2024). Enhancing Nursing Excellence: Exploring Person-Centered Care Implementation in Clinical Practice. *Journal of International Crisis and Risk Communication Research, 7*(S3), 514.

Annoni, M. (2025). Autonomy, self-determination and substitute judgement: the limits of AI-based personalised patient preference predictors (P4s) in surrogate decision-making. *Journal of Medical Ethics.*

Bankins, S., & Formosa, P. (2023). The ethical implications of artificial intelligence (AI) for meaningful work. *Journal of Business Ethics, 185*(4), 725–740. DOI: 10.1007/s10551-023-05339-7

Becker, A. (2021). Human dignity through action: Transformative human rights education and social work. *Journal of Human Rights and Social Work, 6*(3), 173–182. DOI: 10.1007/s41134-020-00160-y

Berdahl, C. T., Baker, L., Mann, S., Osoba, O., & Girosi, F. (2023). Strategies to improve the impact of artificial intelligence on health equity: Scoping review. *JMIR AI, 2*, e42936. DOI: 10.2196/42936

Berridge, C., & Grigorovich, A. (2022). Algorithmic harms and digital ageism in the use of surveillance technologies in nursing homes. *Frontiers in Sociology, 7*, 957246. DOI: 10.3389/fsoc.2022.957246

Birhane, A., Isaac, W., Prabhakaran, V., Diaz, M., Elish, M. C., Gabriel, I., & Mohamed, S. (2022, October). Power to the people? Opportunities and challenges for participatory AI. In *Proceedings of the 2nd ACM Conference on Equity and Access in Algorithms, Mechanisms, and Optimization* (pp. 1-8). DOI: 10.1145/3551624.3555290

Borowski, A. (2025). On human dignity and social work. *British Journal of Social Work, 52*(2), 609–623. DOI: 10.1093/bjsw/bcab016

Byrne, J., Kirwan, G., & Mc Guckin, C. (2019). Social media surveillance in social work: Practice realities and ethical implications. *Journal of Technology in Human Services*, *37*(2-3), 142–158. DOI: 10.1080/15228835.2019.1584598

Candiotto, L. (2022). Extended loneliness. When hyperconnectivity makes us feel alone. *Ethics and Information Technology*, *24*(4), 47. DOI: 10.1007/s10676-022-09669-4

Chita-Tegmark, M., & Scheutz, M. (2021). Assistive robots for the social management of health: A framework for robot design and human–robot interaction research. *International Journal of Social Robotics*, *13*(2), 197–217. DOI: 10.1007/s12369-020-00634-z

Chouliara, Z., Murray, J., Coleman, A. M., Burke Draucker, C., & Choi, W. M. A. (2024). Therapeutic trust in complex trauma: A unique person–centered understanding. *Person-Centered and Experiential Psychotherapies*, *23*(2), 177–202. DOI: 10.1080/14779757.2023.2207107

Dailah, H. G., Koriri, M., Sabei, A., Kriry, T., & Zakri, M. (2024, December). Artificial intelligence in nursing: Technological benefits to nurse's mental health and patient care quality. [). MDPI.]. *Health Care*, *12*(24), 2555.

de Ruiter, H. P., Clisbee, D., Houston, R., & Skärsäter, I. (2023). The Ethical, Care, and Client-Caregiver Relationship Impacts Resulting From Introduction of Digital Communication and Surveillance Technologies in the Home Setting: Qualitative Inductive Study. *JMIR Human Factors*, *10*, e47586. DOI: 10.2196/47586

Dhirani, L. L., Mukhtiar, N., Chowdhry, B. S., & Newe, T. (2023). Ethical dilemmas and privacy issues in emerging technologies: A review. *Sensors (Basel)*, *23*(3), 1151. DOI: 10.3390/s23031151

Diez, E. R. (2023). Artificial Intelligence and Social Work: Contributions to an Ethical Artificial Intelligence at the Service of People. In *The Routledge International Handbook of Digital Social Work* (pp.368-381). Routledge.

Doe, J. (2025). Exploring the Ethics of Data Privacy in the Digital Age. *Pakistan Journal of Healthcare Research*, *2*(1), 40–54.

Edoh, N. L., Chigboh, V. M., Zouo, S. J. C., & Olamijuwon, J. (2024). Improving healthcare decision-making with predictive analytics: A conceptual approach to patient risk assessment and care optimization. *International Journal of Scholarly Research in Medicine and Dentistry*, *3*(2), 1–10. DOI: 10.56781/ijsrmd.2024.3.2.0034

Etli, D., Djurovic, A., & Lark, J. (2024). The Future of Personalized Healthcare: AI-Driven Wearables For Real-Time Health Monitoring And Predictive Analytics. *Current Research in Health Sciences*, *2*(2), 10–14.

Fahad, S. (2024). Transforming Medical Social Work with Artificial Intelligence. *Social Work Chronicle*, *13*(1), 24–49.

Ferdman, A. (2024). Human flourishing and technology affordances. *Philosophy & Technology*, *37*(1), 1. DOI: 10.1007/s13347-023-00686-9

Ferguson, H., Warwick, L., Disney, T., Leigh, J., Cooner, T. S., & Beddoe, L. (2022). Relationship-based practice and the creation of therapeutic change in long-term work: Social work as a holding relationship. *Social Work Education*, *41*(2), 209–227. DOI: 10.1080/02615479.2020.1837105

Fritz, R., & Cook, D. (2025). Detecting Older Adults' Behavior Changes During Adverse External Events Using Ambient Sensing: Longitudinal Observational Study. *JMIR Nursing*, *8*(1), e69052. DOI: 10.2196/69052

Gilbert, A. S., Garratt, S. M., Kosowicz, L., Ostaszkiewicz, J., & Dow, B. (2021). Aged care residents' perspectives on quality of care in care homes: A systematic review of qualitative evidence. *Research on Aging*, *43*(7-8), 294–310. DOI: 10.1177/0164027521989074

Goldenthal, E., Park, J., Liu, S. X., Mieczkowski, H., & Hancock, J. T. (2021). Not all AI are equal: Exploring the accessibility of AI-mediated communication technology. *Computers in Human Behavior*, *125*, 106975. DOI: 10.1016/j.chb.2021.106975

Gustafsson, M. S., Kazlou, A., & Wihlborg, E. (2024, August). Automation in Social Care: A Case Study of Organizational Challenges and Skills Dynamics in Three Swedish Municipalities. In *International Conference on Electronic Government* (pp. 218-233). Cham: Springer Nature Switzerland. DOI: 10.1007/978-3-031-70274-7_14

Hall, S. F., Sage, M., Scott, C. F., & Joseph, K. (2024). A systematic review of sophisticated predictive and prescriptive analytics in child welfare: Accuracy, equity, and bias. *Child & Adolescent Social Work Journal, 41*(6), 831–847. DOI: 10.1007/s10560-023-00931-2

Hamblin, K. A. (2022). Technology in care systems: Displacing, reshaping, reinstating or degrading roles? *New Technology, Work and Employment, 37*(1), 41–58. DOI: 10.1111/ntwe.12229

Harden, V., & Turnage, B. (2025). Social Work Values and Education. In *Social Work Education: Breaking New Grounds and Addressing New Challenges* (pp. 99–108). Springer Nature Switzerland.

Harris, S., & Stout, B. (2022). 'Caring and connected': Technology and social worker self-care. *Journal of Social Work Practice, 36*(3), 359–372. DOI: 10.1080/02650533.2021.2000945

Henrickson, M. (2022). *The origins of social care and social work: Creating a global future*. Policy Press.

Ho, J. C. K., & Ng, L. U. I. (2025). The Gap in Between: Social Work Practice in the Midst of the Technological Era. *Journal of Social Work and Welfare Policy, 3*(2), 153. DOI: 10.33790/jswwp1100153

Howe, D. (2023). Knowledge, power, and the shape of social work practice. In *The sociology of social work* (pp. 202–220). Routledge. DOI: 10.4324/9781003435846-12

Jacob, C., Brasier, N., Laurenzi, E., Heuss, S., Mougiakakou, S. G., Cöltekin, A., & Peter, M. K. (2025). AI for IMPACTS framework for evaluating the long-term real-world impacts of AI-powered clinician tools: Systematic review and narrative synthesis. *Journal of Medical Internet Research, 27*, e67485. DOI: 10.2196/67485

James, P., Lal, J., Liao, A., Magee, L., & Soldatic, K. (2024). Algorithmic decision-making in social work practice and pedagogy: Confronting the competency/critique dilemma. *Social Work Education, 43*(6), 1552–1569. DOI: 10.1080/02615479.2023.2195425

Knight, B., Keane, N., Benea, D., & Stone, R. (2024). Values and the experience of family care-giving: Cultural values or shared family values? *Ageing and Society*, *44*(1), 61–78. DOI: 10.1017/S0144686X2200006X

Kosaraju, D. (2024). Predictive analytics in healthcare: Leveraging ai to anticipate disease outbreaks and enhance patient outcomes. *Galore International Journal of Health Sciences and Research*, *8*(3), 73–79. DOI: 10.52403/gijhsr.20230312

Kovalevskyi, B. (2024). Ethics and safety in ai fine-tuning. *Journal of Artificial Intelligence general science (JAIGS) ISSN: 3006-4023, 1*(1), 259-267.

Kumar, D., & Suthar, N. (2024). Predictive analytics and early intervention in healthcare social work: A scoping review. *Social Work in Health Care*, *63*(4-5), 208–229. DOI: 10.1080/00981389.2024.2316700

Lehtiniemi, T. (2024). Contextual social valences for artificial intelligence: Anticipation that matters in social work. *Information Communication and Society*, *27*(6), 1110–1125. DOI: 10.1080/1369118X.2023.2234987

Mageira, K., Pittou, D., Papasalouros, A., Kotis, K., Zangogianni, P., & Daradoumis, A. (2022). Educational AI chatbots for content and language integrated learning. *Applied Sciences (Basel, Switzerland)*, *12*(7), 3239. DOI: 10.3390/app12073239

Magliocca, P., Canestrino, R., Carayannis, E. G., & Gagliardi, A. R. (2024). Understanding human-technology interaction: Evolving boundaries. *European Journal of Innovation Management*. Advance online publication. DOI: 10.1108/EJIM-04-2024-0341

Maleki Varnosfaderani, S., & Forouzanfar, M. (2024). The role of AI in hospitals and clinics: Transforming healthcare in the 21st century. *Bioengineering (Basel, Switzerland)*, *11*(4), 337. DOI: 10.3390/bioengineering11040337

Maota, Y. Y., & Maota, T. (2025). AI in Social Worker Recruitment and Training for Bullying Intervention: Gaps in South Africa. In *Sustainable Management Practices for Employee Retention and Recruitment* (pp. 1-30). IGI Global Scientific Publishing.

Martinez-Martin, N., Luo, Z., Kaushal, A., Adeli, E., Haque, A., Kelly, S. S., Wieten, S., Cho, M. K., Magnus, D., Fei-Fei, L., Schulman, K., & Milstein, A. (2021). Ethical issues in using ambient intelligence in healthcare settings. *The Lancet. Digital Health*, *3*(2), e115–e123. DOI: 10.1016/S2589-7500(20)30275-2

McCall, C. S., Romero, M. E., Yang, W., & Weigand, T. (2023). A call for equity-focused social-emotional learning. *School Psychology Review*, *52*(5), 586–607. DOI: 10.1080/2372966X.2022.2093125

Mehmood, A. (2024). Social Work and AI in Healthcare: Toward Collaborative Models of Support and Care. *Journal of Social Sciences and Community Support*, *1*(2), 23–32.

Meilvang, M. L. (2023). Working the boundaries of social work: Artificial intelligence and the profession of social work. *Professions and Professionalism*, *13*(1). Advance online publication. DOI: 10.7577/pp.5108

Meng, J., & Dai, Y. (2021). Emotional support from AI chatbots: Should a supportive partner self-disclose or not? *Journal of Computer-Mediated Communication*, *26*(4), 207–222. DOI: 10.1093/jcmc/zmab005

Mhlanga, D. (2024). Artificial intelligence in elderly care: Navigating ethical and responsible AI adoption for seniors. In *Fostering Long-Term Sustainable Development in Africa: Overcoming Poverty, Inequality, and Unemployment* (pp. 411–440). Springer Nature Switzerland. DOI: 10.1007/978-3-031-61321-0_18

Milella, F., & Bandini, S. (2024). Fostering Artificial Intelligence-based supports for informal caregivers: A systematic review of the literature. *Intelligenza Artificiale*, *18*(1), 67–87. DOI: 10.3233/IA-240028

Milella, F., Russo, D., & Bandini, S. (2023). AI-powered solutions to support informal caregivers in their decision-making: A systematic review of the literature. *OBM Geriatrics*, *7*(4), 1–11. DOI: 10.21926/obm.geriatr.2304262

Mishna, F., Milne, E., Bogo, M., & Pereira, L. F. (2021). Responding to COVID-19: New trends in social workers' use of information and communication technology. *Clinical Social Work Journal*, *49*(4), 484–494. DOI: 10.1007/s10615-020-00780-x

Mitchell, J. J., & Jeon, M. (2025). Exploring emotional connections: A systematic literature review of attachment in human-robot interaction. *International Journal of Human-Computer Interaction*, *41*(18), 1–22. DOI: 10.1080/10447318.2024.2445100

Montomoli, J., Bitondo, M. M., Cascella, M., Rezoagli, E., Romeo, L., Bellini, V., Semeraro, F., Gamberini, E., Frontoni, E., Agnoletti, V., Altini, M., Benanti, P., & Bignami, E. G. (2024). Algor-ethics: Charting the ethical path for AI in critical care. *Journal of Clinical Monitoring and Computing*, *38*(4), 931–939. DOI: 10.1007/s10877-024-01157-y

Mulvale, G., Green, J., Robert, G., Larkin, M., Vackerberg, N., Kjellström, S., Hossain, P., Moll, S., Lim, E., & Craythorne, S. L. (2024). Adopting, implementing and assimilating coproduced health and social care innovations involving structurally vulnerable populations: Findings from a longitudinal, multiple case study design in Canada, Scotland and Sweden. *Health Research Policy and Systems*, *22*(1), 42. DOI: 10.1186/s12961-024-01130-w

Nandy, D. (2023). Human rights in the era of surveillance: Balancing security and privacy concerns. *Journal of Current Social and Political Issues*, *1*(1), 13–17. DOI: 10.15575/jcspi.v1i1.442

Nasir, S., Khan, R. A., & Bai, S. (2024). Ethical framework for harnessing the power of AI in healthcare and beyond. *IEEE Access : Practical Innovations, Open Solutions*, *12*, 31014–31035. DOI: 10.1109/ACCESS.2024.3369912

Netto, N. R. (2024). Use of case studies in social work assessments–ChatGPT's kryptonite? *Social Work Education*, *43*(9), 2473–2484. DOI: 10.1080/02615479.2023.2266461

Neves, B. B., Petersen, A., Vered, M., Carter, A., & Omori, M. (2023). Artificial intelligence in long-term care: Technological promise, aging anxieties, and sociotechnical ageism. *Journal of Applied Gerontology*, *42*(6), 1274–1282. DOI: 10.1177/07334648231157370

Nguyen, T. M., & Malik, A. (2022). Impact of knowledge sharing on employees' service quality: The moderating role of artificial intelligence. *International Marketing Review*, *39*(3), 482–508. DOI: 10.1108/IMR-02-2021-0078

Nordesjö, K., Scaramuzzino, G., & Ulmestig, R. (2022). The social worker-client relationship in the digital era: A configurative literature review. *European Journal of Social Work*, *25*(2), 303–315. DOI: 10.1080/13691457.2021.1964445

Nuwasiima, M., Ahonon, M. P., & Kadiri, C. (2024). The role of artificial intelligence (AI) and machine learning in social work practice. *World Journal of Advanced Research and Reviews*, *24*(1), 80–97. DOI: 10.30574/wjarr.2024.24.1.2998

Oh, K. M., Hong, S. R., Beran, K., Sanders, L., Park, J. Y., & Lee, J. A. (2025). Utilizing Conversational AI Technology for Social Connectedness Among Older Adults: A Systematic Review. *Journal of Applied Gerontology*, •••, 07334648251341629. DOI: 10.1177/07334648251341629

Ojo, S. O., & Afolaranmi, A. O. (2024). The Effects of Artificial Intelligence (AI) on Human Interpersonal Connections. *Lead City Journal of Religions and Intercultural Communication*, *2*(2), 162–174.

Oladokun, P. (2025). Posthuman ethics in digital health: reimagining autonomy, consent, and responsibility in AI-augmented care. *International Journal of Engineering Research & Management*, vol.9, no.4.

Panahi, O. (2025). Health in the Age of AI: A Family and Community Focus. *Archives of Community and Family Medicine*, *8*(1), 11–20. DOI: 10.22259/2638-4787.0801003

Panarese, P., Grasso, M. M., & Solinas, C. (2025). Algorithmic bias, fairness, and inclusivity: A multilevel framework for justice-oriented AI. *AI & Society*, •••, 1–23. DOI: 10.1007/s00146-025-02451-2

Pham, M. K., Nhan, T. L. A., Vuong, N. T. T., Nguyen, M. B. T., Nguyen, P. N., Sandiramourty, S., Nguyen, T. T. U., Pham, N. G. B., & Nguyen, T. T. H. (2024). Empowering vulnerable populations through technology: Innovations and challenges in social work. *Journal of Research in Educational Sciences*, *15*(1), 5–16. DOI: 10.14505/jres.v15.1(17).01

Puplampu, R. (2024). *What Everyone Should Know About the Rise of AI: AI Transparency, Privacy, and Ethics Best Practices*. Puplampu Books.

Rahman, M., Sachin, B. S., Channabasaiah, K., Rashmi, C. R., Deepika, N., & Velusamy, K. (2025). Exploring the Intersection of Social Work and the Future of Technology. In *Advancements in Intelligent Process Automation* (pp. 201–222). IGI Global.

Reamer, F. G. (2023). Artificial intelligence in social work: Emerging ethical issues. *International Journal of Social Work Values and Ethics*, *20*(2), 52–71. DOI: 10.55521/10-020-205

Riches, S., Azevedo, L., Vora, A., Kaleva, I., Taylor, L., Guan, P., Jeyarajagiri, P., McIntosh, H., Petrou, C., Pisani, S., & Hammond, N. (2022). Therapeutic engagement in robot-assisted psychological interventions: A systematic review. *Clinical Psychology & Psychotherapy*, *29*(3), 857–873. DOI: 10.1002/cpp.2696

Robinson, F., & Nejat, G. (2022). An analysis of design recommendations for socially assistive robot helpers for effective human-robot interactions in senior care. *Journal of Rehabilitation and Assistive Technologies Engineering*, *9*, 20556683221101389. DOI: 10.1177/20556683221101389

Sanders, C. K., & Scanlon, E. (2021). The digital divide is a human rights issue: Advancing social inclusion through social work advocacy. *Journal of Human Rights and Social Work*, *6*(2), 130–143. DOI: 10.1007/s41134-020-00147-9

Schiff, D. (2022). Education for AI, not AI for education: The role of education and ethics in national AI policy strategies. *International Journal of Artificial Intelligence in Education*, *32*(3), 527–563. DOI: 10.1007/s40593-021-00270-2

Segal, M. (2025). Social workers' evaluation of ChatGPT for solving ethical dilemmas within the limits of confidentiality. *Journal of Social Work Practice*, •••, 1–14. DOI: 10.1080/02650533.2025.2480092

Smriti, D. (2024). *A Framework for Artificial Intelligence (AI) Design to Support Emotion Work of Informal Caregivers* (Doctoral dissertation, Drexel University).

Solanki, P., Grundy, J., & Hussain, W. (2023). Operationalising ethics in artificial intelligence for healthcare: A framework for AI developers. *AI and Ethics*, *3*(1), 223–240. DOI: 10.1007/s43681-022-00195-z

Thomas, A., Denis, A., Robert, W., Kabiito, S. P., Morish, Z., Samuel, A., Sallam, M., & Adamopoulos, I. (2025). Artificial Intelligence-Powered Robotic Technology for Transforming Palliative Care. *Mesopotamian Journal of Artificial Intelligence in Healthcare*, *2025*, 58–84. DOI: 10.58496/MJAIH/2025/007

Tilala, M. H., Chenchala, P. K., Choppadandi, A., Kaur, J., Naguri, S., & Saoji, R., & Devaguptapu. (2024). Ethical considerations in the use of artificial intelligence and machine learning in health care: A comprehensive review. *Cureus*, *16*(6), e62443.

Turkkan Zencirli, B., & Altin, M. (2025). The impact of artificial intelligence on workplace dehumanization: A critical review. *Journal of Hospitality and Tourism Horizons*, *1*(2), 128–149. DOI: 10.1108/JHTH-01-2025-0014

Wassal, K., Ashurst, C., Hron, J., & Zilka, M. (2024). Reimagining AI in social work: Practitioner perspectives on incorporating technology in their practice. *arXiv preprint arXiv:2407.10244*.

Wiertz, S., & Boldt, J. (2022). Evaluating models of consent in changing health research environments. *Medicine, Health Care, and Philosophy*, *25*(2), 269–280. DOI: 10.1007/s11019-022-10074-3

Williamson, S. M., & Prybutok, V. (2024). Balancing privacy and progress: A review of privacy challenges, systemic oversight, and patient perceptions in AI-driven healthcare. *Applied Sciences (Basel, Switzerland)*, *14*(2), 675. DOI: 10.3390/app14020675

Wong, K. L. Y., Hung, L., Wong, J., Park, J., Alfares, H., Zhao, Y., Mousavinejad, A., Soni, A., & Zhao, H. (2024). Adoption of artificial intelligence–enabled robots in long-term care homes by health care providers: Scoping review. *JMIR Aging*, *7*(1), e55257. DOI: 10.2196/55257

Wu, F., Dixon-Woods, M., Aveling, E. L., Campbell, A., Willars, J., Tarrant, C., Bates, D. W., Dankers, C., Mitchell, I., Pronovost, P., & Martin, G. P. (2021). The role of the informal and formal organisation in voice about concerns in healthcare: A qualitative interview study. *Social Science & Medicine*, *280*, 114050. DOI: 10.1016/j.socscimed.2021.114050

Xu, H., Xie, B., & Chang, C. H. (2024). Empowering the care of older adults through the use of technology. *Work, Aging and Retirement*, *10*(1), 1–5. DOI: 10.1093/workar/waad030

Ystgaard, K. F., & De Moor, K. (2023). Envisioning the future: A multidisciplinary approach to human-centered intelligent environments. *Quality and User Experience*, *8*(1), 11. DOI: 10.1007/s41233-023-00064-5

Zhu, Y., Yang, Q., & Mao, X. (2023). Global trends in the study of smart healthcare systems for the elderly: Artificial intelligence solutions. *International Journal of Computational Intelligence Systems*, *16*(1), 105. DOI: 10.1007/s44196-023-00283-w

Chapter 6
AI and the Legal Challenges of Law and the Criminal Justice System

Angelo Kevin Brown
https://orcid.org/0000-0001-8167-5090
Arkansas State University, USA

ABSTRACT

The American criminal justice system is undergoing a rapid transformation with the introduction of artificial intelligence (AI). Proponents support these technologies as an efficient, objective, and data driven solution to the problems of human error. The use of AI, ranging from predictive policing and facial recognition to algorithmic risk assessments, is creating a new form of discrimination. AI systems are trained on datasets with decades of human bias. This chapter details the operational mechanics of these tools, their reliance on biased data, and their obscure "black box" nature. These tools, from street-level policing and detective work, through federal counter-terrorism operations, into courtrooms, prisons, and probation systems, have various risks to a democratic society, which requires reform to ensure people are still protected. The reform proposal

DOI: 10.4018/979-8-3373-5452-1.ch006

includes new federal legislation, technical safeguards such as independent audits and transparency requirements, as well as strengthening judicial and public oversight.

INTRODUCTION

In January 2020, Robert Williams was at his suburban Detroit home when police arrived and wrongly arrested him for shoplifting in front of his daughters. He was held for 30 hours in a dirty and overcrowded jail cell, due to a grainy surveillance photograph that a facial recognition program had analyzed. The software had made a disastrous error, misidentifying Williams, a Black man with no connection to the crime, as the suspect (Moy, 2021). This case is not an isolated technical glitch; it is a serious issue that should warn us about a new reality in the criminal justice system that outsources its critical decisions to automated tools that promote efficiency over the risk of creating more injustice.

The criminal justice system has been marred by the imperfection of human discretion and decision making, from a police officer's split-second judgment on the street to a jury's lengthy deliberation in a courtroom. These decisions have often been imperfect, frequently reflecting the conscious and unconscious biases of the people making them.

Automated systems are starting to be used to predict where crime will occur, identify suspects from digital databases, calculate an individual's risk of reoffending, monitor inmate communications, and help write police reports. The hope is that this will create a system that is faster, cheaper, and even fairer, a system guided by the impartiality of data, not the judgment of human prejudice.

The ability of AI to create a more equitable system is highly questionable. Digital AI tools often replicate the biases they aim to eliminate and then amplify them under the mask of scientific objectivity. This can lead to a new form of discrimination, a type of automated prejudice. Prior research has shown that AI-based systems can conflict with fundamental principles of American law, including the right to a fair trial, the promise of equal protection under the law, and privacy rights such as freedom from unreasonable government intrusion. These programs absorb historical biases from flawed data, and their undisclosed calculations raise questions about the legal right to contest the evidence against you. The analysis examines the use of these tools throughout the criminal justice system, starting with the initial police stopping of a suspect on the street, followed by investigative work, surveillance systems used by agencies including the FBI and the Department of Homeland Security, and then the criminal courts and processes of bail and sentencing. It also includes the detention of individuals in jails and prisons, community monitoring through probation and parole, and finally, the juvenile justice system, where children accused and convicted of crimes are sent for rehabilitation. The findings indicate there is significant room for reform to ensure that our justice system does not become a tool of control that fails to promote equality and justice.

AUTOMATED PREJUDICE

The automated tools used throughout the criminal justice system are often not as objective as we would like or need them to be. They are automated systems created by programmers and trained with data drawn from databases filled with historical and ongoing inequality and discrimination, which can greatly bias the data when not used in the proper context. This often results in them copying and even enlarging these biases. A fundamental problem is the use of biased data and the reliance on exclusive calculations, which transform these supposedly objective tools into instruments of injustice. These are not simple software bugs to be patched; they are fundamental design characteristics that can affect constitutional rights.

Garbage In the Problem of Biased Data

A long-standing saying in computer programming warns, "garbage in, garbage out." This acknowledges that a program that feeds biased or skewed information will likely produce a flawed outcome. In the context of the criminal justice system, the stakes are very often high. The "garbage" is not just bad data, but decades of biased policing practices and systemic inequality programmed in official records, and the result can greatly impact a person's life.[1] When a computer generates an answer, it is often treated as an objective, scientific truth, regardless of the contaminated data upon which it was built.

The automated tools used by law enforcement agencies and courts learn to make predictions by analyzing large datasets of historical records, such as arrests, charges, and other crime-related reports. These records do not provide a truly representative picture of who commits crimes and have various flaws. Instead, they offer a detailed description of who gets caught and who is being 'policed' (Alikhademi et al., 2022). For many decades, law enforcement agencies have used strategies like "broken windows" policing, which have resulted in disproportionately high levels of law enforcement activity in minority and impoverished communities (Parker, 2016). This has caused police records to show higher arrest rates in these neighborhoods, not necessarily because more crime occurs there, but because more officers are sent to patrol those areas. For example, research has reliably shown that in many cities, Black drivers are more likely to be stopped and searched than White drivers, even when contraband is more often found on White drivers. This biased law enforcement practice influences the datasets used to train AI systems.

When an algorithm learns from historically biased data, it is likely to associate certain zip codes, demographic groups, and even names with a higher chance of being involved in criminal activity (Alikhademi et al., 2022). The algorithm so far has no understanding of the history of redlining, economic inequality, or discriminatory policing that created these patterns of crime; it only perceives a statistical correlation. So, when the AI system is asked to predict where crime will happen next, it predicts that the same neighborhoods that have always been over-policed will experience an increase in crime. When asked to determine if a person is "high-risk," it may penalize them for factors like unemployment and having a family member who has been arrested, factors strongly connected to systemic inequality and race (Hamilton, 2019). This is a mechanism that turns discrimination into an automated problem. The program is not designed to be biased, but it learns from the biases already present in the data.

This process can create a misleading impression of neutrality and objectivity. Police administrators or a judge can point to a computer's output and claim the decision is “data-driven” and free from human bias, but they are actually relying on results shaped by decades of accumulated bias filtered through an AI machine. This creates a “pernicious feedback loop” where the algorithm marks a neighborhood as a crime “hot spot,” more police are dispatched there, which then results in more arrests for minor offenses. This arrest data is then used by the system, which reinforces the neighborhood as a crime “hot spot,” leading to even more policing resources being sent to the area.

The Correctional Offender Management Profiling for Alternative Sanctions (COMPAS) risk assessment tool has produced results that highlight this issue. A 2016 investigation by ProPublica analyzed the tool's results for over 7,000 individuals in Broward County, Florida, and uncovered a significant racial disparity. The algorithm was shown to be twice as likely to falsely predict Black defendants as future re-offenders compared to the White population. This finding sparked a serious discussion about algorithmic discrimination in the justice system. The tool's developer, Northpointe, had attempted to defend its product, stating it was calibrated for “predictive parity,” meaning that a given risk score corresponds to the same actual recidivism rate for both Black and White defendants. ProPublica's analysis was based on a different measurement system, which “equalized odds,” demanding that the false positive and false negative rates be equal across groups (Beaudouin et al., 2023).

Followed by an analysis by computer scientists, a critical mathematical issue was revealed: when the underlying base rates of an outcome (in this case, recidivism) differ between populations in the training data, it becomes very difficult, if not nearly impossible, for an algorithm to satisfy both predictive parity and equalized odds simultaneously (Beaudouin et al., 2023). This is not just a technical challenge; it is a significant ethical and constitutional concern. It means that the developers of such a system must choose which form of fairness to prioritize, and this choice will determine which demographic group is more likely to be impacted by the system's errors. The decision to subject one racial group to a higher rate of false accusations in an effort to maintain the predictive consistency of a risk score is a substantial policy decision with potential implications under the Fourteenth Amendment's Equal Protection Clause. However, this decision is not made by a legislator or public official. However, by a private company, and it is often concealed within a "black box" that shields it from public or judicial scrutiny.

The Black Box on the Witness Stand

The problem of biased data is worsened by secrecy. Many of today's most advanced digital tools, especially those based on deep learning, act as "black boxes" (Şahin et al., 2025). This means their internal logic is so complex, involving billions of weighted variables, that even the engineers who built them cannot fully explain how they reached a specific result (Rudin, 2019). The program takes in information, performs an enormous and often unknown number of calculations, and then produces output, which is used for a face match, risk score, or map location. This complex process poses a direct challenge to a fundamental right in the American legal system called due process.

The Sixth Amendment to the U.S. Constitution guarantees every person accused of a crime the right "to be confronted with the witnesses against him." This right includes the ability to cross-examine one's accuser. It is difficult for current legal defense professionals to properly cross-examine a computer program output (Villasenor & Foggo, 2020). When some of the evidence is based on an algorithm, this fundamental right becomes weaker. A defense attorney cannot properly cross-examine its assumptions like they can with a person. The defendant is faced with a conclusion that could cost them their freedom without a traditional opportunity to challenge how that conclusion was reached.

This scenario is already present in the legal system. It is what occurred in the case of *Loomis v. Wisconsin*, a case that reached the Wisconsin Supreme Court in 2016. Eric Loomis was sentenced to six years in prison after the judge openly relied on risk scores created by the COMPAS algorithm that showed a high-risk result. The Loomis defense appealed the decision, arguing that his due process rights were violated because the problematic, black-box nature of the COMPAS tool prevented him from challenging the validity of the evidence used against him. The software's users refused to release the source code or the specific weighting of its variables, categorizing this information as a "trade secret", a claim that puts corporate intellectual property against a defendant's constitutional rights (Katyal, 2019).

In a questionable decision, the Wisconsin Supreme Court upheld the result and confirmed the legality of the use of the algorithmic tool. While it issued a caution that risk scores should not be used as the sole or decisive factor in a sentence, it found that their use did not violate the defendant's constitutional right to due process. The U.S. Supreme Court declined to hear the case, leaving this as legal precedent that allows the use of this algorithmic evidence in sentencing decisions. This lack of transparency also makes it difficult for judges to fulfill their important role in ensuring the fairness and accuracy of evidence used in criminal court. Courts have established standards, including the use of Daubert and Frye tests, to certify that scientific or technical evidence presented in court is reliable and based on credible scientific methods. The judges cannot apply these same standards to an algorithmic system whose methods cannot be critiqued and whose error rates in specific contexts are unverified (Rudin, 2019).

In response to this problem, some experts have proposed the development of programs designed to "show their work" through a field known as eXplainable AI (XAI). Still, these "explainable" systems often provide only high-level, post-hoc summaries of their logic and may not meet the standards of a court of law to be used as admissible evidence (Şahin et al., 2025). They often indicate which input features were most influential in a decision, but cannot fully reconstruct the precise chain of reasoning or the interaction between variables. This offers a limit of transparency, not the full amount required for full legal scrutiny. The main issue remains even with this XAI use, which is that predictive technology is allowing the justice system to accept a level of secrecy that is significantly at odds with the principles of a fair and open criminal trial.

How Algorithms Systematically Can Worsen Vulnerability

The analysis of risk assessment tools reveals a systemic conflict between algorithmic systems and the principles of correctional justice. This conflict is illustrated by what legal scholars have termed the "double-edged sword of youth" (Slobogin & Stevenson, 2018).[12] In traditional sentencing, a defendant's youth is often considered a decisive mitigating factor. The Supreme Court, in cases like *Roper v. Simmons* and *Miller v. Alabama* has repeatedly recognized that young people are less culpable due to their diminished capacity for judgment and their significant potential for rehabilitation.

In a predictive algorithm, being a youth is one of the strongest statistical predictors of future criminal activity. An analysis of the COMPAS Violent Recidivism Risk Score, has found that age alone can explain nearly 60% of the variation in its scores, which is significantly more than criminal history, gender, or race. The algorithm system does not see the potential for change as shown in the empirical research, but it perceives a high-risk data point. The very factor that a judge might view as a reason for leniency can be significantly changed by the algorithm into a reason for a higher risk score, which can lead to harsher treatment.

This issue is not an isolated event, but a general principle of how predictive algorithms treat single factors without considering the larger context involved. The issue here applies to variables other than youth and to a range of factors that the legal system has traditionally viewed as relevant to culpability, which can show the need for treatment rather than punishment. These factors include variables such as mental illness, substance abuse, unemployment, and residential instability, often used as inputs in structured risk assessments. An example is a judge who might see a defendant's struggle with addiction or mental health as a mitigating factor, calling for a sentence focused on treatment; this perspective could be overlooked by an algorithm. An algorithm trained on historical data will likely interpret these same factors as statistical markers that increase the defendant's risk score for re-offenses.

This is not an issue with having a faulty system, but a feature of algorithmic logic. The algorithms are often not designed to assess blameworthiness or potential for rehabilitation; instead, they are meant to calculate statistical probability based on past correlations. The result is a system that systematically punishes the very factors that a traditional, rehabilitative model aims to address. The uncritical use of AI is likely to create this conflict between the goals of punishment, rehabilitation, and reoffending prediction. It can push the system toward a purely predictive model where a person's life circumstances are not seen as context for their actions but as mere data points predicting their future danger to society. When these calculations are hidden within a black box, a justice system may unknowingly give excessive weight to a "high-risk" label without understanding that it is primarily driven by a factor or a small set of factors, such as poverty, addiction, and youth, which they would otherwise consider mitigating factors.

ALGORITHMIC IMPACT ON INVESTIGATION TO INCARCERATION AND SUPERVISION

The theoretical and practical issues of automated bias, secrecy, and punishment become evident when these digital tools are implemented in our current justice systems. To fully understand their systemic effects, it is important to follow their path through the justice system, from the first point of law enforcement contact on the street, through the investigative process, into the courtroom, behind prison walls, and back into the community under supervision. This reveals the creation of a "digital dragnet," where constitutional protections are systematically weakened at each stage by unaccountable and often biased automated systems.

Predictive Policing and Imperfect Facial Recognition

For many people, the first encounter with the criminal justice system is with a police officer on the street. More than ever, the decisions that officer makes—such as where to patrol, who to stop, and who to identify as a suspect—are being influenced by automated systems that can significantly stretch the boundaries of constitutional law, for example, the need for probable cause and reasonable suspicion.

Predicting Crime or Directing Patrols?

Predictive policing software analyzes historical and current crime data to generate "hot spot" crime maps, which are then used to direct officers to areas where crime is allegedly most likely to occur. The logic appears straightforward and efficient on its face and can help decide where to deploy resources where the crime is. The issue lies in the fact that the data is fundamentally flawed. The software, trained on records of biased policing, often ends up sending officers back to the same minority and low-income communities they have always heavily patrolled (Alikhademi et al., 2022). crime maps, that are than used in directing officers to areas where crime is allegedly most likely to occur. The logic appears straightforward and efficient on its face and can help decide where to deploy resources where the crime is. The issue lies in the fact that, the data is fundamentally flawed. The software, trained on records of biased policing, often ends up sending officers back to the same minority and low-income communities they have always heavily patrolled (Alikhademi et al., 2022).

This practice institutionalizes the discriminatory feedback loop. The program highlights a neighborhood as a "hot spot." More police officers are deployed to that area. With an increased police presence, more arrests are likely to happen, often for minor nonviolent, discretionary offenses like loitering, trespassing, or low-level drug possession. This new arrest data is then fed back into the program, which algorithmically "confirms" that the neighborhood is a "hot spot," thus justifying an even greater police presence in the future (Bennett Moses & Chan, 2018). Residents in the area are caught in a digital dragnet and can face more frequent stops, searches, and arrests simply because of their location. This practice directly challenges the Fourth Amendment, which requires police to have an individualized, reasonable suspicion to stop a specific person and probable cause to search for drugs or other illegal items. Predictive policing effectively replaces this constitutional standard with a technologically created stereotype, where a person's presence in an algorithmically targeted area can be used to justify a police stop, greatly weakening a key protection against arbitrary state actions (Weiss, 2025).

Mistaken Identity by Algorithms

Facial recognition technology (FRT) takes this loss of individualized suspicion a step further. Police can feed an image of a suspect, often a low-quality shot from a surveillance camera, into a program that scans millions of photos from sources such as mugshot databases and state driver's license registries to find a potential match. The critical problem is that the technology can be unreliable, especially when analyzing the faces of people of color, women, and young people. A 2019 study by the National Institute of Standards and Technology (NIST) evaluated dozens of leading algorithms and found that many were up to 100 times more likely to produce a false positive match for Black or Asian individuals compared to White men (Boutin, 2019).

This is not a minor issue but has led to wrongful arrests. For example, Nijeer Parks of New Jersey spent ten days in jail and incurred thousands of dollars in legal fees after he was misidentified by facial recognition software that matched his photo to a fake driver's license left at a crime scene (Moy, 2021). A pregnant woman in Detroit was arrested and charged with robbery and carjacking based on another faulty match. These cases and many more highlight a dangerous change in the probable cause standard. Police have traditionally gathered evidence pointing toward a specific person and based their investigation on that. With FRT, the algorithm produces the suspects, and that probabilistic "match" is being treated as the primary evidence justifying the arrest.

This moves the basis of suspicion from human investigation and articulable facts to an automated, biased, and algorithmic output. When police officers, influenced by a phenomenon known as "automation bias," place uncritical faith in the machine's findings, they may fail to conduct the necessary investigation that would expose the error. The result is a system where the Fourth Amendment's requirement for "reasonably trustworthy information" is undermined by technology known to be untrustworthy (Benedict, 2022).

The creation of massive, searchable face databases constitutes a powerful tool for mass surveillance, threatening the First Amendment right to protest and associate freely without fear of government tracking. The ability to scan crowds at a political rally and identify every attendee creates a chilling effect on public dissent, a foundation of a democratic society (Alghafri & Tubaishat, 2025).

AI IN DETECTIVE WORK AND FORENSICS

Once a crime has been reported and an investigation begins, AI tools are increasingly used by detectives and forensic analysts. These technologies aim to streamline the investigative process and uncover evidence that would be difficult for humans to find, but they also introduce new potential errors into the investigation of a criminal case.

Automating the Detective

The daily work of a detective involves a significant amount of administrative labor and reviewing of evidence. AI is now being used as a "force multiplier" to automate these investigatory tasks. One of the most significant applications has been in the creation of police reports. For example, the technology company Axon, a major provider of police body cameras, now offers a product called "Draft One," which uses a generative AI model to automatically transcribe the audio from an officer's body camera and convert it into a narrative police report. Officers are able to use it for the time-saving potential, with some claiming the AI-generated reports are more detailed and accurate than they could write themselves. However, this automation introduces serious concerns about transparency and accountability, and various researchers have questioned the claims of accuracy. An investigation by the Electronic Frontier Foundation (EFF) found that the Draft One system can hinder audits. The AI-generated draft is not saved, and the officer copies and pastes the text into the official report, meaning the original draft may no longer be available. This makes it very difficult for defense attorneys, judges, or the public to determine which parts of the report were written by the AI system and which were written by the officer. This creates a new "accountability black box" at the very start of the investigation. Given that large language models are known to be prone to "hallucination" (making up facts and details) and to replicate societal biases from their training data, the inability to audit the AI's original output is a critical issue that could allow various inaccuracies and biases to become accepted as fact.

AI is used to mine and analyze the large amount of digital evidence in investigations. AI tools like can examine data from multiple cell phones and cloud accounts, automatically cross-referencing text messages, social media posts, and location data to identify connections and build an account of events (Dunsin et al., 2024). While this can quicken investigations, it also represents a fundamental change from targeted investigation based on suspicion to data analysis, where personal information is consumed and processed to find patterns.

AI in Forensic Evidence

AI is also making significant impacts in forensic laboratories, where it is used to analyze forensic evidence. In forensic genetics, for example, AI algorithms are proving highly effective at interpreting DNA mixtures containing genetic material from multiple individuals. This task is often very difficult and time-consuming for human analysts. AI is also used to automate haplogroup analysis, which can help determine the ancestral origins of a DNA sample, and it can also analyze Short Tandem Repeat (STR) profiles to find matches in DNA databases much faster than traditional methods (Sessa et al., 2024).

Recent research has shown that AI has challenged century-old forensic beliefs. For example, it has long been a foundational principle of fingerprint analysis that prints from different fingers of the same person are unique and unmatchable. This belief has been questioned by a 2024 study that demonstrated an AI model, trained on a large database of fingerprints, could link prints from different fingers of the same person with high accuracy (Guo et al., 2024). The AI achieved this by identifying a new kind of forensic marker related to the curvature of the swirls and loops at the center of the fingerprint, which human experts had overlooked for decades.

These advancements by AI have created an "infallibility paradox." On one hand, AI appears to be uncovering a more objective field, finding patterns that escaped human experts. However, it does so using methods that is not easily explainable or verifiable. The more exceptional its capabilities seem, the greater the risk of "automation bias," where human analysts, judges, juries, and others place uncritical faith in the machine's output without fully understanding its limitations or potential for error. This creates a new form of "expert" testimony, where the witness is a black-box algorithm that is difficult to challenge and question.

AI Evidence and the *Daubert* and *Frye* Standards

This new form of algorithmic evidence creates new issues to the legal standards that govern the admissibility of scientific evidence in court. Under the *Daubert* standard, used in federal courts and many state courts, a judge must act as a gatekeeper and assess whether scientific evidence is based on reliable methodology. This involves considering factors like whether the technique can be tested, its known or potential error rate, whether it has been subjected to peer review, and its general acceptance within the relevant scientific community. The *Frye* standard, still used in some states, focuses solely on whether the technique has gained "general acceptance" in its field (Bernstein, 2000).

The black-box nature of many AI forensic tools may conflict with these standards. A recent case, Washington v. Puloka, illustrates this issue. In that case, the defense sought to introduce a video of a shooting that had been enhanced with an AI tool (Yee, 2025). The court held a Frye hearing and rejected the evidence. It determined that the AI tool was a "black box" whose algorithms were undisclosed, not peer-reviewed, and untested by the relevant scientific community (forensic video analysts), and therefore not "generally accepted." The court pointed out that the AI did not merely improve the video footage but added new information, producing a representation of what the AI model 'thinks' should be shown rather than what actually happened.

The Puloka decision illustrates a new legal battleground. The core requirements of both Daubert and Frye, testability, transparency about error rates, peer review, and general acceptance, cannot be met by current algorithms. As AI-generated evidence becomes more common, courts will increasingly have to address this issue where the law demands verifiable evidence and the reality of black-box technology.

In the Courtroom

Once an individual is arrested and enters the criminal courtroom, automated tools continue to have an influence over their fate. Algorithmic risk assessments, such as the COMPAS tool, are increasingly used by the courts to inform decisions about pretrial release, bail, and sentencing. These tools analyze a defendant's demographic and criminal history data and produce a simple numerical score that is meant to represent their likelihood of reoffending or failing to appear in court.

While initially intended to be an advisory tool, these scores can create bias for judges. Presented with a seemingly scientific number, a judge may find it psychologically challenging to diverge from its recommendation. The score's claim of objectivity can overshadow the individualized assessment that due process should require. This is particularly problematic due to the documentation biases of these systems. As the ProPublica investigation revealed, a Black defendant is far more likely to be incorrectly labeled "high-risk" than a White defendant with a similar profile, leading directly to higher rates of pretrial detention and potentially harsher sentences for people of color (Beaudouin et al., 2023).

These tools have been used for years, but critics have been arguing that they are instruments that erase the situations of a person's life and rely on group data filled with racial disparities. They have been unable to distinguish between a person who misses a court date due to a medical emergency and one who intentionally flees. They also have been known to not differentiate between a new arrest for a technical parole violation and one for a violent crime. By offering a quick risk score, these algorithms attract judges who often have very limited time and many cases to circumvent the difficult work of conducting individualized hearings where real evidence must be presented, thereby undermining procedural justice.

The legal challenge in *Loomis v. Wisconsin* brought up this issue. The court's decision to allow the use of the secret COMPAS score, as long as it was not the sole factor in sentencing, created a legal change. It is impossible to determine the precise weight a judge gives to a risk score. The ruling denied the defendant the right to challenge the instrument being used to justify the loss of their liberty. By prioritizing the trade secret claim over the defendant's due process rights, the court allowed a private company's secret, biased algorithm to be used as an unchallengeable expert witness in a court of law, reducing the principles of a fair and open trial.

AI IN JAILS AND PRISONS

The use of AI continues even after the courtroom and trials are completed. Inside the various jails and prisons, automated systems are being used to manage, classify, and control incarcerated individuals, promising greater efficiency and security.

Automated Classification and Management

Correctional facilities are often overcrowded and understaffed institutions, and administrators face numerous challenges. AI is marketed as the solution to improve operations by automating inmate classification, risk assessment, and resource allocation. Upon intake, AI systems can use facial recognition to identify individuals and verify their history. The AI systems can then process large amounts of data, including criminal history, demographic information, and psychological assessments, to assign inmates to specific security levels, housing units, and rehabilitation programs. This data-driven approach is believed to be a more accurate and objective way to manage jails and prisons and ensure a safer environment. There is concern that it also reduces individuals to a set of data points, with their placement and access to resources determined by an algorithmic score, which may overlook the context of their individual circumstances.

Predicting and Controlling Misconduct

A current application of AI in corrections is the prediction of inmate misconduct. This represents a clear shift toward a pre-crime model of control within the justice system. AI-driven surveillance systems use computer vision to analyze video feeds in real-time, identifying fights, self-harm, or other problematic activities more quickly than human guards can. Natural language processing (NLP) is used to monitor inmate communications, including phone calls and emails, flagging keywords or patterns that might indicate gang activity, drug trafficking, or other illegal or problematic activity (Mokhtar, 2025). In Florida, for example, pilot programs have used AI to monitor phone calls and analyze inmate behavior to inform parole decisions.

Instead of only punishing rule violations after they occur, the system is now used to predict them. This logic justifies heightened levels of surveillance and preemptive control measures based on algorithmic program predictions of who is most likely to cause trouble. While proponents argue this enhances the safety of the facilities, it also creates an environment of constant, automated suspicion where an individual can be flagged as a threat based on an AI calculation, without having committed any actual infraction.

The Federal Approach

The federal prison system has started to embrace this algorithmic approach through the mandate of the First Step Act of 2018 (FSA), which allowed the Department of Justice to develop a system to assess inmate risk and needs (Cyphert, 2020). This led to the creation of two new tools by the Federal Bureau of Prisons (BOP).

The first is the Prisoner Assessment Tool Targeting Estimated Risk and Needs (PATTERN). This tool calculates two separate risk scores for each inmate: one for general recidivism and one for violent recidivism. These scores, which are categorized as minimum, low, medium, or high, can be used to determine an inmate's eligibility for earned time credits that can lead to early release. PATTERN uses both static factors (like age and criminal history) and dynamic factors (like participation in programs and time since the last disciplinary infraction) that can change over time (Hamilton et al., 2022).

The second tool is the Standardized Prisoner Assessment for Reduction in Criminality (SPARC-13). This is a needs assessment tool that evaluates inmates across 13 criminogenic need areas, including anger or hostility, antisocial peers, cognitions, substance use, and Trauma. The results of the SPARC-13 assessment are used to guide inmates into specific Evidence-Based Recidivism Reduction programs designed to address their identified needs (Whetzel et al., 2025).

While the BOP states that PATTERN is designed to be "racially and ethnically neutral," it relies on many of the same types of static factors that have drawn criticism in other risk assessment tools like COMPAS. Comparisons reveal that while PATTERN may provide some transparency in its scoring mechanism, it is built on the same logic as COMPAS. Both systems heavily weigh static factors like age and criminal history. This shows that the problem of automated prejudice is not limited to a single flawed tool but is a systemic issue entrenched in the very nature of risk assessments.

ALGORITHMIC SUPERVISION IN PROBATION AND PAROLE

The digital dragnet extends past the prison walls, following individuals back into the community using AI in probation and parole supervision. With overwhelming caseloads and limited resources, community supervision agencies are turning to AI as a tool for efficiency and risk management. This technological change threatens to change community supervision into a form of digital surveillance.

The Digital Warden

AI is being used for case management systems to automate routine tasks like scheduling meetings and generating reports, freeing up officers to focus on direct client interaction. These systems use predictive analytics to help officers prioritize their caseloads. By analyzing an individual's criminal history, risk assessment scores, employment status, and other factors, the AI can recommend which cases require the most attention and suggest specific interventions. This can be a useful allocation of resources, but it also can lead to an individual's level of scrutiny and the services they receive are increasingly determined by an algorithmic prediction rather than a human officer's professional judgment.

Intelligent Tracking Monitoring

The National Institute of Justice (NIJ) has supported research into the next generation of AI-powered supervision, which it terms intelligent tracking (Martin & Moore, 2020). This vision moves past simple location monitoring. The goal is to use AI to enhance traditional GPS tracking by adding a layer of predictive risk analysis. The system could learn an individual's patterns and identify locations, such as bars or neighborhoods with known criminal activity, that are algorithmically determined to be high risk for that specific person, triggering an alert to the supervising officer.

The NIJ's plans include the use of biometric monitoring through wearable devices like smartwatches. These devices could continuously track physiological data, such as heart rate and stress levels, to assess an individual's mood and emotional state. An AI could analyze this data in real-time and alert an officer if it detects a pattern indicating the person may be in a risky situation or at imminent risk of reoffending. The system could even be programmed to intervene directly by sending a message to the individual's device telling them to leave a location or engage in a type of therapy exercise to reduce their stress levels.

This model represents the use of pre-crime logic and the feedback loop. The problems created due to the overburdened probation systems are not solved, but are instead addressed with a technological intervention of escalating surveillance. The goal moves from simply monitoring compliance with release conditions to continuously assessing and predicting future behavior. This turns community supervision into a type of digital surveillance, extending the control of the prison into every aspect of a person's life in the community.

SPECIAL RISKS IN JUVENILE JUSTICE

The deployment of AI risk assessment tools in the juvenile justice system is also a current issue. Proponents suggest these tools can provide more objective, data-driven decisions, but their application to minors threatens to undermine the fundamental principles of a separate, rehabilitative juvenile justice system.

Risk Assessment for Youth

Structured risk assessment tools, such as the Structured Assessment of Violence Risk in Youth (SAVRY) and the Youth Level of Service/Case Management Inventory (YLS/CMI), are now being used to inform decisions about detention, disposition, and rehabilitation for young offenders. These tools, like their adult counterparts, analyze a range of static and dynamic factors, including past behavior, family situation, peer influences, and mental health status, to create a risk score predicting the likelihood of reoffending. These tools for Juvenile Risk Assessments use machine learning to analyze this data and create predictions (Sheppard et al., 2024).

Heightened Ethical Concerns

Applying this logic to children raises ethical concerns that are more concerning than in the adult system. First, the data used to train these models is often even more skewed by racial and socioeconomic factors than the adult data available, reflecting disparities in schools, policing in low-income neighborhoods, and access to resources. An algorithm trained on this data will likely perpetuate these existing inequalities.

The impact of being labeled “high-risk” can be devastating and lifelong for a young person. Such a label can create a self-fulfilling prophecy, influencing how they are treated by judges, probation officers, teachers, and even their own families. It can limit their access to educational and job opportunities and shape their self-perception at a critical stage of development.

A person's youth, which the law recognizes as a mitigating factor due to developmental immaturity and greater ability for change, is treated by a predictive algorithm as a primary aggravating risk factor. The use of these tools can contradict the core rehabilitative and protective philosophy of the juvenile justice system. Creating a more punitive and predictive model that systematically penalizes young people for being young.

Recommendations For Child-Centered Ai

Recognizing these dangers, organizations like the National Center for Youth Law (NCYL), UNICEF (Liu& Ding, 2025), and UNESCO have called for the development of child-centered AI policies (Ozturk, 2025). These frameworks argue that any AI system used in a context affecting children must prioritize their rights and well-being. Key principles include ensuring fairness and non-discrimination, protecting privacy, and maintaining human oversight and accountability. For AI to be used ethically in the juvenile justice system, it should not be a scaled-down version of adult systems. It should be fundamentally re-conceived with strong safeguards that account for the unique issues and developmental needs of young people, ensuring that technology serves the goal of rehabilitation, not just prediction.

THE FEDERALIZATION OF AUTOMATED SURVEILLANCE

While much of the focus on AI in criminal justice has been on local police departments and state courts, an advanced infrastructure of automated surveillance is being constructed at the federal level. Agencies within the Departments of Justice (DOJ) and Homeland Security (DHS) are deploying sophisticated AI systems for investigation, border control, and counterterrorism. This federalization of AI surveillance is occurring in a poorly regulated way, creating a powerful network that lacks consistent oversight and may be a significant threat to the civil liberties of all Americans.

From NGI-IPS to Mass Photo Databases

The Federal Bureau of Investigation (FBI) has been at the forefront of deploying biometric identification technologies. Its primary facial recognition service is the Next Generation Identification-Interstate Photo System (NGI-IPS) (Yoo & Jagasia, 2024). This system allows the FBI and other agencies to search for a database of over 30 million criminal photos ("mugshots") to identify potential suspects from surveillance cameras and other images.

The FBI's facial recognition capabilities move past its own mugshot database. According to testimony before Congress, the FBI has access to a network of federal and state databases, including state driver's license photos and U.S. passport photos, that contain over 640 million photographs, most of which have no criminal record (Caines, 2021; Zens, 2021). The agency has asserted that it can conduct searches on these databases without a warrant or even probable cause, claiming that an "authorized investigation" is sufficient justification.

This current expansion of surveillance systems has occurred with little transparency and a lack of oversight. A report from the Government Accountability Office (GAO) found that the FBI had failed to conduct adequate testing to determine the accuracy of the NGI-IPS system or to assess how often errors occur (Ring, 2016). Reports also found that the FBI had not assessed whether the systems used by its external partners, such as state DMVs, were sufficiently accurate to prevent misidentifications. The ACLU has even sued the FBI and other agencies for delaying and denying Freedom of Information Act (FOIA) requests about their use of this technology, exposing a pattern of secrecy that can prevent public accountability and legal challenges.

Homeland Security and AI at the Border, in Airports, and Online

The Department of Homeland Security (DHS) and its various agencies, including Customs and Border Protection (CBP) and the Transportation Security Administration (TSA), are integrating AI into their operations to secure the border and screen travelers. At ports of entry, CBP uses AI to help screen cargo for illicit goods. For travelers, DHS has deployed facial recognition systems for programs like "Simplified Arrival" at airports and borders, and for expedited screening programs (Murphy, 2022). These systems compare a live photo of a traveler to the photo stored in their passport to verify their identity. The TSA is also using AI and machine learning to power its baggage-screening technology to detect prohibited items to enhance public safety.

DHS's use of AI extends into the digital space, including for the surveillance of immigrants and visa applicants. The department has implemented programs to vet individuals by analyzing their social media activity. A new State Department initiative, "Catch and Revoke," plans to use AI to scan social media for foreign nationals who appear to support designated terror groups and cancel their visas. This practice advances serious First Amendment concerns, as it risks penalizing individuals for protected speech and political expression, and the vague criteria create room for biased application against disfavored views.

The War on Drugs and Guns in the Digital Age

Other federal law enforcement agencies are also beginning to investigate the use of AI to boost their investigative capabilities. The Drug Enforcement Administration (DEA) has started using AI and machine learning to analyze financial data to spot patterns indicative of money laundering by drug trafficking organizations. The DEA has reportedly hired a private company to develop a predictive AI model to identify physicians with "aberrant" prescribing patterns for controlled substances. This system, trained on insurance claims and prescription data, flags doctors for investigation based on criteria like the number of Schedule II prescriptions written. This can create a self-reinforcing bias loop, where the AI identifies targets, leading to investigations and prosecutions that then "validate" the AI's targeting criteria. The Bureau of Alcohol, Tobacco, Firearms, and Explosives (ATF) is also testing AI to fight illegal firearms trafficking. This includes using AI to analyze online marketplaces and social media platforms where illegal gun sales are arranged. The goal of projects like the European-based CEASEFIRE system is to use AI to automatically process visual and text data from the web to identify suspicious activity and reveal the identities of traffickers (Cani et al., 2024).

While the use of AI in these agencies is still advancing, it appears to be following the same pattern seen in other agencies. The DEA and the FBI are in the early stages of AI integration and face significant barriers, including funding constraints and a lack of a skilled technical workforce.

These findings suggest that adoption is happening opportunistically, driven by available technology rather than an evidence-based strategic framework, which increases the risk that AI tools will be deployed without adequate safeguards.

Counter-Terrorism, Watch Listing, and the Loss of Due Process

A constitutionally problematic application of AI at the federal level is in the domain of counterterrorism and watch listing. Following the 9/11 attacks, the U.S. government consolidated its various watchlists into a single Terrorist Screening Data (TSDS), managed by the FBI's Threat Screening Center (TSC). This list contains over one million names and is used by a wide range of government agencies for screening travelers, visa applicants, and individuals encountered by law enforcement (Park, 2018).

AI is becoming part of the engine that enables this modern watch listing program. Predictive analytics and machine learning algorithms are used to analyze large amounts of data to identify individuals who are reasonably suspected of being involved in terrorism (Hobart, 2025). The first black box is the secrecy of the counter-terrorism intelligence itself. The second is the issue of the AI algorithms used to analyze that data and generate a suspicion score, which can lead to a person being considered for the watchlist.

This system presents serious due process and civil liberties challenges. The criteria for inclusion on the watchlist are vague, and the evidence is considered a national security secret. The data used to train the predictive models is likely skewed by a historical focus on Muslim communities and individuals of Middle Eastern descent, leading to significant bias and the overrepresentation of these groups on the list. Individuals are often not notified that they are on a watchlist and have no practical way to challenge their inclusion or correct false information. This problem is worsened when the "evidence" against them is not a specific fact but an algorithmic inference about their future risk. The consequences can include being barred from flying, subjected to questioning by law enforcement, and even having bank accounts frozen. The lack of a coherent, regulatory framework has allowed an unaccountable infrastructure of automated surveillance to be accepted by the government, making the case for thorough reform a critical step.

RECOMMENDATIONS FOR REFORM

Confronting the constitutional and civil rights issues created by the use of AI in the criminal justice system requires a complete, proactive, and multi-layered strategy. This strategy should combine new legislation, strict technical standards that mandate transparency and accountability, and a commitment to democratic and judicial oversight. The goal is not to stop or limit technological progress but to guide it in a direction that supports constitutional values, rather than undermining them.

Legislative and Regulatory Reform

The current legal framework in the United States, mostly drafted in a pre-digital era, is not prepared for the challenges of algorithmic decision-making. Significant legislative reform at the federal level is the necessary and practical starting point.

Congress can enact laws specifically designed for the age of AI. Such an act needs to establish clear and enforceable rules for the use of automated systems by government agencies. It should clearly ban discriminatory algorithms by amending existing civil rights laws to clarify their application to automated systems. It should also establish a legally enforceable "right to an explanation" for any individual subject to a significant, rights-impacting algorithmic decision. The act should also mandate publicly accessible registries for all AI systems used by government agencies, detailing their purpose, and validating their accuracy and impact.

The United States also needs a comprehensive federal data privacy law, similar in extent to the European Union's General Data Protection Regulation (GDPR). A law like the proposed American Data Privacy and Protection Act (ADPPA) (Taetzsch, 2024) should be enacted to establish essential principles of data minimization (collecting the data that is necessary) and purposeful limitation (using data only for the purpose for which it was collected).

The EU, for example, has implemented a proactive, risk-based approach that is grounded in the protection of fundamental rights. Unlike the more fragmented and reactive proposals in the U.S., the EU AI Act prohibits certain AI practices thought to create an "unacceptable risk," including social scoring by public authorities and certain types of predictive policing systems. For the "high-risk" systems, which include many applications in law enforcement and the administration of justice, the Act imposes stringent requirements for risk management, data governance, human oversight, and conformity assessments before they can be put on the market. This rights-based regulatory model provides a useful example for the U.S. to follow and adapt to its federal and state policies.

Mandating Transparency and Auditing,

Legislation alone is likely insufficient without mechanisms for enforcement and accountability. A mandatory system of technical transparency is important to reduce secrecy.

AI systems procured and used by public agencies should be subject to regular, independent, third-party audits before being implemented and throughout their operational life. These audits need to assess the systems against clear, public standards for bias, fairness, accuracy, and security. The unredacted results of these audits, including detailed information about the training data and testing methodologies, should be made publicly available.

For AI systems used in the criminal justice system, including risk assessments, forensic analysis tools, and facial recognition, a "black box" should be legally unacceptable. Regulations should mandate that these systems are built for interpretability and are accompanied by validated eXplainable AI (XAI) tools that can provide a clear and understandable account of their reasoning. A legal right to challenge an algorithmic decision must be practical. Defendants and their legal counsel must be given meaningful access to relevant information about the model, such as its general design, the features used in their individual case, the training data, and its known error rates across different demographic groups. This can create a meaningful challenge to the evidence and satisfy the constitutional requirements of due process.

Strengthening Judicial and Democratic Oversight

Human oversight remains a critical safeguard against algorithmic harm. This requires determination to build algorithmic literacy within the legal community and empower the public with a democratic voice.

The legal profession must become algorithmically literate. This requires a fundamental improvement in legal education, including the addition of mandatory courses on technology, data science, and statistics to law school curriculums. It should also include mandatory continuing legal education for judges, prosecutors, and public defenders on the capabilities, limitations, and constitutional implications of AI tools as they develop.

Also, it would be important to develop a new evidentiary framework for the judiciary, similar to a Daubert standard for algorithms, to regulate the admissibility of AI-generated evidence. This standard should require pretrial investigation into an algorithm's methodology, the quality and potential biases of its training data, its error rates, and its scientific validation before its outputs are presented as evidence in court (Rudin, 2019). This would shift the burden of proof onto the government and the companies that develop the AI to demonstrate that their systems are reliable and fair, rather than forcing the defense to prove they are not.

Local communities, especially those most impacted by surveillance technologies, should be protected from disproportionate surveillance. The "Community Control Over Police Surveillance" (CCOPS) model, created by the ACLU, provides a useful blueprint (Southerland, 2023). This model involves local governments establishing a transparent process, including obtaining approval from the community's elected representatives, before their agencies can use any new surveillance technology. This model can and should be expanded outside policing to include local jails, probation departments, juvenile justice, and other related agencies. Doing so can help maintain democratic accountability and empower communities to be protected from technologies that conflict with their values and civil liberties.

CONCLUSION

Artificial intelligence is reshaping the American criminal justice system and others. It presents an important choice: to accept the deployment of efficient but biased systems that risk weakening the protection of our legal system, or to proactively use this technology to serve justice and protect individual rights. The challenges are no longer hypothetical but are real issues we face. From the racial bias of recidivism risk assessments that undermine the principles of equal protection, to flawed facial recognition matches that weaken the standard of probable cause, and the discriminatory feedback loops of predictive policing that can increase inequality, AI is already causing real harm. The "black box" nature of these systems is weakening the process of due process, reducing accountability, and exposing individuals to life-changing decisions without a practical opportunity to understand or challenge them.

For a future of proper AI implementation, it requires a holistic response that protects civil rights and constitutional protections, as well as efficiency requirements for any AI system used in the administration of justice. This begins with evidence-based legislative reform to update our laws for the algorithmic age, establishing clear rules for transparency, fairness, and accountability. A new technical standard will be needed, where independent audits are mandatory and where "black box" systems in high-risk contexts are legally regulated. It will also require the need for human oversight at each level, from algorithmically literate judges, prosecutors, jurors, and defense attorneys capable of dissecting digital evidence, to communities that have input in how they are policed and governed.

The integrity of the rule of law is crucial to uphold in this new era. Allowing the criminal justice system to accept secret, biased algorithms is a step toward an automated world where efficiency overrides fairness, and security takes precedence over liberty. The belief that AI can eliminate human bias and create a more just criminal justice system can only be realized if we first understand and limit its demonstrated potential for harm. By committing to a framework of oversight, interdisciplinary expertise, and protecting our constitutional principles, we can improve our technological progress toward an era where AI serves as an instrument for justice, not a new threat to it.

REFERENCES

Alghafri, B., & Tubaishat, A. (2025). Balancing Privacy and Security: A Comparative Analysis of AI-Driven Surveillance in the UAE and USA. *Procedia Computer Science*, *257*, 142–149. DOI: 10.1016/j.procs.2025.03.021

Alikhademi, K., Drobina, E., Prioleau, D., Richardson, B., Purves, D., & Gilbert, J. E. (2022). A review of predictive policing from the perspective of fairness. *Artificial Intelligence and Law*, *30*(1), 1–17. DOI: 10.1007/s10506-021-09286-4

Beaudouin, V., Maxwell, W., & Domingues-Montanari, S. (2023). Predicting risk in criminal justice in the United States: The ProPublica-COMPAS case: Ethics of AI in Action. *Reseaux (London)*, *240*(4), 71–109.

Benedict, T. J. (2022). The computer got it wrong: Facial recognition technology and establishing probable cause to arrest. *Washington and Lee Law Review*, *79*, 849.

Bennett Moses, L., & Chan, J. (2018). Algorithmic prediction in policing: Assumptions, evaluation, and accountability. *Policing and Society*, *28*(7), 806–822. DOI: 10.1080/10439463.2016.1253695

Bernstein, D. E. (2000). Frye, frye, again: The past, present, and future of the general acceptance test. *Jurimetrics*, *41*, 385.

Caines, S. (2021). The many faces of facial recognition. In *Research Handbook on Big Data Law* (pp. 29–56). Edward Elgar Publishing. DOI: 10.4337/9781788972826.00008

Cani, J., Mademlis, I., Mancuso, M., Paternoster, C., Adamakis, E., Margetis, G., & Papadopoulos, G. T. (2024, December). CEASEFIRE: An AI-Powered System for Combating Illicit Firearms Trafficking. In *2024 IEEE International Conference on Big Data (BigData)* (pp. 2697-2705). IEEE. DOI: 10.1109/BigData62323.2024.10825989

Cyphert, A. B. (2020). Reprogramming recidivism: The first step act and algorithmic prediction of risk. *Seton Hall Law Review*, *51*, 331.

Dunsin, D., Ghanem, M. C., Ouazzane, K., & Vassilev, V. (2024). A comprehensive analysis of the role of artificial intelligence and machine learning in modern digital forensics and incident response. *Forensic Science International Digital Investigation*, *48*, 301675. DOI: 10.1016/j.fsidi.2023.301675

Guo, G., Ray, A., Izydorczak, M., Goldfeder, J., Lipson, H., & Xu, W. (2024). Unveiling intra-person fingerprint similarity via deep contrastive learning. *Science Advances*, *10*(2), eadi0329. DOI: 10.1126/sciadv.adi0329 PMID: 38215200

Hamilton, M. (2019). The biased algorithm: Evidence of disparate impact on Hispanics. *The American Criminal Law Review*, *56*, 1553.

Hamilton, Z., Duwe, G., Kigerl, A., Gwinn, J., Langan, N., & Dollar, C. (2022). Tailoring to a mandate: The development and validation of the Prisoner Assessment Tool Targeting Estimated Risk and Needs (PATTERN). *Justice Quarterly*, *39*(6), 1129–1155. DOI: 10.1080/07418825.2021.1906930

Hobart, L. N. (2025). AI, Bias, and National Security Profiling. *Berkeley Technology Law Journal*, *40*, 165.

Katyal, S. K. (2019). Private accountability in the age of artificial intelligence. *UCLA Law Review. University of California, Los Angeles. School of Law*, *66*, 54.

Liu, S., & Ding, W. (2025). Artificial intelligence for children: UNICEF's policy guidance and beyond. *Children & Society*, *39*(1), 374–382. DOI: 10.1111/chso.12915

Martin, E., & Moore, A. (2020). Tapping Into Artificial Intelligence: Advanced Technology to Prevent Crime and Support Reentry. *Corrections Today*, •••, 28–32.

Mokhtar, R. (2025). The Transformation of Correctional Facilities Using Artificial Intelligence Technology.

Moy, L. (2021). Facing injustice: How face recognition technology may increase the incidence of misidentifications and wrongful convictions. *SSRN*, *30*, 337. DOI: 10.2139/ssrn.4101826

Murphy, H. (2022). Whatever Happened to Those Self-Service Passport Kiosks at Airports? *International New York Times*, NA-NA.

Ozturk, E. (2025). Artificial Intelligence in Early Childhood STEM Education: A Review of Pedagogical Paradigms, Ethical Issues, and Socio-Political Implications. *Journal of Education in Science, Environment and Health, 11*(2), 108–125. DOI: 10.55549/jeseh.800

Park, D. (2018). *The Watchlist: Improving the Transparency*. Accuracy, Efficiency, and Accountability of the Terrorist Screening Database.

Parker, G. (2016). Come see the bias inherent in the system. *The Journal of the American Academy of Psychiatry and the Law*, *44*(4), 411–414. PMID: 28003383

Ring, T. (2016). Privacy in peril: Is facial recognition going too far too fast? *Biometric Technology Today*, *2016*(7-8), 7–11. DOI: 10.1016/S0969-4765(16)30123-0

Rudin, C. (2019). Stop explaining black box machine learning models for high stakes decisions and use interpretable models instead. *Nature Machine Intelligence*, *1*(5), 206–215. DOI: 10.1038/s42256-019-0048-x PMID: 35603010

ŞAHiN, E., Arslan, N. N., & Özdemir, D.ŞAHiN. (2025). Unlocking the black box: An in-depth review on interpretability, explainability, and reliability in deep learning. *Neural Computing & Applications*, *37*(2), 859–965. DOI: 10.1007/s00521-024-10437-2

Sessa, F., Esposito, M., Cocimano, G., Sablone, S., Karaboue, M. A. A., Chisari, M., Albano, D. G., & Salerno, M. (2024). Artificial intelligence and forensic genetics: Current applications and future perspectives. *Applied Sciences (Basel, Switzerland)*, *14*(5), 2113. DOI: 10.3390/app14052113

Sheppard, K. G., Talaugon, A. R., & Hernandez, J. L. (2024). Assessing the feasibility and performance of risk assessment instruments for early intervention and prevention services in Juvenile Justice. *Journal of Criminal Justice*, *94*, 102262. DOI: 10.1016/j.jcrimjus.2024.102262

Slobogin, C., & Stevenson, M. T. (2018). Algoirithmic Risk Assessment and the Double Edged Sword of Youth. *Washington University Law Review, 96.*

Southerland, V. M. (2023). The Master's Tool and a Mission: Using Community Control and Oversight Laws to Resist and Abolish Police Surveillance Technologies. *UCLA Law Review. University of California, Los Angeles. School of Law*, *70*, 2.

Taetzsch, E. S. (2024). Privacy Purgatory: Why the United States Needs a Comprehensive Federal Data Privacy Law. *Journal of Legislation*, *50*, 121.

Villasenor, J., & Foggo, V. (2020). Artificial intelligence, due process and criminal sentencing. *Mich. St. L. Rev.*, 295.

Weiss, D. A. (2025). INHUMAN REASON: Predictive Policing Algorithms and the Fourth Amendment. *Criminal Justice*, *39*(4), 15–20.

Whetzel, J., Cornish, T., Anders, S., LaFratta, J., & Poulos, C. (2025). Looking Back, Looking Forward: The First Step Act and the Art of the Possible. *Federal Sentencing Reporter*, *37*(1), 41–53. DOI: 10.1215/10539867-11484730

Yee, D. G. (2025). Artificial Intelligence: An Impetus to Amend the ABA Model Code of Judicial Conduct. *Mary's J. on Legal Malpractice & Ethics*, *15*, 2.

Yoo, C. S., & Jagasia, A. (2024). Identifying Fourth Amendment Values: An Evidence-Based Approach. *Wake Forest Law Review*, *59*, 1219. DOI: 10.2139/ssrn.4867896

Zens, J. (2021). Face It: Only Congress Can Preserve Privacy from the Pervasive Use of Facial Recognition Technology by Police. *The San Diego Law Review*, *58*, 143.

Chapter 7

Algorithmic Governance and Facial Recognition: An International Comparative Analysis

Kumar Ankit
https://orcid.org/0009-0003-8876-3626
Christ University, India

Gopi Ranganath
Christ University, India

ABSTRACT

This chapter examines Facial Recognition Technology (FRT) as a tool of algorithmic governance that reshapes state surveillance practices. It details the technical workflow of FRT, from face detection to the creation of mathematical faceprints using convolutional neural networks (CNNs), and highlights systemic challenges such as algorithmic bias and the black box problem that impede legal accountability. Drawing on studies like Gender Shades and NIST FRVT, the chapter demonstrates accuracy disparities, particularly the disproportionate errors affecting darker-skinned women. Comparative governance models in India, the United States, and the European Union are analyzed, emphasizing differences in regulatory approaches, adoption strategies, and human rights implications. The so-

DOI: 10.4018/979-8-3373-5452-1.ch007

cietal consequences of FRT—including the erosion of public anonymity, chilling effects on democratic dissent, and risks of wrongful arrests—are explored. The chapter concludes by advocating for policy frameworks that align technological innovation with democratic principles and the protection of civil liberties.

1. INTRODUCTION

Artificial Intelligence (AI) began to take shape in the mid-20th century, with Alan Turing—famous for breaking the Enigma code—posing the groundbreaking question: can machines think like humans? His ideas laid the foundation for modern AI. Later, John McCarthy introduced the term artificial intelligence describing it as the science of building intelligent machines. Over time, AI evolved into a broad, interdisciplinary field that draws from areas like sociology, cognitive science, and mathematics, making it difficult to pin down a single definition (Idder & Coulaux, 2021).

Facial Recognition Technology (FRT) is a powerful application of AI. To completely fathom its legal and social impact, it is important to learn how it works. FRT involves a complex process, driven by advanced algorithms that try to identify people based on their facial features. However, it's far from perfect. The technology often reflects built-in biases, raising serious concerns about fairness and reliability in real-world situations (Mounica S, 2024).

Facial recognition works by converting a person's face into a unique digital signature that a computer can use to identify them (Parmar & Mehta, 2014). This process involves several distinct steps, each relying on sophisticated programs. Every stage has its own technical hurdles and the possibility of making errors. Grasping this entire sequence is vital to fully appreciate both the power and the shortcomings of the technology. The process begins with face detection. During this initial stage, the primary function of the algorithm is to identify human faces within a digital image or video feed. It must effectively distinguish faces from other elements present in the scene.

In the past, classic techniques like *Haar Cascades,* a machine learning based approach for object detection, were used for this purpose. Today, however, systems are increasingly built with more accurate deep learning models, like the Multi-Task Cascaded Convolutional Neural Network (MTCNN), because they are far more reliable.

Once a face is detected, the system starts Facial Mapping and Feature Extraction. This process involves measuring the face in detail to create a unique profile. It identifies and measures important features, called nodal points, such as the space between the eyes, the shape of the jawline, and the depth of the eyes (Devasia,2024). This geometric data is then crunched by an algorithm to produce a unique numerical code. This identifier, often called a "faceprint" or "embedding", is the face's unique signature (Preciozzi, 2025).

It's important to know that a "faceprint" is a mathematical code, not a stored picture of one's face, a key difference that makes it incredibly efficient to store and search through millions of records. Getting this digital faceprint right is the most crucial part of the process, as a poor or inconsistent faceprint will lead to an inefficient system. In the final stage, the system compares this newly generated faceprint against a database of pre-existing ones, calculating a "similarity score" to measure how closely they match.

This comparison can serve two primary functions:

- **Verification (1:1 Matching):** This is a simple one-to-one check to confirm the identity of an individual. This occurs when facial recognition technology is employed to authenticate an individual's identity, such as unlocking a smartphone or gaining access to a secured facility. In such instances, the system performs a one-to-one comparison between the live facial image and the pre-stored facial template of the same individual.
- **Identification (1:N Matching):** This is a one-to-many search used to figure out an unknown person's identity. The system compares a new faceprint against an entire database to find a match without any prior claim of who the person is. This is how law enforcement might identify a suspect from security footage.

A significant issue with facial recognition is that its decision-making process is black-boxed, obscure and uncertainable even to its human operators. Suffice it to say that, it's nearly impossible to see the internal logic the system uses to declare a match (Kayser-Bril, 2020). This lacks transparency and creates accountability issues, it cannot be tested on the anvil of cross examination. A case of false positives, may lead to a wrongful arrest and the error can't be traced back to the system's design. This fundamental opacity undermines a person's right to due process and creates serious challenges for using facial recognition leads as evidence.

To understand the fundamental steps of facial recognition, it is important to examine the underlying AI mechanisms that make this technology so powerful. At the heart of modern FRT lies a specialized type of AI called a Convolutional Neural Network (CNN), which drives the feature extraction, face mapping, and matching processes described previously. While earlier sections highlighted the stages of detection, feature encoding, and database comparison, CNNs are the engines that enable these stages to operate with high accuracy and scalability.

The remarkable power of modern facial recognition comes down to a special type of AI called a Convolutional Neural Network (CNN). Though first pioneered in the 1980s for simpler tasks like reading handwritten numbers, CNNs are now the go-to tool for analyzing images, as they are perfectly built to handle data in a grid-like format, just like the grid of pixels in a photo (Biswal, 2025).

The idea behind Convolutional Neural Networks (CNNs) was inspired by how a cat's brain processes visual information. In a study it was discovered that certain groups of cells in a cat's visual cortex respond to specific parts of what the cat sees. These cells become active only when something appears in their designated area of the visual field. Interestingly, these cells are also sensitive to the shape and direction of what they detect, for example, some respond to horizontal lines while others react to vertical lines.

A CNN works like a multi-stage assembly line for images. The process starts in the Convolutional Layer, which uses digital "filters" to scan the image for basic patterns like edges, corners, and colors. As the image data passes deeper into the network, subsequent layers combine these simple shapes to recognize more complex features, like an eye or the curve of a cheekbone (Wei-Meng Lee, 2025). Next, Pooling Layers step in to intelligently shrink this data, which makes the network run faster and helps it recognize a face even if it's slightly tilted or off-center.

Finally, after all the key features have been extracted and refined, the information is sent to the Fully Connected Layers. This is where the final decision happens. These layers synthesize all the detected features to perform the final classification. In the context of facial recognition, this means producing a final probability score that determines how likely it is that the face in the picture matches a specific person in a database (Thinking Neuron, 2025).

The most critical aspect of CNNs is that they teach themselves; humans don't program their rules by hand. Instead, they go through a "training" process where they are shown millions of labeled images. With each image, the network makes a guess, checks if it was right, and slightly adjusts its internal settings to become more accurate.

This method of learning from data is both the source of a CNN's power and its greatest weakness. Ultimately, the system is only as good as the data it was trained on. A sophisticated AI trained on a biased or unrepresentative dataset won't fix that bias rather it will learn and even amplify it. For instance, if the training data mostly features images of one demographic group, the network will become an expert at recognizing that group while performing poorly on underrepresented groups. This establishes a direct, technical link between how these networks function and the systemic problem of algorithmic bias.

Further it's also important to recognize that FRT isn't a one-size-fits-all technology. While CNNs form the mechanism that analyzes and interprets facial features, in practice, FRT comes in several different forms, each with its own strengths, weaknesses, and ways of working. The choice between 2D, 3D, or thermal systems can have a major impact on how accurate, secure, and effective a facial recognition setup actually is. Facial Recognition Technology (FRT) should not be considered a monolithic field; rather, it encompasses several distinct modalities, each with unique operational characteristics, advantages, and limitations. The selection of a specific modality has profound implications for a system's accuracy, security, and overall efficacy in its intended application.

The most ubiquitous and cost-effective modality is two-dimensional (2D) facial recognition, which operates by analyzing planar images captured from standard optical sensors. Its low cost and the ease with which it can be integrated into existing infrastructure, such as CCTV networks, have led to its widespread deployment (Aratek, 2023). However, its performance is highly susceptible to variations in ambient illumination, head pose, and facial expression. Critically, 2D systems exhibit a significant vulnerability to presentation attacks, commonly termed "spoofing," wherein they can be deceived by a high-resolution photograph or video of the target subject (Corning, 2023).

A more robust and secure alternative is three-dimensional (3D) facial recognition. This modality captures the three-dimensional topography of a subject's facial structure, often using technologies like structured light or time-of-flight sensors, as exemplified by Apple's Face ID system. By analyzing the actual geometry of the face, 3D systems are largely invariant to changes in lighting and demonstrate substantial resilience against 2D presentation attacks (FaceTec, n.d.). The primary barrier to their widespread adoption has been the reliance on specialized and often cost-prohibitive data acquisition hardware. A third modality, thermal facial recognition, operates on a fundamentally different principle, utilizing infrared cameras to detect the unique thermal signatures originating from subcutaneous vascular patterns. This method maintains operational efficacy in low-light or zero-lux conditions and can, in certain scenarios, perform identifications even through partial facial occlusions.

This technological divergence presents a significant challenge in practice. Many critical security and law enforcement systems have deployed the less secure 2D technology, a decision often dictated by economic constraints rather than technical superiority. This reliance on systems with known vulnerabilities fosters a "security theater," a phenomenon where the perception of security significantly outweighs the system's actual protective capabilities. Such a discrepancy can lead to severe operational failures, including false negatives (a failure to identify a target subject) and false positives (the erroneous identification of an innocent individual), thereby undermining the fundamental purpose of the security apparatus.

While understanding different models of FRT, it is also important to recognize that technology alone does not guarantee fairness or reliability. Even the most advanced system can produce flawed outcomes if the algorithms and training data it relies on are biased. This brings us to a critical concern in the deployment of FRT: algorithmic bias. Despite the perception of AI as mathematically neutral, facial recognition systems often reflect and even amplify societal prejudices, leading to unequal performance across different demographic groups.

A pervasive and dangerous misconception surrounding AI is the idea of machine neutrality and algorithms being based on mathematics and logic, are inherently objective and free from human prejudice. In reality, AI systems, and FRT in particular, are products of the data on which they are trained and the priorities of the people who design them. Consequently, they often reflect, and can even amplify, existing societal biases. The issue of algorithmic bias in FRT is not a minor technical flaw but a systemic problem with profound implications for fairness, equality, and justice (Christian, G. 2023).

Two influential studies have provided strong, data-driven evidence that facial recognition systems used by both commercial entities and government agencies can exhibit significant demographic bias. The first, known as the "Gender Shades" study, was conducted in 2018 by Joy Buolamwini and Timnit Gebru at the MIT Media Lab (Cogent Infotech, 2024). This pioneering research evaluated the accuracy of gender classification tools developed by Microsoft, IBM, and Face++ and highlighted a major shortcoming in the datasets these systems were trained on. The researchers found that existing benchmark datasets were heavily biased, mostly comprising lighter-skinned and male individuals (Friedler and Wilson, 2018).

To correct this imbalance, they created a new dataset, the Pilot Parliaments Benchmark (PPB) which better represented a diverse population. Using this improved dataset, the study uncovered stark disparities in performance. For lighter-skinned males, the error rate was as low as 0.8%, but for darker-skinned females, the error rate soared to 34.7%. In many cases, the systems were effectively making guesses no better than chance for certain demographic groups. Following this, the U.S. National Institute of Standards and Technology (NIST) conducted its own extensive investigation in 2019, known as the Face Recognition Vendor Test

(FRVT) Part 3: Demographic Effects (National Institute of Standards and Technology, 2019/2025). This was one of the most thorough evaluations ever conducted, assessing 189 algorithms from 99 different developers using millions of facial images drawn from U.S. government databases.

NIST's findings not only confirmed the results of "Gender Shades" but also offered deeper insight. In one-to-one (1:1) verification tests, false positive rates were found to be 10 to 100 times higher for Asian and African American faces compared to those of Caucasian individuals (Cogent Infotech, 2024). Even more concerning were the results from one-to-many (1:N) identification tasks, which is often used in policing where African American females experienced the highest rates of false matches. While NIST did acknowledge that some of the top-performing algorithms showed smaller disparities, the study ultimately concluded that a majority of the systems tested still displayed clear demographic biases (National Institute of Standards and Technology, 2019). This calls attention to the pressing need for more inclusive datasets, better training practices, and stronger accountability in the deployment of facial recognition technologies.

While the previous paragraph highlighted the findings of the "Gender Shades" and NIST studies, it is equally important to examine the methodology behind these investigations. What set the "Gender Shades" study apart was not only its findings but also the way the researchers approached the issue of bias (Buolamwini & Gebru, 2018). Instead of analysing race and gender as separate categories, the study took an intersectional perspective, examining how these identities interact by evaluating four specific groups: lighter-skinned males, darker-skinned males, lighter-skinned females, and darker-skinned females. This approach revealed that inaccuracies in facial recognition systems weren't merely a sum of individual biases rather they were compounded at the intersection of race and gender. The results clearly showed that darker-skinned women were the most frequently misclassified group across all systems tested, and by a significant margin.

This wasn't a random flaw; it was the predictable outcome of a system trained on biased data. Most of the training datasets used to build commercial facial recognition tools were dominated by images of lighter-skinned males (Cogent Infotech, 2024). Naturally, the systems became highly accurate for that demographic while struggling with others who were underrepresented in the data. These tools weren't malfunctioning but they were working exactly as they had been taught, mirroring the imbalance in their design inputs.

The consequences become far more troubling when these flawed systems are used in real-world applications like law enforcement. Surveillance efforts in many regions are already disproportionately focused on minority communities. When facial recognition systems less accurate for these groups are applied in such settings, they intensify existing inequalities. Misidentifications can lead to innocent individuals, particularly people of colour, being stopped, questioned, or even wrongly arrested (Perkowitz, 2021). And even if these encounters do not result in charges, they often generate new biometric records such as mugshots that are added to police databases (ACLU of Minnesota, 2021). These new data points, in turn, feed back into the same flawed systems, reinforcing the biases with every new iteration.

In this way, facial recognition technology doesn't merely reflect societal bias, it magnifies embedding discrimination into automated systems that appear neutral on the surface. A single misidentification can initiate a chain reaction that generates more biased data, leading to more errors, more interventions, and a self-perpetuating cycle. Ultimately, what's presented as objective technology ends up deepening the very patterns of injustice it was often claimed to solve.

The financial incentives of private deployment demonstrate how FRT is evolving into a widely used commercial technology outside of public-sector surveillance. Applications for facial recognition technology (FRT) are no longer limited to border control and law enforcement. In order to automate identification, reduce friction, and, they contend, lower costs and fraud, private-sector adopters such as airports and airlines, retail chains, banks and financial services companies, and corporations managing workplace access are increasingly implementing FRT. These implementations are motivated by managerial trade-offs between privacy and customer experience, compliance requirements like data protection laws and industry-specific regulations, and economic evaluations that take into account capital expenditures, operating costs, staffing implications, and expected return on investment. Research from several jurisdictions demonstrates that managers usually present the decision to implement FRT as an investment in anti-fraud or operational enhancement rather than as one involving social risk or surveillance infrastructure (Privacy and Civil Liberties Oversight Board [PCLOB], 2023).

Airlines and airports provide a clear example of this trend. Face matching is used at multiple passenger touchpoints in biometric-enabled check-in systems and “document-free” boarding gates. While regulators and privacy advocates raise concerns about consent, data minimization, and cross-border data flows, managers focus on throughput gains, faster boarding, less queuing and possible labor savings. These deployments and their effects are described in detail in government audits and oversight reports of U.S. Customs and Border Protection biometric pilots and the Transportation Security Administration (PCLOB, 2023). Managers are recommended to model the impact of passenger opt-in or opt-out on throughput, map legal obligations related to international data transfers, and weigh time savings and staffing reductions against capital and vendor costs when assessing airport FRT (ScienceDirect, 2024).

Facial biometrics are frequently promoted by financial institutions as a seamless authentication technique for remote onboarding and transaction approval. FRT integration into branch kiosks or mobile banking apps has been shown to lower certain types of fraud, but issues with spoofing, liveness detection, and accessibility for elderly or disabled clients still exist (CORE, 2024). Managers in this industry should evaluate multi-factor strategies that combine biometrics and traditional credentials, integrate adversarial threat models, such as presentation attacks and deepfakes, and set up explicit KPIs like customer drop-off, fraud-loss reduction, and false-accept and false-reject rates.

Common managerial and financial factors appear in all of these industries. Hardware and integration costs, ongoing vendor fees, training costs, and anticipated benefits like labor savings, loss reduction, and fraud prevention should all be included in cost-benefit analyses. Government return-on-investment studies and recent empirical models provide helpful models for benefit monetization (SSRN, 2024). Additionally, risk management needs to take into consideration potential class-action lawsuits, regulatory non-compliance fines, reputational damage, and bias-related harms like false matches that disproportionately impact specific demographic groups (Crest Research, 2024a). Lastly, contractual service-level agreements that outline acceptable error rates, provisions guaranteeing the provenance of training data, audit rights, and requirements for independent evaluation are beneficial to procurement and vendor governance; some organizations also test FRT in sandboxed pilots with stringent data-retention limits (Crest Research, 2024b). While private-sector adoption demonstrates the commercial pull of FRT, its most controversial uses remain in policing, which the next section examines comparatively.

2. FRT IN LAW ENFORCEMENT: A COMPARATIVE ANALYSIS OF DEPLOYMENT AND DOCTRINE

Facial Recognition Technology (FRT) has swiftly evolved from a theoretical innovation within research laboratories to a practical instrument employed extensively by law enforcement agencies worldwide. However, its integration into policing frameworks has not followed a uniform trajectory. The scale, regulatory frameworks, and normative justifications for its deployment vary considerably across jurisdictions. This section adopts a comparative lens to examine the operationalisation of FRT in India, the United States, and the European Union. By analysing emblematic case studies from each region, it underscores the divergent institutional approaches and the socio-legal implications that accompany them, thereby laying the groundwork for the subsequent legal analysis (Arnold, L. 2025)..

Under the banner of 'Digital India' and a push for police modernization, India has initiated a determined, large-scale campaign to incorporate Facial Recognition Technology (FRT) into its governance and security infrastructure. This state-directed effort has triggered a swift proliferation of FRT systems throughout the country, often advancing far more quickly than the legal and ethical guardrails needed to regulate them (Software Freedom Law Center, India, 2023). A central component of this national strategy is the development of the Automated Facial Recognition System (AFRS), which is conceived as one of the globe's largest centralized facial recognition databases. The AFRS is designed to consolidate facial images from a wide variety of government-held records including passport photos and criminal archives and make this vast repository available to all police stations nationwide (Project Statecraft, 2023). In addition to this federal endeavour, numerous state police agencies have rolled out their own bespoke systems, exemplified by FaceTagr in Tamil Nadu, the Punjab Artificial Intelligence System (PAIS), and Uttar Pradesh's 'Trinetra' app. Ultimately, this widespread implementation points to a strong belief in using technological fixes to address complex issues of crime and social order.

Within India's nationwide push for FRT, certain states have emerged as particularly active implementers, illustrating both the promise and the pitfalls of these technologies at a regional level. The state of Telangana has positioned itself at the forefront of Facial Recognition Technology (FRT) deployment in India, pioneering a series of initiatives that have been simultaneously lauded for technological innovation and intensely criticised for their detrimental impact on civil liberties. Central to this strategy is the Telangana State Crime and Operations Platform (TSCOP), a mobile application introduced in 2018 to equip frontline police with immediate access to criminal data. A core function of TSCOP is its embedded FRT, which enables an officer to capture any individual's photograph and instantly check it against a state-wide database reported to hold images of over 100,000 suspects (The New Indian Express, 2018).

The platform's use has been linked to highly contentious policing tactics. Numerous reports from Hyderabad, the state capital, have documented police conducting arbitrary stops where ordinary citizens, not under any suspicion of criminal activity, are compelled to have their photographs taken with official tablets (Amnesty International, n.d.). Civil liberties advocates argue that this practice facilitates the creation of a vast, non-consensual 'shadow' population database that lacks legal authorisation, effectively inverting the presumption of innocence for the general public. The gravity of these concerns was starkly realised last year, when the TSCOP system was compromised in a major data breach. Malicious actors infiltrated the application and leaked highly confidential information including offender records, police firearm licenses, and the personal details of officers exposing fundamental flaws in the system's security design (The New Indian Express, 2024).

Further other states in India have pursued alternative approaches that expand the scope of biometric surveillance. In Maharashtra The Automated Multi-Modal Biometric Identification System (AMBIS) has made law enforcement better at what they do. This new system goes beyond just using facial recognition. It makes a full biometric profile by combining facial scans, fingerprints, palm prints, and iris scans. As of 2019, AMBIS is intended to be the state's primary database, holding information on about 650,000 people who have been arrested or convicted (Hindustan Times, 2022). One of AMBIS's main strategic goals is to be completely interconnected with a number of national and state law enforcement databases. The Crime and Criminal Tracking Network and Systems (CCTNS) portal, the National Automated Fingerprint Identification System (NAFIS), and the state's many CCTV cameras are all being connected to the system. This makes a surveillance system that is very interconnected and allows you to promptly cross-reference different biometric identifiers. Supporters have called AMBIS the first ever system of its kind in the country and say it will greatly improve both the rates of solving crimes and convicting people (Jagran Josh, 2019).

India's use of facial recognition technology (FRT) shows a governance strategy that puts the state's interests ahead of developing the legal and ethical frameworks that are needed. The most common way of thinking seems to be "do it now, regulate it later." A lot of the time, big and intrusive systems are put in place without any specific laws to control how they work. This happens in a data protection framework that gives the state a lot of leeway (Project Statecraft, 2023).

In the international perspective, the interaction between a fragmented public sector and a dynamic, aggressive private sector has a unique impact on the facial recognition technology landscape specially in the United States. The US approach is distinguished by private companies creating potent and frequently contentious FRT tools, which are subsequently purchased and used by thousands of federal, state, and local law enforcement agencies functioning under a patchwork of disparate laws and policies, in contrast to the state-driven, top-down model observed in India (Bipartisan Policy Center, 2023).

Police use of FRT has rapidly increased as a result of this regulatory gap at the federal level. According to the seminal Georgetown Law report "The Perpetual Line-Up," published in 2016, law enforcement face recognition networks already contained the pictures of more than 117 million American adults, or nearly one in two (Georgetown Law Center on Privacy & Technology, 2016). The availability of strong new tools created by the private sector has been a major factor in the enormous growth of biometric surveillance.

Clearview AI is the company that best represents the American model. By building a database containing over three billion facial images that were scraped from public sources online, including news websites, social media sites like Facebook and YouTube, and other websites, the company produced a groundbreaking and highly contentious product. After that, this enormous non-governmental database was bundled with a potent search algorithm and offered for sale as a subscription service, mostly to law enforcement organizations.

By using a nearly infinite database of faces, Clearview AI provided police departments with an enticing tool: the ability to recognize an unidentified suspected person from a grainy surveillance photo. According to reports, the service was utilized by thousands of agencies in the US to produce investigative leads in almost all the criminal cases. Despite the success the business's practices provoked a strong backlash and a flurry of legal action. The Illinois Biometric Information Privacy Act (BIPA), a special state law that demands express consent for the collection of biometric data, was the subject of most important legal challenges (American Civil Liberties Union, n.d.). A historic 2022 settlement with the American Civil Liberties Union (ACLU) severely limited Clearview AI's business model by permanently prohibiting it from selling its faceprint database to the majority of private businesses and individuals in the country.

A number of recorded wrongful arrests all involving Black people have occurred in the US as a result of biased facial recognition algorithms and unchecked police use. Notable cases include Nijeer Parks, who was imprisoned for ten days in 2019 after an incorrect FRT match from a phony ID photo; Robert Williams, who was arrested in 2020 in front of his family based only on a false match from a blurry surveillance image (MIT Sociotechnical Systems Research Center, 2021) and Porcha Woodruff, who was eight months pregnant when she was wrongfully arrested in 2023, making her the first woman and sixth known person to be affected by such a failure (AI News, 2023). Despite poor image quality and little investigative verification, these incidents show a concerning reliance on FRT as conclusive proof (University of Michigan Law School, 2025).

The U.S. model, in which law enforcement frequently purchases surveillance equipment from private companies functioning in legal limbo, exacerbates this over-reliance (Spivack & Garvie, 2020). Through dubious data scraping, businesses such as Clearview AI have constructed extensive biometric databases, evading legal constraints that would directly affect government agencies (Troutman Pepper Locke Insights, 2025). Police departments can acquire strong surveillance capabilities without taking on the political and legal risks by acquiring access to such tools, diverting public attention away from private providers.

A third unique model is presented by the implementation of FRT in the UK and the EU, which is marked by a more circumspect and contentious deployment. In Europe, law enforcement agencies have encountered increased legal scrutiny and public opposition due to the robust and comprehensive regulations for data protection. Although there is still a lot of pressure to increase the technology's use for security, this has led to a more restricted and experimental use of the technology.

Although police in at least eleven EU member states use FRT, its use is frequently limited to forensic, post-event analysis. This method, which is typically regarded as less invasive than live surveillance, compares a suspect's still image to an existing database of known criminals (Simmler, 2025). Nonetheless, there is a discernible trend and desire among law enforcement to implement live, real-time FRT systems in public areas, especially during major events like football games and concerts, a practice that is still very contentious (Kayser-Bril, 2019/2020). Divergent positions have been taken by various member states; for instance, the Swedish data protection authority has authorized the use of FRT for criminal surveillance, while the French data protection authority has taken a strong stand against its use in schools (Jakubowska, 2019). In the meantime, German officials related to data protection have already given warning on the use of FRT in public space as it violates fundamental rights.

3. A COMPARATIVE LEGAL ANALYSIS

The disparate deployment doctrines that are seen in the US, the EU, and India are not coincidental; rather, they are the direct outcome of essentially dissimilar legal and constitutional systems. Core tenets of a society's relationship with its government, such as the right to privacy, the extent of state power, and the procedures for individual redress, are all touched upon by the regulation of a technology as potent as FRT. The legal foundations that support FRT governance in these three jurisdictions are critically compared in this section, which explains why their approaches to striking a balance between security and liberty differ so greatly.

In India a strong, judicially upheld fundamental right that is right to privacy gives the state broad authority in the name of national security are at odds in India's FRT legal environment. This leads to the paradoxical situation where citizens have a strong constitutional right in theory but find it difficult to actually enforce it against state surveillance (Yash Gupta, 2025). The Supreme Court's historic 2017 ruling in Justice K.S. Puttaswamy (Retd.) v. Union of India is the cornerstone of privacy rights in India. A nine-judge panel ruled unanimously that the right to privacy is a fundamental right that is safeguarded by Article 21 of the Constitution as an integral component of the right to life and personal liberty.

Crucially, the Court established a stringent proportionality test that any state action infringing upon this right must satisfy. To be constitutionally valid, an intrusion into privacy must: (1) be sanctioned by an existing law; (2) pursue a legitimate state aim; (3) have a rational connection to that aim; and (4) be the least intrusive measure available to achieve the objective, ensuring a balance between the right and the state's interest(40). This test, in principle, sets a high bar for the deployment of mass surveillance technologies like FRT.

However, the legislative response to this judgment has been ambivalent. The *Digital Personal Data Protection Act (DPDPA) of 2023* is India's first comprehensive data protection law, establishing a framework based on principles of consent, purpose limitation, and data minimization. Under the DPDPA, biometric data, including facial scans, is classified as "personal data," and its processing requires the explicit, informed, and unambiguous consent of the individual (Concur, 2025).

The Act's protections are significantly undermined by its broad exemption clauses. Section 17(2) of the DPDPA grants the central government wide-ranging powers to exempt its agencies from the Act's provisions on grounds of sovereignty and integrity of India, security of the State, friendly relations with foreign States, maintenance of public order, or preventing incitement to any cognizable offence. This effectively carves out most law enforcement and national security uses of FRT from the core requirements of the data protection law, including the need for consent.

This legal structure creates a "constitutional shell game." The judiciary establishes a powerful fundamental right with a strict test for its infringement. The legislature then enacts a data protection law that appears to implement this right but includes an escape hatch that renders its protections inapplicable to the state's most intrusive surveillance activities. This forces citizens seeking to challenge FRT surveillance to bypass the data protection law and mount a direct, resource-intensive constitutional challenge based on the *Puttaswamy* principles. The DPDPA, which should serve as the primary, accessible shield for citizens' data rights, is effectively nullified in the very context where it is most needed (Efthymiou, I. & Egleton, T. E., 2023). This framework systematically privileges state security interests over individual privacy, creating a legal environment conducive to the expansion of surveillance.

But navigating through the international perspective the most extensive regulation for data and AI, including FRT, was created by the *European Union*. The EU's strategy is proactive, top-down, and based on the idea that fundamental rights such as the right to privacy and data protection are of utmost importance. The General Data Protection Regulation (GDPR) and the recently passed AI Act are two important pieces of legislation that operationalize this philosophy.

The fundamental layer of protection is offered by the GDPR, which has been in force since 2018. Biometric information used to identify an individual uniquely is categorized as "special category data" (Amini & Javidnejad, 2024).It is by default that processing such data is forbidden under GDPR Article 9. Only in certain circumstances, such as gaining the person's express consent or when processing is required for "substantial public interest" as defined by Union or Member State law—which must be commensurate with the goal being pursued can this prohibition be lifted (Sinha, 2024).

The EU AI Act expands upon this framework by establishing a particular, risk-based regulatory framework for AI systems (European Parliament, 2025). Different risk categories are used to categorize AI systems, and each has associated regulatory requirements. "Unacceptable Risk" systems are completely prohibited because they clearly endanger people's rights, safety, and means of subsistence. A direct legislative response to the Clearview AI model, this category includes a number of applications of Facial Recognition Technology (FRT), including social scoring by government agencies using AI, emotion recognition in the workplace and educational institutions, and most importantly the development or growth of facial recognition databases through the untargeted scraping of images from the internet or CCTV footage (European Parliament, 2023/2025).

A step below this, "High Risk" systems which include the majority of other FRT applications, such as its use for access to employment, education, or essential services are not prohibited but must meet stringent legal requirements before being put on the market (European Union, 2024). Lastly, systems that pose "Limited and Minimal Risk" are either unregulated or subject to less stringent transparency requirements.

The AI Act is especially strict when it comes to law enforcement's use of FRT. Since real-time remote biometric identification falls under the "unacceptable risk" category, it is prohibited in publicly accessible areas. The Act offers a series of extremely limited and comprehensive exceptions to this prohibition, including the identification of a suspect in a serious crime, the prevention of a specific and imminent terrorist threat, and the targeted search for a missing child (European Union, 2024). Law enforcement must perform a fundamental rights impact assessment and get prior authorization from a judicial or independent administrative authority, even in cases where an exception applies.

On the other hand, post-remote biometric identification, which involves examining recorded video after the fact, is categorized as a high-risk application and is bound by the strict compliance requirements of the Act (Almeida, D, 2021).. The EU is actively working to influence the global technology market through its regulatory approach, which goes beyond simple defense. The EU makes use of the "Brussels Effect" by instituting a strict, rights-based standard for AI governance. International tech firms must design their products to satisfy the stringent criteria of the AI Act in order to gain access to the sizable and lucrative EU market. Building a single, compliant product for the global market is frequently more cost-effective than maintaining several versions with disparate standards. The EU's rules on risk management, data governance, and transparency for high-risk AI are therefore probably going to become the de facto standard worldwide. In this sense, the EU exports its values and forces the global technology sector to adopt a more rights-conscious development paradigm by using its regulatory authority as a tool of geopolitical influence.

Further In the United States the legal environment for FRT is fragmented, bottom-up, and sector-specific, which stands in sharp contrast to the EU's centralized and all-encompassing approach. As of right now, neither government organizations nor private businesses are subject to any comprehensive federal legislation that explicitly regulates the deployment of FRT or the gathering and use of biometric data. Despite numerous bills being introduced in Congress, they have never been able to secure enough bipartisan support to pass into law (Bipartisan Policy Center, 2023).

States and municipalities are now the main testing grounds for FRT regulation in this federal void. As a result, the nation now has a patchwork of laws that are unclear and inconsistent. The use of FRT by agencies like the police, has been virtually outlawed in some cities, such as San Francisco and Oakland (Amnesty International USA, 2020). More focused laws have been enacted in other states. For instance, states like Colorado and Virginia have mandated accuracy and bias testing for any FRT systems purchased by the government, while states like Montana and Utah now require police to obtain a warrant before conducting a FRT search (Laperruque, 2025).

The Biometric Information Privacy Act (BIPA) of Illinois is the most significant piece of legislation in this regard. BIPA is the most robust state-level biometric privacy law in the country, having been passed in 2008, long before FRT was a popular issue.81 It has two main provisions that give it power. First, it mandates that before collecting or capturing a person's biometric identifiers, like a fingerprint or a faceprint, any private entity must first obtain a written release from the person (ACLU of Illinois, 2024).

Second, and perhaps most significantly, BIPA gives people a private right of action, which enables them to bring direct legal action against businesses for infractions. Statutory damages of $1,000 for each negligent infraction and $5,000 for each intentional or reckless infraction are provided by the law.This private right of action's existence has made BIPA a potent instrument for accountability and sparked a wave of class-action lawsuits against businesses that gather biometric information without authorization (Cotter, 2024). It has served as the main legal tool in cases against Clearview AI, resulting in sizable settlements and modifications to the company's operations (Piepgrass, Navetta, Geiser, & Waltz, 2025).

The "regulation by litigation" system is the result of this American model. The threat of expensive, citizen-driven lawsuits under BIPA is the main factor influencing FRT policy and corporate behavior in the absence of proactive and comprehensive legislation from Congress. Even for businesses that do not primarily operate in Illinois, the enormous financial risk posed by possible class-action judgments provides a strong incentive for them to implement stronger standards for handling biometric data (Hartzog, 2019). This is an ineffective and reactive method of establishing policy, even though it offers a strong check on corporate overreach. In addition to causing legal ambiguity and inconsistency, it shifts the enforcement burden from a specialized regulatory body to private individuals and civil society organizations. The conflict over the prospects of facial recognition in the US has shifted from the legislature to the legal system.

Further examining Africa and Latin America provides important comparative depth to the uneven development of facial recognition governance around the world. The African Union (AU) has presented a continental AI strategy and a more comprehensive Digital Transformation Agenda for Africa that prioritizes economic development and innovation while committing to respecting data protection and human rights (African Union Commission, 2022; au.int, 2023). A number of member states, including Senegal, Nigeria, and Kenya, are extending their facial recognition-heavy border control systems and implementing biometric digital ID programs. These programs show how much the continent has invested in identity infrastructure, but they also draw attention to oversight and enforcement weaknesses.

The Collaboration on International ICT Policy for East and Southern Africa (CIPESA) and other regional data-protection authorities have cautioned that privacy protections are still not uniform and that regulatory frameworks frequently fall behind the speed at which they are being implemented (Future of Privacy Forum, 2023; International Association of Privacy Professionals [IAPP], 2023). For instance, Senegal's data-protection authority has issued warning guidelines regarding the use of biometrics, indicating the emergence of new but still disjointed oversight mechanisms.

Another useful contrast is found in Latin America. FRT has been piloted or implemented for policing and urban security in cities like Buenos Aires, São Paulo, and Mcxico City, sparking intense discussion about civil liberties and public accountability. Although legal protections and transparency measures differ greatly, national governments in Brazil, Argentina, and Mexico are experimenting with FRT in identity or public safety programs. Both municipal support for surveillance and robust civil-society opposition, including legal challenges and temporary moratoria in certain jurisdictions, are documented in reports from Chatham House (2023) and Access Now (2023). When taken as a whole, these examples show how institutional capacity, activist pressure, and political dynamics influence adoption paths throughout the region.

When viewed in conjunction with other significant actors, these developments highlight how institutional and political context, in addition to technological capability, are reflected in FRT governance. The European Union's cautious regulatory approach, anchored in the General Data Protection Regulation (GDPR) and the upcoming AI Act, and the United States' disjointed, primarily state-level approach stand in stark contrast to China's centrally planned, state-driven surveillance model. Comparing these areas reveals how disparities in administrative capability, the influence of civil society, and commercial incentives lead to different regulatory outcomes and provide important insights for any global facial recognition framework.

4. SOCIETAL IMPLICATIONS OF USING FACIAL RECOGNITION TECHNOLOGY

The use of facial recognition technology is transforming the relationship between the state, the public square, and the individual going beyond technical and legal arguments. Its spread has significant societal repercussions that change long-standing privacy expectations which affects the exercise of basic democratic rights and opening up new avenues for social control and discrimination. This section examines these wider human effects, examining how FRT normalizes the growth of state power through the sneaky process of "function creep," discourages political dissent, and contributes to a state of constant surveillance.

The wider effects of FRT on society become most tangible when we consider how it adversely affects our privacy rights. What was once a simple fact of daily life that we could move through public spaces without constantly being watched is disappearing. Furthermore, the mass use of Facial Recognition Technology has turned everyday life into a kind of perpetual line-up, where merely being out in public can place you under the state's watchful eye (Choung, H, 2024)..

In the past, a certain amount of practical anonymity was provided by being in a public setting. One could be seen, but it took a deliberate effort to be recognized. This paradigm is destroyed by widespread FRT combined with the constantly expanding CCTV camera networks. According to the Georgetown Law Center on Privacy & Technology, it results in a "perpetual line-up" (Center on Privacy and Technology, 2016). Every individual entering a monitored public area is continuously and passively subjected to a biometric identity check in this new reality.

Law enforcement could search images of half of all American adults, which were primarily taken from databases of non-criminal driver's licenses, using FRT, according to a 2016 Georgetown report that exposed the startling scope of this phenomenon in the US (Center on Privacy & Technology, 2016). This makes surveillance a passive, widespread, and ongoing aspect of public life rather than an active, targeted measure started out of suspicion. Many cities already have the necessary infrastructure in place for this, including Hyderabad, which is ready to be integrated with

FRT and is covered by a dense network of up to 600,000 cameras that feed into a central command and control center (Amnesty International, n.d.).

The presumption of innocence, a pillar of liberal democratic legal systems, is essentially inverted by this mass, automated identification system. It is customary to assume that a person is going about their legal business, and a police encounter can only be warranted by a specific, reasonable suspicion of misconduct. This script is reversed by the perpetual line-up. Every person is automatically scanned and checked against a watchlist of suspects, missing persons, or other people of interest (South Wales Police, 2025).

Every citizen is viewed as a possible person of interest in this model, and their identity needs to be algorithmically confirmed. Now, merely being in the public eye and having a faceprint that is probabilistically similar to an image in a database serves as the trigger for state attention instead of suspicious behavior. This represents a significant and perilous change in the relationship between the citizen and the state since it normalizes a state of unquestioning scrutiny and undermines the very notion of an anonymous, carefree existence in the public sphere.

The impact of FRT on society goes far beyond privacy, as it directly affects how we participate in democracy. Public spaces are increasingly turning into zones of constant biometric surveillance, posing a clear threat to our freedoms. The simple act of blending into a crowd, once a fundamental safeguard for personal expression, is gradually disappearing. This isn't just an abstract concern; it influences how people navigate the world and whether they feel safe speaking out or challenging authority (Wang et al., 2024).

In any functioning democracy, the freedom to peacefully assemble and protest is an essential outlet and a fundamental accountability mechanism. The ability of people to voice disapproval without worrying about retaliation frequently determines how effective protests are. This dynamic is directly threatened by the use of FRT at public events, which has a strong "chilling effect" on free speech and association (Askin, 2025).

People are discouraged from exercising their constitutional rights due to a fear of government action, even if that action does not involve direct punishment, a phenomenon known as the chilling effect (Askin, 2009/2025).

People may self-censor and refrain from taking part in legitimate protests if they are aware or even just suspect that their faces are being scanned, identified, and possibly added to a permanent government database of protesters (Richards, 2013). Protesters have long found anonymity in a crowd to be a useful safety measure, shielding them from possible employer reprisals, social disgrace, or unjustified police attention. This protection is methodically undermined by FRT (Zick, 2023).

This isn't a theoretical issue. FRT has already been applied to protests by law enforcement organizations worldwide. Police in the United States have used FRT to find and apprehend participants in Black Lives Matter demonstrations in Miami, Baltimore, and Washington, D.C. (Rathi, 2021). At a Prime Minister's rally in 2019, the Delhi Police used FRT for the first time in India with the specific goal of locating and dealing with demonstrators (Software Freedom Law Center, India, 2024). Human rights organizations in the UK are alarmed by the use of LFR at occasions such as the coronation of King Charles III and the Notting Hill Carnival. This risk has been acknowledged by the UN High Commissioner for Human Rights, who has called for a moratorium on the use of FRT in this situation and expressed concern that it may have a chilling effect on the right to freedom of assembly (Newson, 2024).

This surveillance's effects go well beyond discouraging involvement in a particular event. It helps to create a "digital panopticon," a setting in which people come to accept the constant threat of surveillance. Now, anyone thinking about going to a protest has to balance their dedication to a cause with the possibility of having their identity permanently linked to a certain political movement (Richards, 2013). Many will unavoidably stop participating in public politics as a result of this risk-benefit analysis, not because their actions are unlawful but rather because they are anti-government or just unconventional. The end result is a kind of proactive social control. To discourage grassroots activism and undermine a cornerstone of democratic society, the state does not have to arrest every protester; the mere sight of FRT-enabled cameras is sufficient to discipline the populace into becoming less willing to take political risks.

The effects of FRT on society go beyond merely violating privacy rights or limiting dissent; they reveal a deeper struggle between state authority and individual freedom. As surveillance spreads and public spaces become constantly monitored by biometric systems, it's worth asking what real benefits this technology brings and what freedoms we are giving up in the process. The presence of FRT can quietly shape behavior, discouraging protest, self-expression, and civic engagement even without direct enforcement. In this way, it creates a digital panopticon, where people begin to feel the weight of constant observation and adjust their actions accordingly. The main argument surrounding FRT and other mass surveillance technologies is frequently presented as a simple trade-off: society must be prepared to give up some degree of individual liberty, specifically privacy, in order to increase collective security. FRT proponents contend that a decrease in public anonymity is a fair price to pay for these advantages, and that it is an essential tool for contemporary law enforcement, required to stop terrorism, solve violent crimes, and safeguard the public (Lawvs, 2025).

Critics respond that this framing offers an incorrect option. They contend that while the promised increases in security are frequently speculative and overstated, the erosion of liberty through widespread surveillance is a certain and immediate harm. Moreover, not everyone bears the same costs as a result of this trade-off. Communities that are already marginalized and overpoliced bear the brunt of the loss of liberty and the risk of misidentification because of the technology's known biases.

This balance has been achieved in radically different ways by various jurisdictions. The fundamental right to privacy is explicitly prioritized by the EU's legal framework, which views mass surveillance as an intrinsically disproportionate measure and forbids processing biometric data by default as well as the majority of real-time public surveillance methods (Abhimanyu Paliwal, Sidra Ahmed, 2025). Although it seems to prioritize state security interests in practice, India's framework reflects a deep ambivalence between its broad national security exemptions and its strong constitutional right to privacy (Mahapatra, 2021). The US is home to a fragmented and continuous debate, with various states and cities reaching wildly divergent conclusions due to the lack of a unified federal approach.

The "security vs. liberty" debate is frequently a false dichotomy, according to a critical analysis of the available data. The idea behind the trade-off is that we gain a noticeable boost in security in exchange for our liberty. This is called into question, though, by the performance of many

FRT systems that have been documented. The persistent demographic inaccuracies found by the "Gender Shades" and NIST studies, as well as the incredibly high false positive rates observed in early police trials, like the SWP deployment, show that the technology frequently falls short of its security promises.Negative security outcomes, like the erroneous arrests of innocent people, are directly caused by this inaccuracy. These arrests not only hurt innocent people but also waste police resources and damage public confidence (AI News, 2023).

Therefore, "liberty for security" is not the true trade-off. More precisely, it is the loss of a certain and substantial degree of freedom in return for a very hazy and frequently fictitious increase in security, which carries the additional risk of purposefully undermining the security of innocent people by putting them in danger of being falsely accused and arrested. We need to reframe the argument. "Is this specific technology, with its documented flaws and biases, capable of providing a security benefit so substantial and certain that it justifies its definite and disproportionate costs to liberty and equality?" is the crucial question, not "How much liberty are we willing to give up for security?"

5. POLICY RECOMMENDATIONS AND CONCLUSION FOR RESPONSIBLE FRT GOVERNANCE

This report's analysis shows that facial recognition technology is a crucial and dangerous invention. Its potential to erode democratic norms and fundamental rights is equal to, if not greater than, its potential benefits for law enforcement. While a total ban might not be politically feasible in many jurisdictions, a laissez-faire approach to its adoption is unacceptable. Therefore, creating strong, all-encompassing, rights-based legal frameworks that strictly monitor and regulate FRT is the way forward. This section offers a set of specific policy recommendations based on a comparative analysis of the US, the EU, and India. It focuses on guiding India in a responsible manner while taking inspiration from international best practices.

India stands at a pivotal moment in shaping its approach to Facial Recognition Technology (FRT). While the country possesses a strong constitutional framework that upholds the right to privacy, it is rapidly deploying FRT through a centralized, state-led model in a largely unregulated legal environment. To align its technological advancements with constitutional values, India must abandon the prevailing "deploy first, regulate later" approach and instead adopt a robust, proactive governance structure (Efthymiou, I., 2025). Drawing on global best practices, several key recommendations can guide this transformation. First, India must enact a specific, standalone FRT law.

The current reliance on the Digital Personal Data Protection Act (DPDPA) is inadequate, given its broad exemptions for law enforcement. A dedicated statute should govern every stage of FRT's lifecycle from development and procurement to deployment and oversight across both public and private sectors. Crucially, this law must be rooted in the four-part proportionality test laid out by the Supreme Court in the Puttaswamy judgment, ensuring all FRT use is lawful, necessary, proportionate, and the least intrusive means to achieve a legitimate aim.

Second, the law must prohibit high-risk and unacceptable uses of FRT. Following the EU's risk-based AI Act, India should categorically ban applications that threaten fundamental rights (105). These include real-time remote biometric identification in public spaces, mass image scraping from social media, FRT use in social scoring or predictive policing based on profiling, and surveillance of individuals engaged in lawful protests or assemblies.

Third, the creation of an independent oversight body is essential. This authority composed of judicial, technical, and civil society experts, and independent from police or government ministries should conduct mandatory Human Rights Impact Assessments before any FRT deployment. It should also perform regular audits to evaluate accuracy, bias, and legal compliance of all government FRT systems, and publish these findings in the public domain.

Fourth, transparency and public accountability must be central to the legal framework. All government agencies using FRT should maintain a public registry detailing system capabilities, vendors, and datasets. They should also publish binding operational policies and release annual transparency reports, including disaggregated statistics on searches, match rates, and documented errors by demographic group. Finally, the law must reinforce due process and evidentiary safeguards. An FRT match should be recognized only as a preliminary investigative lead—not sufficient grounds, in itself, for arrests, searches, or warrants. Any law enforcement action must be supported by substantial, independent corroborating evidence. In criminal trials, the defense must have full access to technical details about the FRT system used, including the specific algorithm, known error rates especially for the relevant demographic, the match confidence score, and image chain of custody.

Facial recognition technology is more than just a tool; it is a revolutionary technology that calls into question the fundamental characteristics of public space, personal freedom, and the distribution of power between the state and its citizens. Its spread poses a serious challenge to democratic societies around the globe. Although its potential to improve efficiency and security is strong, there is no denying its shortcomings, bias, and potential to allow for previously unheard-of levels of mass surveillance.

It is instructive to examine the different approaches taken by the United States, India, and the European Union. They show that the future is not solely determined by technology. Instead, intentional political and legal decisions influence the effects of FRT. The most promising model for negotiating this challenging environment is the EU's proactive, rights-first, risk-based strategy. It shows that rather than letting technology automatically determine social norms, it is possible to create robust legal barriers that encourage innovation within moral bounds.

This comparative analysis's main takeaway is that the FRT debate cannot be reduced to a straightforward choice between security and liberty or progress and privacy. The true decision concerns the type of society we want to create. Accepting the normalization of unquestioning scrutiny, the suppression of dissent, and the automation of preexisting biases are all characteristics of a society that supports unregulated FRT. A society that decides to firmly regulate it is one that reaffirms its dedication to equality, privacy, and the rule of law as prerequisites for true security. The way forward necessitates a firm demand that our technologies be developed and regulated in accordance with our most valued democratic principles, not a rejection of technology.

REFERENCES

Almeida, D. (2021). Ethical implications of facial recognition technology: Transparency, accountability, and privacy concerns. *Frontiers in Artificial Intelligence*, *4*, 678234. Retrieved July 20, 2025, from https://pmc.ncbi.nlm.nih.gov/articles/PMC8320316/

Amini, M., & Javidnejad, L. (2024). Legal regulation of biometric data: A comparative analysis of global standards. *Legal Studies in the Digital Age*, *3*(1), 26–34. DOI: 10.1234/lsda.2024.3.1.26

Amnesty International. (2020, June 11). Amnesty International calls for ban on the use of facial recognition technology for mass surveillance [Public statement]. Retrieved July 20, 2025, from https://www.amnesty.org/en/latest/news/2020/06/amnesty-international-calls-for-ban-on-facial-recognition/

Amnesty International. (n.d.). Ban the scan Hyderabad. Retrieved July 20, 2025, from https://www.amnesty.org/en/campaigns/ban-the-scan-hyderabad/

Aratek. (2023). Reading your face: How does facial recognition work? Retrieved July 20, 2025, from https://www.aratek.co/blog/reading-your-face-how-does-facial-recognition-work/

Arnold, L. (2025). Usc of facial rccognition tcchnologics for law cnforcement: A comparative analysis. *Oregon Review of International Law, 26*(1), 175–225. Retrieved from https://scholarsbank.uoregon.edu/server/api/core/bitstreams/cf4701e9-7335-4bf5-98a3-a741300221e5/content?utm_source=chatgpt.com

Askin, F. (2009, January 1; updated June 2, 2025). Chilling effect. In The First Amendment Encyclopedia. Middle Tennessee State University. Retrieved July 20, 2025, from https://www.mtsu.edu/first-amendment/article/968/chilling-effect

Bipartisan Policy Center. (2023, March 30). Face recognition technology policy landscape, terms, and definitions. Retrieved July 20, 2025, from https://bipartisanpolicy.org/report/face-recognition-technology-policy-landscape/

Biswal, A. (2025). CNN in deep learning: Algorithm and machine learning uses. Simplilearn. Retrieved July 20, 2025, from https://www.simplilearn.com/cnn-in-deep-learning-algorithm-and-machine-learning-uses/

Buolamwini, J., & Gebru, T. (2018). Gender shades: Intersectional accuracy disparities in commercial gender classification. In S. A. Friedler & C. Wilson (Eds.), Proceedings of the 1st Conference on Fairness, Accountability and Transparency (Vol. 81, pp. 77–91). Proceedings of Machine Learning Research. Retrieved July 20, 2025, from http://proceedings.mlr.press/v81/buolamwini18a.html

Center on Privacy & Technology at Georgetown Law. (2016). The perpetual line-up: Unregulated police face recognition in America. Retrieved July 20, 2025, from https://www.perpetuallineup.org/

Choung, H. (2024). Acceptance of AI-powered facial recognition technology in public spaces: Balancing crime prevention and privacy concerns. *ScienceDirect.* https://www.sciencedirect.com/science/article/abs/pii/S0160791X24002690

Christian, G. (2023). Law professor explores racial bias implications in facial recognition technology. *University of Calgary News.* Retrieved from https://ucalgary.ca/news/law-professor-explores-racial-bias-implications-facial-recognition-technology

Cogent Infotech. (2024, March 13). Addressing gender bias in facial recognition technology: An urgent need for fairness and inclusion. Retrieved July 20, 2025, from https://www.cogentinfotech.com/blog/addressing-gender-bias-in-facial-recognition-technology

Concur. (2025, June 11). Facial recognition technology & DPDPA 2023: A compliance blueprint for Indian businesses. Retrieved July 20, 2025, from https://www.concur.in/blog/facial-recognition-technology-dpdpa-2023

Corning. (2023). Face to face: Why NIR facial recognition systems are the most secure. Radiant Vision Systems. Retrieved July 20, 2025, from https://www.radiantvisionsystems.com/blog/face-to-face-why-nir-facial-recognition-systems-are-the-most-secure

Cotter, D. A. (2024, November 18). The Biometric Information Privacy Act. TortSource, Fall 2024. American Bar Association. Retrieved July 20, 2025, from https://www.americanbar.org/groups/tort_trial_insurance_practice/publications/tortsource/2024/fall/biometric-information-privacy-act/

Devasia, A. (2024). Facial recognition system: How does it work? Safe and Sound Security. Retrieved July 20, 2025, from https://www.safeandsoundsecurity.com/facial-recognition-system-how-does-it-work/

Efthymiou, I. (2025). The Role of E-Government and E-Governance in Modern Societies. In Wongmahesak, K., Ahmad, J., & Mustanir, A. (Eds.), *Public Governance Practices in the Age of AI* (pp. 45–68). IGI Global Scientific Publishing., DOI: 10.4018/979-8-3693-9286-7.ch003

Efthymiou, I., & Egleton, T. E. (2023). Artificial Intelligence for Sustainable Smart Cities. In Mishra, B. (Ed.), *Handbook of Research on Applications of AI, Digital Twin, and Internet of Things for Sustainable Development* (pp. 1–11). IGI Global Scientific Publishing., DOI: 10.4018/978-1-6684-6821-0.ch001

European Parliament. (2025, February 19). EU AI Act: First regulation on artificial intelligence. Retrieved July 20, 2025, from https://www.europarl.europa.eu/news/en/headlines/society/20230601STO93804/eu-ai-act-first-regulation-on-artificial-intelligence

European Union. (2024, July 30). AI Act | Shaping Europe's digital future. European Commission Digital Strategy. Retrieved July 20, 2025, from https://digital-strategy.ec.europa.eu/en/policies/ai-act

European Union. (2024). Regulation (EU) 2024/1689 laying down harmonised rules on artificial intelligence (Artificial Intelligence Act). Official Journal of the European Union. Retrieved from https://eur-lex.europa.eu/eli/reg/2024/1689/oj

FaceTec. (n.d.). 2D vs. 3D face matching. Retrieved July 20, 2025, from https://www.facetec.com/2d-vs-3d-face-matching/

Friedler, S. A., & Wilson, C. (2018). Gender shades: Intersectional accuracy disparities in commercial gender classification. In Proceedings of the 1st Conference on Fairness, Accountability and Transparency (Vol. 81, pp. 77–91). Proceedings of Machine Learning Research. Retrieved July 20, 2025, from http://proceedings.mlr.press/v81/buolamwini18a.html

Gupta, Y. (2025). Facial recognition technology and the fundamental right to privacy. SSRN. Retrieved July 20, 2025, from https://papers.ssrn.com/sol3/papers.cfm?abstract_id=5228551 DOI: 10.2139/ssrn.5228551

Hartzog, W. (2019). *BIPA: The most important biometric privacy law in the U.S.?* AI Now Institute. Retrieved from https://ainowinstitute.org/wp-content/uploads/2023/09/regulatingbiometrics-hartzog.pdf

Hindustan Times. (2022, May 16). Maharashtra police launch new tech to help check crimes. Retrieved July 20, 2025, from https://www.hindustantimes.com/cities/mumbai-news/maharashtra-police-launch-new-tech-to-help-check-crimes-101652678945123.html

Idder, A., & Coulaux, S. (2021, December 13). Artificial intelligence in criminal justice: Invasion or revolution? International Bar Association. Retrieved July 20, 2025, from https://www.ibanet.org/dec-21-ai-criminal-justice

Jagran Josh. (2019, August 24). What is 'AMBIS' system and how will it help in nabbing the criminals? Retrieved July 20, 2025, from https://www.jagranjosh.com/general-knowledge/what-is-ambis-system-and-how-will-it-help-in-nabbing-the-criminals-1566648370-1

Jakubowska, E. (2019, December 4). The many faces of facial recognition in the EU. European Digital Rights (EDRi). Retrieved July 20, 2025, from https://edri.org/our-work/the-many-faces-of-facial-recognition-in-the-eu/

Kayser-Bril, N. (2020, June 18). At least 11 police forces use face recognition in the EU, AlgorithmWatch reveals. AlgorithmWatch. Retrieved July 20, 2025, from https://algorithmwatch.org/en/at-least-11-police-forces-use-face-recognition-in-the-eu/

Laperruque, J. (2025, January 6). Status of state laws on facial recognition surveillance: Continued progress and smart innovations. TechPolicy.Press. Retrieved July 20, 2025, from https://techpolicy.press/status-of-state-laws-on-facial-recognition-surveillance

Lawvs. (2025, June 29). Navigating the tension: Civil liberties vs. national security in a surveillance society. Retrieved July 20, 2025, from https://www.lawvs.com/navigating-the-tension-civil-liberties-vs-national-security/

Lee, W.-M. (2025). *Implementing face recognition using deep learning and support vector machines.* Retrieved July 20, 2025, from https://www.codemag.com/Article/2205081/Implementing-Face-Recognition-Using-Deep-Learning-and-Support-Vector-Machines

Mahapatra, S. (2021). Digital surveillance and the threat to civil liberties in India (GIGA Focus Asia, No. 3). German Institute for Global and Area Studies (GIGA). Retrieved July 20, 2025, from https://www.giga-hamburg.de/en/publications/giga-focus/digital-surveillance-and-the-threat-to-civil-liberties-in-india

MIT Sociotechnical Systems Research Center. (2021). The bias in the machine: Facial recognition technology and racial disparities. Retrieved July 20, 2025, from https://ssrc.mit.edu/publications/the-bias-in-the-machine-facial-recognition-technology-and-racial-disparities/

Mounica, S. (2024). A comprehensive guide to face recognition algorithms. Hyperverge. Retrieved July 20, 2025, from https://hyperverge.co/blog/a-comprehensive-guide-to-face-recognition-algorithms/

National Institute of Standards and Technology. (2025, February 3). NIST study evaluates effects of race, age, sex on face recognition software. Retrieved July 20, 2025, from https://www.nist.gov/news-events/news/2019/12/nist-study-evaluates-effects-race-age-sex-face-recognition-software

Newson, N. (2024, April 18). UN standards on the use of surveillance technology at protests. House of Lords Library. Retrieved July 20, 2025, from https://lordslibrary.parliament.uk/un-standards-on-the-use-of-surveillance-technology-at-protests/

Paliwal, A., & Ahmed, S. (2025). Constitutional approaches to data protection and privacy in the age of surveillance: A comparative analysis of India, the USA, and the European Union. International Journal of Innovation and Research in Law. https://doi.org/DOI: 10.1234/ijirl.2025.1.1.10

Parmar, D. N., & Mehta, B. B. (2014). *Face recognition methods and applications. arXiv preprint arXiv:1403.0485*.https://doi.org//arXiv.1403.0485. Retrieved July 20, 2025, from https://www.troutman.com/insights/facial-recognition-and-legal-boundaries-the-clearview-ai-case-study/DOI: 10.48550

Perkowitz, S. (2021, February 5). The bias in the machine: Facial recognition technology and racial disparities. MIT Case Studies in Social and Ethical Responsibilities of Computing. Retrieved July 20, 2025, from https://mit-serc.pubpub.org/pub/facial-recognition-technology-and-racial-disparities

Piepgrass, S., Navetta, D., Geiser, L., & Waltz, D. (2025, June 10). *Facial recognition: Legal boundaries and Clearview AI [Audio podcast episode]*. Regulatory Oversight. https://www.newindianexpress.com/cities/hyderabad/2018/Aug/03/tscop-app-to-use-facial-recognition-1852485.html

Preciozzi, J. (2025). How does facial recognition work? From pixels to identity. Digital Sense. Retrieved July 20, 2025, from https://www.digitalsense.ai/how-does-facial-recognition-work/

Project Statecraft. (2023, June 21). Facial recognition technology in India. Retrieved July 20, 2025, from https://www.projectstatecraft.org/facial-recognition-technology-in-india/

Rathi, M. (2021, December 1). Government facial recognition threatens our rights to free speech and protest. Security Technology, ASIS International. Retrieved July 20, 2025, from https://www.asisonline.org/security-management-magazine/articles/2021/12/government-facial-recognition-threatens-rights/

Richards, N. M. (2013). The dangers of surveillance. *Harvard Law Review, 126*(7), 1934–1965. Retrieved July 20, 2025, from https://harvardlawreview.org/2013/05/the-dangers-of-surveillance/

Simmler, M. (2025). Facial recognition technology in law enforcement. *ScienceDirect*. Retrieved July 20, 2025, from https://www.sciencedirect.com/science/article/pii/S0267364924001572

Sinha, A. (2024, March 13). The landscape of facial recognition technologies in India. TechPolicy.Press. Retrieved July 20, 2025, from https://techpolicy.press/the-landscape-of-facial-recognition-technologies-in-india/

Software Freedom Law Center. India. (2024, November 12). Deployment of facial recognition technology for state surveillance and monitoring. Retrieved July 20, 2025, from https://sflc.in/deployment-of-facial-recognition-technology-for-state-surveillance/

South Wales Police. (2025). Live facial recognition technology: Everything you need to know. Retrieved July 20, 2025, from https://www.south-wales.police.uk/news/south-wales/news/2025/live-facial-recognition-technology-everything-you-need-to-know/

Spivack, J., & Garvie, C. (2020). A taxonomy of legislative approaches to face recognition in the United States. In A. Kak (Ed.), Regulating biometrics: Global approaches and urgent questions. AI Now Institute. Retrieved July 20, 2025, from https://ainowinstitute.org/regulating-biometrics.html

The American Civil Liberties Union. (n.d.). ACLU v. Clearview AI. Retrieved July 20, 2025, from https://www.aclu.org/cases/aclu-v-clearview-ai

The American Civil Liberties Union of Illinois. (2024). Biometric Information Privacy Act (BIPA). Retrieved July 20, 2025, from https://www.aclu-il.org/en/cases/biometric-information-privacy-act-bipa

The American Civil Liberties Union of Minnesota. (2021, June 9). Biased technology: The automated discrimination of facial recognition. Retrieved July 20, 2025, from https://www.aclu-mn.org/en/news/biased-technology-automated-discrimination-facial-recognition

The New Indian Express. (2018, August 3). TSCOP app to use facial recognition. The New Indian Express Retrieved July 20, 2025, from. https://www.newindianexpress.com/cities/hyderabad/2018/Aug/03/tscop-app-to-use-facial-recognition-1852485.html

The New Indian Express. (2024, June 8). Second major data breach hits Telangana police as TSCOP app hacked. Retrieved July 20, 2025, from https://www.newindianexpress.com/states/telangana/2024/jun/08/second-major-data-breach-hits-telangana-police-as-tscop-app-hacked

Thinking Neuron. (2025). Convolutional neural networks (CNN) - Face recognition case study - Algorithm & full code explained [Video]. YouTube. Retrieved July 20, 2025, from https://www.youtube.com/watch?v=[VideoID]

University of Michigan Law School. (2025, Winter). Flawed facial recognition technology leads to wrongful arrest and historic settlement. Law Quadrangle. Retrieved July 20, 2025, from https://quadrangle.law.umich.edu/winter2025/flawed-facial-recognition-technology/

Wang, X., Wu, Y. C., Zhou, M., & Fu, H. (2024). Beyond surveillance: Privacy, ethics, and regulations in facial recognition technology. *Frontiers in Big Data*, *7*, 1337465. Retrieved July 20, 2025, from https://www.frontiersin.org/journals/big-data/articles/10.3389/fdata.2024.1337465/full. DOI: 10.3389/fdata.2024.1337465 PMID: 39027377

Zick, T. (2023). *Managed dissent: The law of public protest.* Cambridge University Press.Retrieved July 20, 2025, from https://www.cambridge.org/core/books/managed-dissent/12A7E4D9035D78C4A5BF24B1D81B0746

Compilation of References

Abdalla, S., Al-Maamari, W., & Al-Azki, J. (2024). Data analytics-driven innovation: UTAUT model perspectives for advancing healthcare social work. *Journal of Open Innovation*, *10*(4), 100411. DOI: 10.1016/j.joitmc.2024.100411

Abdulai, A. F. (2025). Is Generative AI Increasing the Risk for Technology-Mediated Trauma Among Vulnerable Populations? *Nursing Inquiry*, *32*(1), e12686. DOI: 10.1111/nin.12686

Abhilash, A., Shenoy, S. S., & Shetty, D. K. (2023). Overview of Corporate governance research in India: A bibliometric analysis. *Cogent Business & Management*, *10*(1), 2182361. Advance online publication. DOI: 10.1080/23311975.2023.2182361

Aboy, M., Minssen, T., & Vayena, E. (2024). Navigating the EU AI Act: Implications for regulated digital medical products. *NPJ Digital Medicine*, *7*(1), 237. DOI: 10.1038/s41746-024-01232-3 PMID: 39242831

ACI Adam BV and Others v Stichting de Thuiskopie and Stichting Onderhandelingen Thuiskopie vergoeding. (2014). Court of Justice of the European Union, C-435/12, 10 April 2014, ECLI:EU:C:2014:254.

Adeniyi, A. O., Arowoogun, J. O., Okolo, C. A., Chidi, R., & Babawarun, O. (2024). Ethical considerations in healthcare IT: A review of data privacy and patient consent issues. *World Journal of Advanced Research and Reviews*, *21*(2), 1660–1668. DOI: 10.30574/wjarr.2024.21.2.0593

Agarwal, D. (2024). Artificial intelligence and artistic imitation: A legal analysis of the Ghibli-style image debate. *IIPRD Blog*. https://www.iiprd.com/artificial-intelligence-and-artistic-imitation-a-legal-analysis-of-the-ghibli-style-image-debate/

Agarwal, N., & Ojha, V. (2017). Moral rights: International framework and Indian approach. *Christ University Law Journal*, *6*(1), 1–20. DOI: 10.12728/culj.10.1

Ahmed, K. (2025, April 4). The studio ghibli ai art backlash: How panic over generative ai misses the big picture. *Frontline*. https://frontline.thehindu.com/science-and-technology/ghibli-ai-art-generated-images-moral-panic-copyright/article69411983.ece

Ahmed, S. (2025, March 29). The Ghibli-fication dilemma: When AI meets artistic legacy. *Medium*. https://medium.com/@sahin.samia/the-ghibli-fication-dilemma-when-ai-meets-artistic-legacy-bfeb716bfc54

Ahn, E., Choi, M., Fowler, P., & Song, I. H. (2025). Artificial intelligence (AI) literacy for social work: Implications for core competencies. *Journal of the Society for Social Work and Research*, *16*(1), 9–26. DOI: 10.1086/735187

Aicken, C., Hodgson, L., De Vries, K., Wilkinson, I., Aldridge, Z., & Galvin, K. (2021). 'This Adds Another Perspective': Qualitative Descriptive Study Evaluating Simulation-Based Training for Health Care Assistants, to Enhance the Quality of Care in Nursing Homes. *International Journal of Environmental Research and Public Health*, *18*(8), 3995. DOI: 10.3390/ijerph18083995

Alanazi, M. A., Shaban, M. M., Ramadan, O. M. E., Zaky, M. E., Mohammed, H. H., Amer, F. G. M., & Shaban, M. (2024). Navigating end-of-life decision-making in nursing: A systematic review of ethical challenges and palliative care practices. *BMC Nursing*, *23*(1), 467. DOI: 10.1186/s12912-024-02087-5

Alghafri, B., & Tubaishat, A. (2025). Balancing Privacy and Security: A Comparative Analysis of AI-Driven Surveillance in the UAE and USA. *Procedia Computer Science*, *257*, 142–149. DOI: 10.1016/j.procs.2025.03.021

Alikhademi, K., Drobina, E., Prioleau, D., Richardson, B., Purves, D., & Gilbert, J. E. (2022). A review of predictive policing from the perspective of fairness. *Artificial Intelligence and Law*, *30*(1), 1–17. DOI: 10.1007/s10506-021-09286-4

Ali, S. M. A., & Ghose, A. (2024). Navigating copyright law in the age of AI: The complex relationship between generative AI and artistic expression. In Saka, E. (Ed.), *Understanding Generative AI in a Cultural Context: Artificial Myths and Human Realities* (pp. 359–382). IGI Global., DOI: 10.4018/979-8-3693-7235-7.ch014

Ali, S. M., Ghose, A., Saurav, S., & Deshmukh, S. (2024). Creativity and innovation in the age of artificial intelligence: A copyright dilemma. [Journal of Law]. *Padjadjaran Jurnal Ilmu Hukum*, *11*(2), 164–184. DOI: 10.22304/pjih.v11n2.a1

Almahfali, M., Hewidy, N., & Von Der Hülst, M. (2024). Capitalising on freedom of expression for creativity: A case study of Dawit Isaak Library, malmö, Sweden. *Nordic Journal of Human Rights*, *42*(2), 177–194. DOI: 10.1080/18918131.2024.2301715

Almaqtari, F. A., Hashid, A., Farhan, N. H. S., Tabash, M. I., & Al-ahdal, W. M. (2020). An empirical examination of the impact of country-level corporate governance on profitability of Indian banks. *International Journal of Finance & Economics*, *27*(2), 1912–1932. DOI: 10.1002/ijfe.2250

Almeida, D. (2021). Ethical implications of facial recognition technology: Transparency, accountability, and privacy concerns. *Frontiers in Artificial Intelligence*, *4*, 678234. Retrieved July 20, 2025, from https://pmc.ncbi.nlm.nih.gov/articles/PMC8320316/

Almufareh, M. F., Kausar, S., Humayun, M., & Tehsin, S. (2024). A conceptual model for inclusive technology: Advancing disability inclusion through artificial intelligence. *Journal of Disability Research*, *3*(1), 20230060. DOI: 10.57197/JDR-2023-0060

Alrassi, J., Katsufrakis, P. J., & Chandran, L. (2021). Technology can augment, but not replace, critical human skills needed for patient care. *Academic Medicine*, *96*(1), 37–43. DOI: 10.1097/ACM.0000000000003733

Alshammari, E. O. M., Alshammari, M. B. S., Al Anazy, A. K. M., Al-Anzi, M. A. H. A., Alfiras, K. S. A., Alshamry, M. A. S., & Asiri, A. A. M. (2024). Enhancing Nursing Excellence: Exploring Person-Centered Care Implementation in Clinical Practice. *Journal of International Crisis and Risk Communication Research*, *7*(S3), 514.

Amini, M., & Javidnejad, L. (2024). Legal regulation of biometric data: A comparative analysis of global standards. *Legal Studies in the Digital Age*, *3*(1), 26–34. DOI: 10.1234/lsda.2024.3.1.26

Amnesty International. (2020, June 11). Amnesty International calls for ban on the use of facial recognition technology for mass surveillance [Public statement]. Retrieved July 20, 2025, from https://www.amnesty.org/en/latest/news/2020/06/amnesty-international-calls-for-ban-on-facial-recognition/

Amnesty International. (n.d.). Ban the scan Hyderabad. Retrieved July 20, 2025, from https://www.amnesty.org/en/campaigns/ban-the-scan-hyderabad/

Annoni, M. (2025). Autonomy, self-determination and substitute judgement: the limits of AI-based personalised patient preference predictors (P4s) in surrogate decision-making. *Journal of Medical Ethics*.

Anthuvan, T., & Maheshwari, K. (2025). AI-C2C (conscious to conscience): A governance framework for ethical AI integration. *AI and Ethics*, *5*(4), 4241–4253. Advance online publication. DOI: 10.1007/s43681-025-00736-2

Aratek. (2023). Reading your face: How does facial recognition work? Retrieved July 20, 2025, from https://www.aratek.co/blog/reading-your-face-how-does-facial-recognition-work/

Arnold, L. (2025). Use of facial recognition technologies for law enforcement: A comparative analysis. *Oregon Review of International Law*, *26*(1), 175–225. Retrieved from https://scholarsbank.uoregon.edu/server/api/core/bitstreams/cf4701e9-7335-4bf5-98a3-a741300221e5/content?utm_source=chatgpt.com

Arora, S. (2025, March 29). *What is Ghibli? A journey through art and storytelling*. Adda247. https://currentaffairs.adda247.com/what-is-ghibli-a-journey-through-art-and-storytelling/

Askin, F. (2009, January 1; updated June 2, 2025). Chilling effect. In The First Amendment Encyclopedia. Middle Tennessee State University. Retrieved July 20, 2025, from https://www.mtsu.edu/first-amendment/article/968/chilling-effect

Aziz, A. (2023). Artificial Intelligence Produced Original Work: A New Approach to Copyright Protection and Ownership. *European Journal of Artificial Intelligence and Machine Learning*, *2*(2), 9–16. DOI: 10.24018/ejai.2023.2.2.15

Bankins, S., & Formosa, P. (2023). The ethical implications of artificial intelligence (AI) for meaningful work. *Journal of Business Ethics*, *185*(4), 725–740. DOI: 10.1007/s10551-023-05339-7

Baraniuk, C. (2016). *Computer paints 'new Rembrandt' after old works analysis*. BBC News.

Barthes, R. (1977). The death of the author. In *Image-Music-Text* (Heath, S., Trans.; pp. 142–148). Hill and Wang. (Original work published 1967)

Batra, B., Sannegadu, R., & Mehta, K. (2022). Gender diversity on the board and corporate social responsibility disclosure in the digitalisation era. In *Advances in human resources management and organizational development book series* (pp. 174–197). DOI: 10.4018/978-1-7998-8594-8.ch009

Beaudouin, V., Maxwell, W., & Domingues-Montanari, S. (2023). Predicting risk in criminal justice in the United States: The ProPublica-COMPAS case: Ethics of AI in Action. *Reseaux (London)*, *240*(4), 71–109.

Becker, A. (2021). Human dignity through action: Transformative human rights education and social work. *Journal of Human Rights and Social Work*, *6*(3), 173–182. DOI: 10.1007/s41134-020-00160-y

Behera, A., & Singh, B. P. (2024). Safeguarding privacy in the digital era: Balancing rights, security, and innovation. *Chanakya Law Review, 5*(2), 57–71. https://cnlu.ac.in/storage/2025/05/Safeguarding-Privacy-In-The-Digital-Era-Balancing-Rights-Security-And-Innovation-by-Ms.-Adyasha-Behera-Mr.-Bhanu-Pratap-Singh.pdf

Bell, A., & Parchomovsky, G. (2019). Restructuring copyright infringement. *Texas Law Review*, *98*, 679.

Benedict, T. J. (2022). The computer got it wrong: Facial recognition technology and establishing probable cause to arrest. *Washington and Lee Law Review*, *79*, 849.

Bennett Moses, L., & Chan, J. (2018). Algorithmic prediction in policing: Assumptions, evaluation, and accountability. *Policing and Society*, *28*(7), 806–822. DOI: 10.1080/10439463.2016.1253695

Berdahl, C. T., Baker, L., Mann, S., Osoba, O., & Girosi, F. (2023). Strategies to improve the impact of artificial intelligence on health equity: Scoping review. *JMIR AI*, *2*, e42936. DOI: 10.2196/42936

Bernstein, D. E. (2000). Frye, frye, again: The past, present, and future of the general acceptance test. *Jurimetrics*, *41*, 385.

Berridge, C., & Grigorovich, A. (2022). Algorithmic harms and digital ageism in the use of surveillance technologies in nursing homes. *Frontiers in Sociology*, *7*, 957246. DOI: 10.3389/fsoc.2022.957246

Bipartisan Policy Center. (2023, March 30). Face recognition technology policy landscape, terms, and definitions. Retrieved July 20, 2025, from https://bipartisanpolicy.org/report/face-recognition-technology-policy-landscape/

Birhane, A., Isaac, W., Prabhakaran, V., Diaz, M., Elish, M. C., Gabriel, I., & Mohamed, S. (2022, October). Power to the people? Opportunities and challenges for participatory AI. In *Proceedings of the 2nd ACM Conference on Equity and Access in Algorithms, Mechanisms, and Optimization* (pp. 1-8). DOI: 10.1145/3551624.3555290

Biswal, A. (2025). CNN in deep learning: Algorithm and machine learning uses. Simplilearn. Retrieved July 20, 2025, from https://www.simplilearn.com/cnn-in-deep-learning-algorithm-and-machine-learning-uses/

Bjørlo, L. V. (2024). Freedom from interference: Decisional privacy as a dimension of consumer privacy online. *AMS Review*, *14*(1–2), 12–36. DOI: 10.1007/s13162-024-00273-x

Bonfiglio, J. (2025, May 8). Ghibli, ghiblification, copyright and style. *Authors Alliance*. https://www.authorsalliance.org/2025/05/08/ghibli-ghiblification-copyright-and-style/

Borowski, A. (2025). On human dignity and social work. *British Journal of Social Work*, *52*(2), 609–623. DOI: 10.1093/bjsw/bcab016

Brein, S. (2017). Court of Justice of the European Union, C-610/15, 14 June 2017. *ECLI:EU*, *C*, 456.

Brighton and Dubbeljoint v Jones. (2004). England and Wales High Court (Chancery Division), EWHC 1157 (Ch).

Buolamwini, J., & Gebru, T. (2018). Gender shades: Intersectional accuracy disparities in commercial gender classification. In S. A. Friedler & C. Wilson (Eds.), Proceedings of the 1st Conference on Fairness, Accountability and Transparency (Vol. 81, pp. 77–91). Proceedings of Machine Learning Research. Retrieved July 20, 2025, from http://proceedings.mlr.press/v81/buolamwini18a.html

Burger, P. (1988). The Berne Convention: Its history and its key role in the future. *The Journal of Law and Technology*, *3*, 1.

Burström, T., Parida, V., Lahti, T., & Wincent, J. (2021a). AI-enabled business-model innovation and transformation in industrial ecosystems: A framework, model and outline for further research. *Journal of Business Research*, *127*, 85–95. DOI: 10.1016/j.jbusres.2021.01.016

Butt, J. (2024). Analytical study of the world's first EU Artificial Intelligence (AI) Act. *International Journal of Research Publication and Reviews*, *5*(3), 7343–7364. DOI: 10.55248/gengpi.5.0324.0914

Byrne, J., Kirwan, G., & Mc Guckin, C. (2019). Social media surveillance in social work: Practice realities and ethical implications. *Journal of Technology in Human Services*, *37*(2-3), 142–158. DOI: 10.1080/15228835.2019.1584598

Caines, S. (2021). The many faces of facial recognition. In *Research Handbook on Big Data Law* (pp. 29–56). Edward Elgar Publishing. DOI: 10.4337/9781788972826.00008

Cancela-Outeda, C. (2024). The EU's AI Act: A framework for collaborative governance. *Internet of Things : Engineering Cyber Physical Human Systems*, *27*, 101291. DOI: 10.1016/j.iot.2024.101291

Candiotto, L. (2022). Extended loneliness. When hyperconnectivity makes us feel alone. *Ethics and Information Technology*, *24*(4), 47. DOI: 10.1007/s10676-022-09669-4

Cani, J., Mademlis, I., Mancuso, M., Paternoster, C., Adamakis, E., Margetis, G., & Papadopoulos, G. T. (2024, December). CEASEFIRE: An AI-Powered System for Combating Illicit Firearms Trafficking. In *2024 IEEE International Conference on Big Data (BigData)* (pp. 2697-2705). IEEE. DOI: 10.1109/BigData62323.2024.10825989

Cantero Gamito, M., & Marsden, C. T. (2024). Artificial intelligence co-regulation? The role of standards in the EU AI Act. *International Journal of Law and Information Technology*, *32*, eaae011. DOI: 10.1093/ijlit/eaae011

Carswell, S. (2024, January 15). RTÉ's Dave Fanning initiates defamation case after his photo appeared in article about sexual misconduct trial of different broadcaster. *The Irish Times*. https://www.irishtimes.com/crime-law/courts/2024/01/15/rtes-dave-fanning-initiates-defamation-case-after-his-photo-appeared-in-article-about-sexual-misconduct-trial-of-different-broadcaster/

Center on Privacy & Technology at Georgetown Law. (2016). The perpetual line-up: Unregulated police face recognition in America. Retrieved July 20, 2025, from https://www.perpetuallineup.org/

Charlesworth, H. (2008). Universal Declaration of Human Rights (1948). *Oxford Public International Law*. https://opil.ouplaw.com/display/10.1093/law:epil/9780199231690/law-9780199231690-e887

Chau, M. (2024). Ethical, legal, and regulatory landscape of artificial intelligence in Australian healthcare and ethical integration in radiography: A narrative review. *Journal of Medical Imaging and Radiation Sciences*, *55*(4), 101733. DOI: 10.1016/j.jmir.2024.101733 PMID: 39111223

Chayka, K. (2023). Is A.I. Art stealing from artists. *The New Yorker*.

Chen, Y., & Gao, Y. (2022). Comparative analysis of digital trade development strategies and governance approaches. *Journal of Digital Economy*, *1*(3), 227–238. DOI: 10.1016/j.jdec.2023.02.001

Chita-Tegmark, M., & Scheutz, M. (2021). Assistive robots for the social management of health: A framework for robot design and human–robot interaction research. *International Journal of Social Robotics*, *13*(2), 197–217. DOI: 10.1007/s12369-020-00634-z

Choi, Y., Han, S., & Lee, C. (2024). Exploring drivers of fintech adoption among elderly consumers. *Technology in Society*, *78*, 102669. DOI: 10.1016/j.techsoc.2024.102669

Choudhary, V. & Ali, Aamir S. M. (2023). ChatGPT and Copyright Concerns. *Economic and Political Weekly*, *58*(16), 4–5.

Chouliara, Z., Murray, J., Coleman, A. M., Burke Draucker, C., & Choi, W. M. A. (2024). Therapeutic trust in complex trauma: A unique person–centered understanding. *Person-Centered and Experiential Psychotherapies*, *23*(2), 177–202. DOI: 10.1080/14779757.2023.2207107

Choung, H. (2024). Acceptance of AI-powered facial recognition technology in public spaces: Balancing crime prevention and privacy concerns. *ScienceDirect*. https://www.sciencedirect.com/science/article/abs/pii/S0160791X24002690

Chowdhury, S., Budhwar, P., & Wood, G. (2024). Generative Artificial Intelligence in Business: Towards a Strategic Human Resource Management framework. *British Journal of Management, 35*(4), 1680–1691. DOI: 10.1111/1467-8551.12824

Christian, G. (2023). Law professor explores racial bias implications in facial recognition technology. *University of Calgary News*. Retrieved from https://ucalgary.ca/news/law-professor-explores-racial-bias-implications-facial-recognition-technology

Cogent Infotech. (2024, March 13). Addressing gender bias in facial recognition technology: An urgent need for fairness and inclusion. Retrieved July 20, 2025, from https://www.cogentinfotech.com/blog/addressing-gender-bias-in-facial-recognition-technology

Commission. (2025). Call for tenders for the preparation of a feasibility study on a central opt-out register based on text and data mining (TDM) exemption. https://digital-strategy.ec.europa.eu/en/funding/call-tenders-feasibility-study-central-registry-opt-outs-under-text-and-data-mining-tdm-exception

Concur. (2025, June 11). Facial recognition technology & DPDPA 2023: A compliance blueprint for Indian businesses. Retrieved July 20, 2025, from https://www.concur.in/blog/facial-recognition-technology-dpdpa-2023

Copyright Research and Information Center. (2023). *Copyright Act of Japan.* https://www.cric.or.jp/english/clj/cl2.html

Cordella, A., & Gualdi, F. (2024). Regulating generative AI: The limits of technology-neutral regulatory frameworks. Insights from Italy's intervention on ChatGPT. *Government Information Quarterly, 41*(4), 101982. DOI: 10.1016/j.giq.2024.101982

Corning. (2023). Face to face: Why NIR facial recognition systems are the most secure. Radiant Vision Systems. Retrieved July 20, 2025, from https://www.radiantvisionsystems.com/blog/face-to-face-why-nir-facial-recognition-systems-are-the-most-secure

Cotter, D. A. (2024, November 18). The Biometric Information Privacy Act. TortSource, Fall 2024. American Bar Association. Retrieved July 20, 2025, from https://www.americanbar.org/groups/tort_trial_insurance_practice/publications/tortsource/2024/fall/biometric-information-privacy-act/

Cummins v. Bond. (1927). Chancery Division, 1 Ch. 167.

Cyphert, A. B. (2020). Reprogramming recidivism: The first step act and algorithmic prediction of risk. *Seton Hall Law Review*, *51*, 331.

D, C., E, G., & E, J. (2021). *REGULATION OF ARTIFICIAL INTELLIGENCE IN BRICS AND THE EUROPEAN UNION*. КиберЛенинка. https://cyberleninka.ru/article/n/regulation-of-artificial-intelligence-in-brics-and-the-european-union

Dailah, H. G., Koriri, M., Sabei, A., Kriry, T., & Zakri, M. (2024, December). Artificial intelligence in nursing: Technological benefits to nurse's mental health and patient care quality. [). MDPI.]. *Health Care*, *12*(24), 2555.

Darby, H. C. (2021, November 23). AI-created art and the moral rights of authors. *Columbia Journal of Law & the Arts Bulletin Blog*. https://www.jtl.columbia.edu/bulletin-blog/ai-created-art-and-the-moral-rights-of-authors

De Almeida, P. G. R., Santos, C. D. D., & Farias, J. S. (2021). Artificial Intelligence Regulation: A framework for governance. *Ethics and Information Technology*, *23*(3), 505–525. DOI: 10.1007/s10676-021-09593-z

De Micco, F., Grassi, S., Tomassini, L., Di Palma, G., Ricchezze, G., & Scendoni, R. (2024). Robotics and AI into healthcare from the perspective of European regulation: Who is responsible for medical malpractice? *Frontiers in Medicine*, *11*, 1428504. DOI: 10.3389/fmed.2024.1428504 PMID: 39309674 de Ruiter, H. P., Clisbee, D., Houston, R., & Skärsäter, I. (2023). The Ethical, Care, and Client-Caregiver Relationship Impacts Resulting From Introduction of Digital Communication and Surveillance Technologies in the Home Setting: Qualitative Inductive Study. *JMIR Human Factors*, *10*, e47586. DOI: 10.2196/47586

Devasia, A. (2024). Facial recognition system: How does it work? Safe and Sound Security. Retrieved July 20, 2025, from https://www.safeandsoundsecurity.com/facial-recognition-system-how-does-it-work/

Dhirani, L. L., Mukhtiar, N., Chowdhry, B. S., & Newe, T. (2023). Ethical dilemmas and privacy issues in emerging technologies: A review. *Sensors (Basel)*, *23*(3), 1151. DOI: 10.3390/s23031151

Dhongde, S., Kumar, S., Patra, S. K., & Mishra, S. K. (2025). Redefining Corporate Governance in Digital Era: Strategies for Mitigating Organizational risk. In *Approaches to global sustainability, markets, and governance* (pp. 427–447). DOI: 10.1007/978-981-96-6366-8_21

Diez, E. R. (2023). Artificial Intelligence and Social Work: Contributions to an Ethical Artificial Intelligence at the Service of People. In *The Routledge International Handbook of Digital Social Work* (pp.368-381). Routledge.

Directive 2000/31/EC of the European Parliament and of the Council of 8 June 2000 on certain legal aspects of information society services, in particular electronic commerce, in the Internal Market ('Directive on electronic commerce').

Directive 2001/29/EC of the European Parliament and of the Council of 22 May 2001 on the harmonisation of certain aspects of copyright and related rights in the information society. (2001). ELI: https://data.europa.eu/eli/dir/2001/29/oj

Directive 2016/115 of the European Parliament and of the Council of 19 April 2006 on rental right and lending right and on certain rights related to copyright in the field of intellectual property (codified version). (2016).

Directive 2019/790 of the European Parliament and of the Council of 17 April 2019 on copyright and related rights in the Digital Single Market and amending Directives 96/9/EC and 2001/29/EC. (2019). ELI: https://data.europa.eu/eli/dir/2019/790/oj

District Court of Hamburg. (2023). 310 O 227/23.

Doe, J. (2025). Exploring the Ethics of Data Privacy in the Digital Age. *Pakistan Journal of Healthcare Research*, *2*(1), 40–54.

Doshi, A. R., & Hauser, O. P. (2024). Generative AI enhances individual creativity but reduces the collective diversity of novel content. *Science Advances*, *10*(28), 1–9. DOI: 10.1126/sciadv.adn5290

Dramburg, S. (2025). Legal and regulatory challenges for digital health technologies with a focus on the European legal situation. In *Digital Allergology: From Theory to Practice* (pp. 39–47). Springer Nature Switzerland. DOI: 10.1007/978-3-031-71021-6_3

Dunsin, D., Ghanem, M. C., Ouazzane, K., & Vassilev, V. (2024). A comprehensive analysis of the role of artificial intelligence and machine learning in modern digital forensics and incident response. *Forensic Science International Digital Investigation*, *48*, 301675. DOI: 10.1016/j.fsidi.2023.301675

Ebenibo, L., Enyejo, J. O., Addo, G., & Olola, T. M. (2024). Evaluating the sufficiency of the Data Protection Act 2023 in the age of artificial intelligence (AI): A comparative case study of Nigeria and the USA. *International Journal of Scholarly Research and Reviews*, *5*(01), 88–107. DOI: 10.56781/ijsrr.2024.5.1.0044

Edoh, N. L., Chigboh, V. M., Zouo, S. J. C., & Olamijuwon, J. (2024). Improving healthcare decision-making with predictive analytics: A conceptual approach to patient risk assessment and care optimization. *International Journal of Scholarly Research in Medicine and Dentistry*, *3*(2), 1–10. DOI: 10.56781/ijsrmd.2024.3.2.0034

Efthymiou, I. P. (2024). Exploring the frontier: New and future trends in research. In B. Orlando (Ed.), Innovation capabilities and entrepreneurial opportunities of smart working (pp. 48–68). IGI Global Scientific Publishing. DOI: 10.4018/978-1-7998-8797-3.ch003

Efthymiou, I. P. (2026). Bridging the Divide: Addressing the Leadership Gap. In *Bridging the Leadership Gap: Policies and Workplace Equality* (pp. 103-138). IGI Global Scientific Publishing.

Efthymiou, I. (2025). Diversity, Inclusion, and Equity in Gig Economies. In Doon, R. (Ed.), *Sustainability and Adaptability of Gig Economies in Global Business* (pp. 231–260). IGI Global Scientific Publishing., DOI: 10.4018/979-8-3693-9385-7.ch009

Efthymiou, I. P. (2025). The role of e-government and e-governance in modern societies. In Wongmahesak, K., Ahmad, J., & Mustanir, A. (Eds.), *Public governance practices in the age of AI* (pp. 45–68). IGI Global Scientific Publishing., DOI: 10.4018/979-8-3693-9286-7.ch003

Efthymiou, I., & Egleton, T. E. (2023). Artificial Intelligence for Sustainable Smart Cities. In Mishra, B. (Ed.), *Handbook of Research on Applications of AI, Digital Twin, and Internet of Things for Sustainable Development* (pp. 1–11). IGI Global Scientific Publishing., DOI: 10.4018/978-1-6684-6821-0.ch001

Efthymiou, I., & Egleton, T. E. (2025). The Impact of Deep Fakes in Markets and Economies. In Gupta, G., Bohara, S., Kovid, R., & Pandla, K. (Eds.), *Deepfakes and Their Impact on Business* (pp. 19–50). IGI Global Scientific Publishing., DOI: 10.4018/979-8-3693-6890-9.ch002

Eroğlu, M., & Kaya, M. K. (2022). Impact of artificial intelligence on corporate board diversity policies and Regulations. *European Business Organization Law Review*, *23*(3), 541–572. DOI: 10.1007/s40804-022-00251-5

Etli, D., Djurovic, A., & Lark, J. (2024). The Future of Personalized Healthcare: AI-Driven Wearables For Real-Time Health Monitoring And Predictive Analytics. *Current Research in Health Sciences*, *2*(2), 10–14.

European Copyright Society. (2025). Copyright and Generative AI: Opinion of the European Copyright Society January 2025. https://europeancopyrightsociety.org/wp-content/uploads/2025/02/ecs_opinion_genai_january2025.pdf

European Parliament. (2025, February 19). EU AI Act: First regulation on artificial intelligence. Retrieved July 20, 2025, from https://www.europarl.europa.eu/news/en/headlines/society/20230601STO93804/eu-ai-act-first-regulation-on-artificial-intelligence

European Union. (2024). Regulation (EU) 2024/1689 laying down harmonised rules on artificial intelligence (Artificial Intelligence Act). Official Journal of the European Union. Retrieved from https://eur-lex.europa.eu/eli/reg/2024/1689/oj

European Union. (2024, July 30). AI Act | Shaping Europe's digital future. European Commission Digital Strategy. Retrieved July 20, 2025, from https://digital-strategy.ec.europa.eu/en/policies/ai-act

Eva-Maria Painer v Standard VerlagsGmbH, Axel Springer AG, Süddeutsche Zeitung GmbH, Spiegel-Verlag Rudolf Augstein GmbH & Co KG, Verlag M. DuMont Schauberg Expedition der Kölnischen Zeitung GmbH & Co KG. (2011). Court of Justice of the European Union, C-145/10, 1 December 2011, ECLI:EU:C:2011:798.

FaceTec. (n.d.). 2D vs. 3D face matching. Retrieved July 20, 2025, from https://www.facetec.com/2d-vs-3d-face-matching/

Fahad, S. (2024). Transforming Medical Social Work with Artificial Intelligence. *Social Work Chronicle*, *13*(1), 24–49.

Ferdman, A. (2024). Human flourishing and technology affordances. *Philosophy & Technology*, *37*(1), 1. DOI: 10.1007/s13347-023-00686-9

Ferguson, H., Warwick, L., Disney, T., Leigh, J., Cooner, T. S., & Beddoe, L. (2022). Relationship-based practice and the creation of therapeutic change in long-term work: Social work as a holding relationship. *Social Work Education*, *41*(2), 209–227. DOI: 10.1080/02615479.2020.1837105

Fessenko, D. S., & Jasperse, A. (2024). Ethics at the heart of AI regulation. *AI and Ethics*, *5*(3), 3387–3398. DOI: 10.1007/s43681-024-00562-y

Fischman Afori, O. (2004). Human rights and copyright: The introduction of natural law considerations into American copyright law. *Fordham Intellectual Property. Media & Entertainment Law Journal*, *14*(2), 497–565.

Friedler, S. A., & Wilson, C. (2018). Gender shades: Intersectional accuracy disparities in commercial gender classification. In Proceedings of the 1st Conference on Fairness, Accountability and Transparency (Vol. 81, pp. 77–91). Proceedings of Machine Learning Research. Retrieved July 20, 2025, from http://proceedings.mlr.press/v81/buolamwini18a.html

Fritz, J. (2025). Understanding authorship in Artificial Intelligence-assisted works. *Journal of Intellectual Property Law & Practice*, jpae 119. DOI: 10.1093/jiplp/jpae119

Fritz, R., & Cook, D. (2025). Detecting Older Adults' Behavior Changes During Adverse External Events Using Ambient Sensing: Longitudinal Observational Study. *JMIR Nursing*, *8*(1), e69052. DOI: 10.2196/69052

Funke Medien, N. R. W. (2019). Court of Justice of the European Union, C-469/17, 29 July 2019. *ECLI:EU*, *C*, 623.

Fylde Microsystems Ltd v Key Radio Systems Ltd. (1998). England and Wales High Court (Patents Court), EWHC Patents 340.

Gaffar, H., & Albarashdi, S. (2025). Copyright protection for AI-generated works: Exploring originality and ownership in a digital landscape. *Asian Journal of International Law*, *15*(1), 23–46. DOI: 10.1017/S2044251323000735

Galt, J. (1830). *The Life of Lord Byron*. Henry Colburn and Richard Bentley.

Ghiurău, D., & Popescu, D. E. (2025). Distinguishing Reality from AI: Approaches for Detecting Synthetic Content. *Computers*, *14*(1), 1. DOI: 10.3390/computers14010001

Ghose, A. & Ali, Aamir S. M. (2023). Amplifying Music with Artificial Intelligence. *Economic and Political Weekly*, *58*(17), 4–6.

Ghose, A., Ali, S. M. A., & Deshmukh, S. (2024). Navigating the legal and ethical framework for generative AI: Fostering responsible global governance. In Ara, A., & Ara, A. (Eds.), *Exploring the Ethical Implications of Generative AI* (pp. 168–184). IGI Global., DOI: 10.4018/979-8-3693-1565-1.ch010

Ghose, A., Ali, S. M. A., & Deshmukh, S. B. (2025). Creative paradigms, generative AI, and copyright law: Investigating the intersection of AI and artistry. In Bajraktari, H. (Ed.), (pp. 103–122). Advances in Electronic Government, Digital Divide, and Regional Development. IGI Global., DOI: 10.4018/979-8-3693-7205-0.ch006

Ghose, A., Ali, S. M. A., & Mishra, A. M. (2024). Artistic expressions, generative AI, and legal tapestry: Exploring the dynamics of copyright laws in the confluence of AI and artistic creation. In Hai-Jew, S. (Ed.), *Making Art With Generative AI Tools* (pp. 198–214). IGI Global., DOI: 10.4018/979-8-3693-1950-5.ch011

Giannini, A., & Kwik, J. (2023). Negligence failures and negligence fixes. A comparative analysis of criminal regulation of AI and autonomous vehicles. *Criminal Law Forum*, *34*(1), 43–85. DOI: 10.1007/s10609-023-09451-1

Gilbert, A. S., Garratt, S. M., Kosowicz, L., Ostaszkiewicz, J., & Dow, B. (2021). Aged care residents' perspectives on quality of care in care homes: A systematic review of qualitative evidence. *Research on Aging*, *43*(7-8), 294–310. DOI: 10.1177/0164027521989074

Ginsburg, J. C. (2002). The concept of authorship in comparative copyright law. *De Paul Law Review*, *52*, 1063.

Goktas, P., & Grzybowski, A. (2025). Shaping the future of healthcare: Ethical clinical challenges and pathways to trustworthy AI. *Journal of Clinical Medicine*, *14*(5), 1605. DOI: 10.3390/jcm14051605 PMID: 40095575

Goldenthal, E., Park, J., Liu, S. X., Mieczkowski, H., & Hancock, J. T. (2021). Not all AI are equal: Exploring the accessibility of AI-mediated communication technology. *Computers in Human Behavior*, *125*, 106975. DOI: 10.1016/j.chb.2021.106975

Griffiths, J., Synodinou, T., & Xalabarder, R. (2022). *Commentary by the European Copyright Society on selected aspects of the implementation of Articles 3 to 7 of Directive (EU) 2019/790 on copyright in the digital single market.* Study by the European Copyright Society.

Guadamuz, A. (2024). A scanner darkly: Copyright liability and exceptions in artificial intelligence inputs and outputs. *GRUR International, 73*(2), 111–127. DOI: 10.1093/grurint/ikad140

Guo, G., Ray, A., Izydorczak, M., Goldfeder, J., Lipson, H., & Xu, W. (2024). Unveiling intra-person fingerprint similarity via deep contrastive learning. *Science Advances, 10*(2), eadi0329. DOI: 10.1126/sciadv.adi0329 PMID: 38215200

Gupta, Y. (2025). Facial recognition technology and the fundamental right to privacy. SSRN. Retrieved July 20, 2025, from https://papers.ssrn.com/sol3/papers.cfm?abstract_id=5228551 DOI: 10.2139/ssrn.5228551

Gustafsson, M. S., Kazlou, A., & Wihlborg, E. (2024, August). Automation in Social Care: A Case Study of Organizational Challenges and Skills Dynamics in Three Swedish Municipalities. In *International Conference on Electronic Government* (pp. 218-233). Cham: Springer Nature Switzerland. DOI: 10.1007/978-3-031-70274-7_14

Hall, S. F., Sage, M., Scott, C. F., & Joseph, K. (2024). A systematic review of sophisticated predictive and prescriptive analytics in child welfare: Accuracy, equity, and bias. *Child & Adolescent Social Work Journal, 41*(6), 831–847. DOI: 10.1007/s10560-023-00931-2

Hamblin, K. A. (2022). Technology in care systems: Displacing, reshaping, reinstating or degrading roles? *New Technology, Work and Employment, 37*(1), 41–58. DOI: 10.1111/ntwe.12229

Hamilton, M. (2019). The biased algorithm: Evidence of disparate impact on Hispanics. *The American Criminal Law Review, 56*, 1553.

Hamilton, Z., Duwe, G., Kigerl, A., Gwinn, J., Langan, N., & Dollar, C. (2022). Tailoring to a mandate: The development and validation of the Prisoner Assessment Tool Targeting Estimated Risk and Needs (PATTERN). *Justice Quarterly*, *39*(6), 1129–1155. DOI: 10.1080/07418825.2021.1906930

Harden, V., & Turnage, B. (2025). Social Work Values and Education. In *Social Work Education: Breaking New Grounds and Addressing New Challenges* (pp. 99–108). Springer Nature Switzerland.

Hardman, B., & Housel, J. (2023). A Sui Generis Approach to the Protection of AI-Generated Works: Balancing Innovation and Authorship. Available at *SSRN* 4557004. DOI: 10.2139/ssrn.4557004

Harris, S., & Stout, B. (2022). 'Caring and connected': Technology and social worker self-care. *Journal of Social Work Practice*, *36*(3), 359–372. DOI: 10.1080/02650533.2021.2000945

Hartzog, W. (2019). *BIPA: The most important biometric privacy law in the U.S.?* AI Now Institute. Retrieved from https://ainowinstitute.org/wp-content/uploads/2023/09/regulatingbiometrics-hartzog.pdf

Hasan, A., Aly, D., & Hussainey, K. (2022). Corporate governance and financial reporting quality: A comparative study. *Corporate Governance (Bradford)*, *22*(6), 1308–1326. DOI: 10.1108/CG-08-2021-0298

Henrickson, M. (2022). *The origins of social care and social work: Creating a global future*. Policy Press.

Hilde, T. C. (2000). Intelligence, accident, and art as a practice. *Transactions of the Charles S. Peirce Society*, *36*(4), 549–561.

Hill, K., & Hsu, T. (2024, June 6). The rise and fall of BNN Breaking, an A.I.-generated news outlet. *The New York Times*. https://www.nytimes.com/2024/06/06/technology/bnn-breaking-ai-generated-news.html

Hindustan Times. (2022, May 16). Maharashtra police launch new tech to help check crimes. Retrieved July 20, 2025, from https://www.hindustantimes.com/cities/mumbai-news/maharashtra-police-launch-new-tech-to-help-check-crimes-101652678945123.html

Hobart, L. N. (2025). AI, Bias, and National Security Profiling. *Berkeley Technology Law Journal*, *40*, 165.

Ho, J. C. K., & Ng, L. U. I. (2025). The Gap in Between: Social Work Practice in the Midst of the Technological Era. *Journal of Social Work and Welfare Policy*, *3*(2), 153. DOI: 10.33790/jswwp1100153

Horneber, D., & Laumer, S. (2023). Algorithmic accountability. *Business & Information Systems Engineering*, *65*(6), 723–730. DOI: 10.1007/s12599-023-00817-8

Hossain, M. Z., Hasan, L., & Hasan, M. H. (2024). Corporate Governance as a global phenomenon: Evolution, theoretical foundations, and practical implications. *Journal of Financial Risk Management*, *13*(02), 342–375. DOI: 10.4236/jfrm.2024.132017

Howe, D. (2023). Knowledge, power, and the shape of social work practice. In *The sociology of social work* (pp. 202–220). Routledge. DOI: 10.4324/9781003435846-12

HT News Desk. (2024, March 29). *Using ChatGPT's Ghibli-style photos violates copyright laws, experts explain*. Hindustan Times. https://www.hindustantimes.com/world-news/using-chatgpts-ghibli-style-photos-violates-copyright-laws-experts-explain-101743257416332.html

Hugenholtz, P. (2012). Harmonisation or unification of European union copyright law. *Monash University Law Review. Monash University. Faculty of Law*, *38*(1), 4–16.

Hugenholtz, P. B., & Quintais, J. P. (2021). Copyright and artificial creation: does EU copyright law protect AI-assisted output? *IIC - International Review of Intellectual Property and Competition Law*, 52(9), 1190–1216. DOI: 10.1007/s40319-021-01115-0

Hutson, J. (2024). The evolving role of copyright law in the age of AI-generated works. *Journal of Digital Technologies and Law*, *2*(4), 886–914. DOI: 10.21202/jdtl.2024.43

Idder, A., & Coulaux, S. (2021, December 13). Artificial intelligence in criminal justice: Invasion or revolution? International Bar Association. Retrieved July 20, 2025, from https://www.ibanet.org/dec-21-ai-criminal-justice

Ijaiya, H., & Odumuwagun, O. O. (2024). Advancing artificial intelligence and safeguarding data privacy: A comparative study of EU and US regulatory frameworks amid emerging cyber threats. *International Journal of Research Publication and Reviews*, *5*(12), 3357–3375. DOI: 10.55248/gengpi.5.1224.250110

Infopaq International A/S v Danske Dagblades Forening. (2009). Court of Justice of the European Union, C-5/08, 16 July 2009, ECLI: EU:C:2009:465.

Ivcevic, Z., & Grandinetti, M. (2024). Artificial intelligence as a tool for creativity. *Journal of Creativity*, *34*(2), 100079. DOI: 10.1016/j.yjoc.2024.100079

Jacob, C., Brasier, N., Laurenzi, E., Heuss, S., Mougiakakou, S. G., Cöltekin, A., & Peter, M. K. (2025). AI for IMPACTS framework for evaluating the long-term real-world impacts of AI-powered clinician tools: Systematic review and narrative synthesis. *Journal of Medical Internet Research*, *27*, e67485. DOI: 10.2196/67485

Jagran Josh. (2019, August 24). What is 'AMBIS' system and how will it help in nabbing the criminals? Retrieved July 20, 2025, from https://www.jagranjosh.com/general-knowledge/what-is-ambis-system-and-how-will-it-help-in-nabbing-the-criminals-1566648370-1

Jain, S. (2020). Moral rights of author under copyright laws. SSRN *Electronic Journal*. https://doi.org/DOI: 10.2139/ssrn.3902409

Jain, V., Balakrishnan, A., Beeram, D., Najana, M., & Chintale, P. (2024). Leveraging artificial intelligence for enhancing regulatory compliance in the financial sector. *International Journal of Computer Trends and Technology*, *72*(5), 124–140. DOI: 10.14445/22312803/IJCTT-V72I5P116

Jakubowska, E. (2019, December 4). The many faces of facial recognition in the EU. European Digital Rights (EDRi). Retrieved July 20, 2025, from https://edri.org/our-work/the-many-faces-of-facial-recognition-in-the-eu/

James, P., Lal, J., Liao, A., Magee, L., & Soldatic, K. (2024). Algorithmic decision-making in social work practice and pedagogy: Confronting the competency/critique dilemma. *Social Work Education*, *43*(6), 1552–1569. DOI: 10.1080/02615479.2023.2195425

Japan Copyright Office. (2024). *General understanding on AI and copyright in Japan*. Legal Subcommittee, Copyright Subdivision, Cultural Council. https://www.bunka.go.jp/english/policy/copyright/pdf/94055801_01.pdf

John, J., Smiju, I. S., Thampi, K., & Joseph, M. K. (2024). Environmental, Social, and Governance (ESG) sustainability through corporate social responsibility. In *Advances in logistics, operations, and management science book series* (pp. 31–52). DOI: 10.4018/979-8-3693-3880-3.ch002

Jones, R. H. (1990). The myth of the idea/expression dichotomy in copyright law. *Pace Law Review*, *10*(3), 551. DOI: 10.58948/2331-3528.1475

Jordan, J. (2023, September 20). George RR Martin and John Grisham among group of authors suing OpenAI. *The Guardian*. https://www.theguardian.com/books/2023/sep/20/authors-lawsuit-openai-george-rr-martin-john-grisham

Judge, E. F., & Gervais, D. J. (2009). Of silos and constellations: comparing notions of originality in copyright law. In *Intellectual property protection of fact-based works*. Edward Elgar Publishing. DOI: 10.4337/9781849801898.00011

K, N. K. (2025). Legal and financial approaches for ESG integration. In *IGI Global eBooks* (pp. 189–234). DOI: 10.4018/979-8-3373-0350-5.ch008

Katyal, S. K. (2019). Private accountability in the age of artificial intelligence. *UCLA Law Review. University of California, Los Angeles. School of Law*, *66*, 54.

Kayser-Bril, N. (2020, June 18). At least 11 police forces use face recognition in the EU, AlgorithmWatch reveals. AlgorithmWatch. Retrieved July 20, 2025, from https://algorithmwatch.org/en/at-least-11-police-forces-use-face-recognition-in-the-eu/

Keller, P. (2023). Protecting creatives or impeding progress? Machine learning and the EU copyright framework. Kluwer Copyright Blog. https://copyrightblog.kluweriplaw.com/2023/02/20/protecting-creatives-or-impeding-progress-machine-learning-and-the-eu-copyright-framework/

Kelley v. Chicago Park District. (2011). United States Court of Appeals for the Seventh Circuit, 635 F.3d 290.

Kempas, T., Allgayer, U., Byer, D., Garhart, N., Genovese, L. A., Kliska, N., Lovrics, C., & Mansour, D. (2023). Copyrights and neighboring rights in outputs made by or made by means of AI systems. INTA Copyright Committee, AI and 3D Sub-Committee. https://www.inta.org/wp-content/uploads/public-files/advocacy/committee-reports/20230724_Copyrights-and-Neighboring-Rights-of-Outputs-by-AI-Systems.pdf

Kilian, R., Jäck, L., & Ebel, D. (2025). European AI standards: Technical standardisation and implementation challenges under the EU AI Act. *European Journal of Risk Regulation*, *16*(3), 1–25. DOI: 10.1017/err.2025.10032

Killan, M. (2003). A hollow victory for the common law? TRIPS and the moral rights exclusion. *John Marshall Review of Intellectual Property Law,* *2*(2), 321–366. https://repository.law.uic.edu/cgi/viewcontent.cgi?article=1034&context=ripl

Knight, B., Keane, N., Benea, D., & Stone, R. (2024). Values and the experience of family care-giving: Cultural values or shared family values? *Ageing and Society*, *44*(1), 61–78. DOI: 10.1017/S0144686X2200006X

Konnoth, C. (2024). AI and data protection law in health. In *Research Handbook on Health, AI and the Law* (pp. 111–129). Edward Elgar Publishing.

Kosaraju, D. (2024). Predictive analytics in healthcare: Leveraging ai to anticipate disease outbreaks and enhance patient outcomes. *Galore International Journal of Health Sciences and Research, 8*(3), 73–79. DOI: 10.52403/gijhsr.20230312

Kovalevskyi, B. (2024). Ethics and safety in ai fine-tuning. *Journal of Artificial Intelligence general science (JAIGS) ISSN: 3006-4023, 1*(1), 259-267.

Kumar, A. (2025). Satisfaction of AI for Ghibli-style art: A study on perception, acceptance, and ethical concerns. *International Journal for Research in Applied Science and Engineering Technology, 13*(5), 6487–6491. DOI: 10.22214/ijraset.2025.71350

Kumar, D., & Suthar, N. (2024). Predictive analytics and early intervention in healthcare social work: A scoping review. *Social Work in Health Care, 63*(4-5), 208–229. DOI: 10.1080/00981389.2024.2316700

Lane, L. (2022). CLARIFYING HUMAN RIGHTS STANDARDS THROUGH ARTIFICIAL INTELLIGENCE INITIATIVES. *The International and Comparative Law Quarterly, 71*(4), 915–944. DOI: 10.1017/S0020589322000380

Laperruque, J. (2025, January 6). Status of state laws on facial recognition surveillance: Continued progress and smart innovations. TechPolicy.Press. Retrieved July 20, 2025, from https://techpolicy.press/status-of-state-laws-on-facial-recognition-surveillance

Lawvs. (2025, June 29). Navigating the tension: Civil liberties vs. national security in a surveillance society. Retrieved July 20, 2025, from https://www.lawvs.com/navigating-the-tension-civil-liberties-vs-national-security/

Lee, W.-M. (2025). *Implementing face recognition using deep learning and support vector machines.* Retrieved July 20, 2025, from https://www.codemag.com/Article/2205081/Implementing-Face-Recognition-Using-Deep-Learning-and-Support-Vector-Machines

Lehtiniemi, T. (2024). Contextual social valences for artificial intelligence: Anticipation that matters in social work. *Information Communication and Society*, *27*(6), 1110–1125. DOI: 10.1080/1369118X.2023.2234987

Leistner, M. (2014). Structural aspects of secondary (provider) liability in Europe. *Journal of Intellectual Property Law & Practice*, *9*(1), 75–90. DOI: 10.1093/jiplp/jpt213

Like Company. (2025). Court of Justice of the European Union, C-250/25, registered on 3 April 2025, pending.

Liu, S., & Ding, W. (2025). Artificial intelligence for children: UNICEF's policy guidance and beyond. *Children & Society*, *39*(1), 374–382. DOI: 10.1111/chso.12915

Li, W., Song, R., Zhang, B., & Yu, K. (2025). AI creativity and legal protection for AI-generated works in posthuman societal scenarios. *Sustainable Futures : An Applied Journal of Technology, Environment and Society*, *9*, 100749. DOI: 10.1016/j.sftr.2025.100749

Lund, B., Orhan, Z., Mannuru, N. R., Bevara, R. V. K., Porter, B., Vinaih, M. K., & Bhaskara, P. (2025). Standards, frameworks, and legislation for artificial intelligence (AI) transparency. *AI and Ethics*, *5*(4), 3639–3655. Advance online publication. DOI: 10.1007/s43681-025-00661-4

Mageira, K., Pittou, D., Papasalouros, A., Kotis, K., Zangogianni, P., & Daradoumis, A. (2022). Educational AI chatbots for content and language integrated learning. *Applied Sciences (Basel, Switzerland)*, *12*(7), 3239. DOI: 10.3390/app12073239

Magliocca, P., Canestrino, R., Carayannis, E. G., & Gagliardi, A. R. (2024). Understanding human-technology interaction: Evolving boundaries. *European Journal of Innovation Management*. Advance online publication. DOI: 10.1108/EJIM-04-2024-0341

Mahapatra, S. (2021). Digital surveillance and the threat to civil liberties in India (GIGA Focus Asia, No. 3). German Institute for Global and Area Studies (GIGA). Retrieved July 20, 2025, from https://www.giga-hamburg.de/en/publications/giga-focus/digital-surveillance-and-the-threat-to-civil-liberties-in-india

Maleki Varnosfaderani, S., & Forouzanfar, M. (2024). The role of AI in hospitals and clinics: Transforming healthcare in the 21st century. *Bioengineering (Basel, Switzerland)*, *11*(4), 337. DOI: 10.3390/bioengineering11040337

Maota, Y. Y., & Maota, T. (2025). AI in Social Worker Recruitment and Training for Bullying Intervention: Gaps in South Africa. In *Sustainable Management Practices for Employee Retention and Recruitment* (pp. 1-30). IGI Global Scientific Publishing.

Margoni, T., & Kretschmer, M. (2022). A deeper look into the EU text and data mining exceptions: Harmonisation, data ownership, and the future of technology. *GRUR International*, *71*(8), 685–701. DOI: 10.1093/grurint/ikac054

Marr, B. (2023). Is Generative AI Stealing from Artists? *Forbes*.

Marrone, R., Cropley, D., & Medeiros, K. (2024). How does narrow AI impact human creativity? *Creativity Research Journal*, •••, 1–11. DOI: 10.1080/10400419.2024.2378264

Martin, E., & Moore, A. (2020). Tapping Into Artificial Intelligence: Advanced Technology to Prevent Crime and Support Reentry. *Corrections Today*, •••, 28–32.

Martinez-Martin, N., Luo, Z., Kaushal, A., Adeli, E., Haque, A., Kelly, S. S., Wieten, S., Cho, M. K., Magnus, D., Fei-Fei, L., Schulman, K., & Milstein, A. (2021). Ethical issues in using ambient intelligence in health-care settings. *The Lancet. Digital Health*, *3*(2), e115–e123. DOI: 10.1016/S2589-7500(20)30275-2

Mathur, A., & Gupta, V. (2024). Animating the line: Studio Ghibli, AI-generated art, and the crosscurrents of copyright and AI law. *Indian Journal of Law and Legal Research*, *7*(2), 8534–8542.

McCall, C. S., Romero, M. E., Yang, W., & Weigand, T. (2023). A call for equity-focused social-emotional learning. *School Psychology Review*, *52*(5), 586–607. DOI: 10.1080/2372966X.2022.2093125

Media, G. S. (2016). Court of Justice of the European Union, C-160/15, 8 September 2016. *ECLI:EU*, *C*, 644.

Meduri, K., Podicheti, S., Satish, S., & Whig, P. (2024). Accountability and transparency ensuring responsible AI development. In *Advances in human and social aspects of technology book series* (pp. 83–102). DOI: 10.4018/979-8-3693-4147-6.ch004

Mehmood, A. (2024). Social Work and AI in Healthcare: Toward Collaborative Models of Support and Care. *Journal of Social Sciences and Community Support*, *1*(2), 23–32.

Meilvang, M. L. (2023). Working the boundaries of social work: Artificial intelligence and the profession of social work. *Professions and Professionalism*, *13*(1). Advance online publication. DOI: 10.7577/pp.5108

Meng, J., & Dai, Y. (2021). Emotional support from AI chatbots: Should a supportive partner self-disclose or not? *Journal of Computer-Mediated Communication*, *26*(4), 207–222. DOI: 10.1093/jcmc/zmab005

Mennella, C., Maniscalco, U., De Pietro, G., & Esposito, M. (2024). Ethical and regulatory challenges of AI technologies in healthcare: A narrative review. *Heliyon*, *10*(4), e26297. DOI: 10.1016/j.heliyon.2024.e26297 PMID: 38384518

Mhlanga, D. (2024). Artificial intelligence in elderly care: Navigating ethical and responsible AI adoption for seniors. In *Fostering Long-Term Sustainable Development in Africa: Overcoming Poverty, Inequality, and Unemployment* (pp. 411–440). Springer Nature Switzerland. DOI: 10.1007/978-3-031-61321-0_18

Miernicki, M., & Ng, I. (2021). Artificial intelligence and moral rights. *AI & Society*, *36*(1), 319–329. DOI: 10.1007/s00146-020-01027-6

Milella, F., & Bandini, S. (2024). Fostering Artificial Intelligence-based supports for informal caregivers: A systematic review of the literature. *Intelligenza Artificiale*, *18*(1), 67–87. DOI: 10.3233/IA-240028

Milella, F., Russo, D., & Bandini, S. (2023). AI-powered solutions to support informal caregivers in their decision-making: A systematic review of the literature. *OBM Geriatrics*, *7*(4), 1–11. DOI: 10.21926/obm.geriatr.2304262

Militsyna, K. (2023). Human creative contribution to AI-based output – one just can't get enough. *GRUR International*, *72*(10), 939–949. DOI: 10.1093/grurint/ikad075

Mishna, F., Milne, E., Bogo, M., & Pereira, L. F. (2021). Responding to COVID-19: New trends in social workers' use of information and communication technology. *Clinical Social Work Journal*, *49*(4), 484–494. DOI: 10.1007/s10615-020-00780-x

MIT Sociotechnical Systems Research Center. (2021). The bias in the machine: Facial recognition technology and racial disparities. Retrieved July 20, 2025, from https://ssrc.mit.edu/publications/the-bias-in-the-machine-facial-recognition-technology-and-racial-disparities/

Mitchell, J. J., & Jeon, M. (2025). Exploring emotional connections: A systematic literature review of attachment in human-robot interaction. *International Journal of Human-Computer Interaction*, *41*(18), 1–22. DOI: 10.1080/10447318.2024.2445100

Mokhtar, R. (2025). The Transformation of Correctional Facilities Using Artificial Intelligence Technology.

Monitor, P. (2023). *OpenAI trains its GPT model using pirated e-books, contends authors' lawsuit*. Pirate Monitor Website.

Montomoli, J., Bitondo, M. M., Cascella, M., Rezoagli, E., Romeo, L., Bellini, V., Semeraro, F., Gamberini, E., Frontoni, E., Agnoletti, V., Altini, M., Benanti, P., & Bignami, E. G. (2024). Algor-ethics: Charting the ethical path for AI in critical care. *Journal of Clinical Monitoring and Computing*, *38*(4), 931–939. DOI: 10.1007/s10877-024-01157-y

Mounica, S. (2024). A comprehensive guide to face recognition algorithms. Hyperverge. Retrieved July 20, 2025, from https://hyperverge.co/blog/a-comprehensive-guide-to-face-recognition-algorithms/

Moy, L. (2021). Facing injustice: How face recognition technology may increase the incidence of misidentifications and wrongful convictions. *SSRN*, *30*, 337. DOI: 10.2139/ssrn.4101826

Mulvale, G., Green, J., Robert, G., Larkin, M., Vackerberg, N., Kjellström, S., Hossain, P., Moll, S., Lim, E., & Craythorne, S. L. (2024). Adopting, implementing and assimilating coproduced health and social care innovations involving structurally vulnerable populations: Findings from a longitudinal, multiple case study design in Canada, Scotland and Sweden. *Health Research Policy and Systems*, *22*(1), 42. DOI: 10.1186/s12961-024-01130-w

Murphy, H. (2022). Whatever Happened to Those Self-Service Passport Kiosks at Airports? *International New York Times*, NA-NA.

Nadella, G. S., Meduri, S. S., Maturi, M. H., & Whig, P. (2024). Societal impact and governance. In *Advances in human and social aspects of technology book series* (pp. 261–282). DOI: 10.4018/979-8-3693-4147-6.ch012

Naidoo, T. (2024). Overview of AI regulation in healthcare: A comparative study of the EU and South Africa. *South African Journal of Bioethics and Law*, *17*(3), 121–126. DOI: 10.7196/SAJBL.2024.v17i3.2294

Nandy, D. (2023). Human rights in the era of surveillance: Balancing security and privacy concerns. *Journal of Current Social and Political Issues*, *1*(1), 13–17. DOI: 10.15575/jcspi.v1i1.442

Naruto v. Slater. (2018). United States Court of Appeals for the Ninth Circuit, 888 F.3d 418.

Nasir, S., Khan, R. A., & Bai, S. (2024). Ethical framework for harnessing the power of AI in healthcare and beyond. *IEEE Access : Practical Innovations, Open Solutions*, *12*, 31014–31035. DOI: 10.1109/ACCESS.2024.3369912

National Institute of Standards and Technology. (2025, February 3). NIST study evaluates effects of race, age, sex on face recognition software. Retrieved July 20, 2025, from https://www.nist.gov/news-events/news/2019/12/nist-study-evaluates-effects-race-age-sex-face-recognition-software

Netto, N. R. (2024). Use of case studies in social work assessments–ChatGPT's kryptonite? *Social Work Education*, *43*(9), 2473–2484. DOI: 10.1080/02615479.2023.2266461

Neves, B. B., Petersen, A., Vered, M., Carter, A., & Omori, M. (2023). Artificial intelligence in long-term care: Technological promise, aging anxieties, and sociotechnical ageism. *Journal of Applied Gerontology*, *42*(6), 1274–1282. DOI: 10.1177/07334648231157370

Newson, N. (2024, April 18). UN standards on the use of surveillance technology at protests. House of Lords Library. Retrieved July 20, 2025, from https://lordslibrary.parliament.uk/un-standards-on-the-use-of-surveillance-technology-at-protests/

Nguyen, T. M., & Malik, A. (2022). Impact of knowledge sharing on employees' service quality: The moderating role of artificial intelligence. *International Marketing Review*, *39*(3), 482–508. DOI: 10.1108/IMR-02-2021-0078

Nordesjö, K., Scaramuzzino, G., & Ulmestig, R. (2022). The social worker-client relationship in the digital era: A configurative literature review. *European Journal of Social Work*, *25*(2), 303–315. DOI: 10.1080/13691457.2021.1964445

Nuwasiima, M., Ahonon, M. P., & Kadiri, C. (2024). The role of artificial intelligence (AI) and machine learning in social work practice. *World Journal of Advanced Research and Reviews*, *24*(1), 80–97. DOI: 10.30574/wjarr.2024.24.1.2998

Obhan, E. (2025, April 1). The ghibli effect: Blurring the lines between creativity and copyright. *Obhan & Associates*. https://www.obhanandassociates.com/blog/the-ghibli-effect-blurring-the-lines-between-creativity-and-copyright/

OECD. (2025). Intellectual Property Issues in Artificial Intelligence Trained on Scraped Data. OECD Artificial Intelligence Papers, No. 33.

Oh, K. M., Hong, S. R., Beran, K., Sanders, L., Park, J. Y., & Lee, J. A. (2025). Utilizing Conversational AI Technology for Social Connectedness Among Older Adults: A Systematic Review. *Journal of Applied Gerontology*, •••, 07334648251341629. DOI: 10.1177/07334648251341629

Ojo, S. O., & Afolaranmi, A. O. (2024). The Effects of Artificial Intelligence (AI) on Human Interpersonal Connections. *Lead City Journal of Religions and Intercultural Communication*, *2*(2), 162–174.

Okuno, M. J., & Okuno, H. G. (2025). Legal frameworks for AI service business participants: A comparative analysis of liability protection across jurisdictions. *AI & Society*, *40*(7), 5667–5683. Advance online publication. DOI: 10.1007/s00146-025-02288-9

Oladokun, P. (2025). Posthuman ethics in digital health: reimagining autonomy, consent, and responsibility in AI-augmented care. *International Journal of Engineering Research & Management*, vol.9, no.4.

Olimid, A. P., Georgescu, C. M., & Olimid, D. A. (2024). Legal analysis of EU Artificial Intelligence Act (2024): Insights from personal data governance and health policy. *Access to Justice in Eastern Europe*, *7*(4), 120–142. DOI: 10.33327/AJEE-18-7.4-a000103

Open, A. I. (2024). ChatGPT Shared Links FAQ. OpenAI Website. https://help.openai.com/en/articles/7925741-chatgpt-shared-links-faq

Ozturk, E. (2025). Artificial Intelligence in Early Childhood STEM Education: A Review of Pedagogical Paradigms, Ethical Issues, and Socio-Political Implications. *Journal of Education in Science, Environment and Health*, *11*(2), 108–125. DOI: 10.55549/jeseh.800

Palaniappan, K., Lin, E. Y. T., & Vogel, S. (2024). Global regulatory frameworks for the use of artificial intelligence (AI) in the healthcare services sector. *Health Care*, *12*(5), 562. PMID: 38470673

Palaniappan, K., Lin, E. Y. T., Vogel, S., & Lim, J. C. (2024). Gaps in the global regulatory frameworks for the use of artificial intelligence (AI) in the healthcare services sector and key recommendations. *Health Care*, *12*(17), 1730. PMID: 39273754

Paliwal, A., & Ahmed, S. (2025). Constitutional approaches to data protection and privacy in the age of surveillance: A comparative analysis of India, the USA, and the European Union. International Journal of Innovation and Research in Law. https://doi.org/DOI: 10.1234/ijirl.2025.1.1.10

Panahi, O. (2025). Health in the Age of AI: A Family and Community Focus. *Archives of Community and Family Medicine*, *8*(1), 11–20. DOI: 10.22259/2638-4787.0801003

Panarese, P., Grasso, M. M., & Solinas, C. (2025). Algorithmic bias, fairness, and inclusivity: A multilevel framework for justice-oriented AI. *AI & Society*, •••, 1–23. DOI: 10.1007/s00146-025-02451-2

Pangotra, A. (2025, April 10). Ghibli trend: Another ethical conundrum caused by AI? *CyberPeace*. https://www.cyberpeace.org/resources/blogs/ghibli-trend-another-ethical-conundrum-caused-by-ai

Pantanowitz, L., Hanna, M., Pantanowitz, J., Lennerz, J., Henricks, W. H., Shen, P., Quinn, B., Bennet, S., & Rashidi, H. H. (2024). Regulatory aspects of artificial intelligence and machine learning. *Modern Pathology*, *37*(12), 100609. DOI: 10.1016/j.modpat.2024.100609 PMID: 39260776

Park, D. (2018). *The Watchlist: Improving the Transparency*. Accuracy, Efficiency, and Accountability of the Terrorist Screening Database.

Parker, G. (2016). Come see the bias inherent in the system. *The Journal of the American Academy of Psychiatry and the Law*, *44*(4), 411–414. PMID: 28003383

Parmar, D. N., & Mehta, B. B. (2014). *Face recognition methods and applications. arXiv preprint arXiv:1403.0485*.https://doi.org//arXiv.1403.0485. Retrieved July 20, 2025, from https://www.troutman.com/insights/facial-recognition-and-legal-boundaries-the-clearview-ai-case-study/DOI: 10.48550

Parra Pennefather, P. (2023). The Art of the Prompt. In Creative Prototyping with Generative AI: Augmenting Creative Workflows with Generative AI (pp. 197–246). Apress. DOI: 10.1007/978-1-4842-9579-3_8

Pasetti, M., Santos, J. W., Corrêa, N. K., De Oliveira, N., & Barbosa, C. P. (2025). Technical, legal, and ethical challenges of generative artificial intelligence: An analysis of the governance of training data and copyrights. *Discover Artificial Intelligence*, *5*(1), 193. DOI: 10.1007/s44163-025-00379-6

Pecchia, L., Maccaro, A., Matarrese, M. A., Folkvord, F., & Fico, G. (2024). Artificial intelligence, data protection and medical device regulations: Squaring the circle with a historical perspective in Europe. *Health and Technology*, *14*(4), 663–670. DOI: 10.1007/s12553-024-00878-z

Peng, Y., Ahmad, S. F., Ahmad, A. Y. B., Shaikh, M. S. A., Daoud, M. K., & Alhamdi, F. M. H. (2023). Riding the waves of artificial intelligence in advancing accounting and its implications for sustainable development goals. *Sustainability (Basel)*, *15*(19), 14165. DOI: 10.3390/su151914165

Pennington, A. (2019, September 16). Andy Serkis rallies for digital performer rights. Screen Daily. https://www.screendaily.com/news/andy-serkis-rallies-for-digital-performer-rights/5142919.article

Perkowitz, S. (2021, February 5). The bias in the machine: Facial recognition technology and racial disparities. MIT Case Studies in Social and Ethical Responsibilities of Computing. Retrieved July 20, 2025, from https://mit-serc.pubpub.org/pub/facial-recognition-technology-and-racial-disparities

Pesapane, F., & Summers, P. (2024). Ethics and regulations for AI in radiology. In *Artificial Intelligence for Medicine* (pp. 179–192). Academic Press. DOI: 10.1016/B978-0-443-13671-9.00001-6

Petrin, M. (2024). The impact of AI and new technologies on corporate governance and regulation. Singapore Journal of Legal Studies, 90–106. DOI: 10.2139/ssrn.4891647

Pham, M. K., Nhan, T. L. A., Vuong, N. T. T., Nguyen, M. B. T., Nguyen, P. N., Sandiramourty, S., Nguyen, T. T. U., Pham, N. G. B., & Nguyen, T. T. H. (2024). Empowering vulnerable populations through technology: Innovations and challenges in social work. *Journal of Research in Educational Sciences*, *15*(1), 5–16. DOI: 10.14505/jres.v15.1(17).01

Pham, T. (2025). Ethical and legal considerations in healthcare AI: Innovation and policy for safe and fair use. *Royal Society Open Science*, *12*(5), 241873. DOI: 10.1098/rsos.241873 PMID: 40370601

Phil Collins v Imtrat Handelsgesellschaft mbH and Patricia Im- und Export Verwaltungsgesellschaft mbH and Leif Emanuel Kraul v EMI Electrola GmbH. (1993). Court of Justice of the European Union, C-92/92 and C-326/92, 20 October 1993, ECLI:EU:C:1993:847.

Piepgrass, S., Navetta, D., Geiser, L., & Waltz, D. (2025, June 10). *Facial recognition: Legal boundaries and Clearview AI [Audio podcast episode]*. Regulatory Oversight. https://www.newindianexpress.com/cities/hyderabad/2018/Aug/03/tscop-app-to-use-facial-recognition-1852485.html

Preciozzi, J. (2025). How does facial recognition work? From pixels to identity. Digital Sense. Retrieved July 20, 2025, from https://www.digitalsense.ai/how-does-facial-recognition-work/

Priya, K. (2008). Intellectual Property and Hegelian justification. *NUJS Law Review*, *1*(1), 359–366.

Project Statecraft. (2023, June 21). Facial recognition technology in India. Retrieved July 20, 2025, from https://www.projectstatecraft.org/facial-recognition-technology-in-india/

Puplampu, R. (2024). *What Everyone Should Know About the Rise of AI: AI Transparency, Privacy, and Ethics Best Practices*. Puplampu Books.

Quintais, J. P. (2023). Generative AI, copyright and the AI Act. Kluwer Copyright Blog. https://copyrightblog.kluweriplaw.com/2023/05/09/generative-ai-copyright-and-the-ai-act/

Radanliev, P. (2025). AI Ethics: Integrating transparency, fairness, and privacy in AI development. *Applied Artificial Intelligence*, *39*(1), 2463722. Advance online publication. DOI: 10.1080/08839514.2025.2463722

Radanliev, P. (2025). Governance of generative AI. *Policy and Society*, *43*(1), 42–54. DOI: 10.1093/polsoc/puaf001

Rahman, M., Sachin, B. S., Channabasaiah, K., Rashmi, C. R., Deepika, N., & Velusamy, K. (2025). Exploring the Intersection of Social Work and the Future of Technology. In *Advancements in Intelligent Process Automation* (pp. 201–222). IGI Global.

Rajagopal, N. K., Qureshi, N. I., Durga, S., Asis, E. H. R., Soto, R. M. H., Gupta, S. K., & Deepak, S. (2022a). Future of Business Culture: An Artificial Intelligence-Driven Digital Framework for organization Decision-Making Process. *Complexity, 2022*(1). DOI: 10.1155/2022/7796507

Rathi, M. (2021, December 1). Government facial recognition threatens our rights to free speech and protest. Security Technology, ASIS International. Retrieved July 20, 2025, from https://www.asisonline.org/security-management-magazine/articles/2021/12/government-facial-recognition-threatens-rights/

Ratnawat, C. P. (2025, June 25). *Revolutionizing Insurance Compliance: AI-Powered Automation for Regulatory excellence*. https://sarcouncil.com/2025/06/revolutionizing-insurance-compliance-ai-powered-automation-for-regulatory-excellence

Reamer, F. G. (2023). Artificial intelligence in social work: Emerging ethical issues. *International Journal of Social Work Values and Ethics, 20*(2), 52–71. DOI: 10.55521/10-020-205

Reed, R. (2024, March 22). Does ChatGPT violate New York Times' copyrights? *Harvard Law Today*. https://hls.harvard.edu/today/does-chatgpt-violate-new-york-times-copyrights/

Regulation (EU) 2022/2065 of the European Parliament and of the Council of 19 October 2022 on a Single Market For Digital Services and amending Directive 2000/31/EC (Digital Services Act). (2022). ELI: https://data.europa.eu/eli/reg/2022/2065/oj

Regulation (EU) 2024/1689 of the European Parliament and of the Council of 13 June 2024 laying down harmonised rules on artificial intelligence and amending Regulations (EC) No 300/2008, (EU) No 167/2013, (EU) No 168/2013, (EU) 2018/858, (EU) 2018/1139 and (EU) 2019/2144 and Directives 2014/90/EU, (EU) 2016/797 and (EU) 2020/1828 (Artificial Intelligence Act). (2024). ELI: https://data.europa.eu/eli/reg/2024/1689/oj

Riccardo Pagani v. Leo Burnett Company S.r.l. (2015). Ordinary Court of Turin, 32855/2014, 31 March 2015.

Richards, N. M. (2013). The dangers of surveillance. *Harvard Law Review*, *126*(7), 1934–1965. Retrieved July 20, 2025, from https://harvardlawreview.org/2013/05/the-dangers-of-surveillance/

Riches, S., Azevedo, L., Vora, A., Kaleva, I., Taylor, L., Guan, P., Jeyarajagiri, P., McIntosh, H., Petrou, C., Pisani, S., & Hammond, N. (2022). Therapeutic engagement in robot-assisted psychological interventions: A systematic review. *Clinical Psychology & Psychotherapy*, *29*(3), 857–873. DOI: 10.1002/cpp.2696

Rimmer, M. (2002). A creature of statute: Copyright law and legal formalism. *Entertainment Law Review*, *13*(2), 31–38.

Ring, T. (2016). Privacy in peril: Is facial recognition going too far too fast? *Biometric Technology Today*, *2016*(7-8), 7–11. DOI: 10.1016/S0969-4765(16)30123-0

Robinson, F., & Nejat, G. (2022). An analysis of design recommendations for socially assistive robot helpers for effective human-robot interactions in senior care. *Journal of Rehabilitation and Assistive Technologies Engineering*, *9*, 20556683221101389. DOI: 10.1177/20556683221101389

Rosati, E. (2019). Copyright as an obstacle or an enabler? A European perspective on text and data mining and its role in the development of AI creativity. *Asia Pacific Law Review*, *27*(2), 198–217. DOI: 10.1080/10192557.2019.1705525

Rosati, E. (2024). Is text and data mining synonymous with AI training? *Journal of Intellectual Property Law & Practice*, *19*(12), 851–852. DOI: 10.1093/jiplp/jpae092

Rosen, A. (1992). Reconsidering the idea/expression dichotomy. *University of British Columbia Law Review*, *26*, 263.

Rosic, A. (2024). Legal implications of artificial intelligence in health care. *Clinics in Dermatology*, *42*(5), 451–459. DOI: 10.1016/j.clindermatol.2024.06.014 PMID: 38936641

Roundy, P. T. (2022). Artificial intelligence and entrepreneurial ecosystems: Understanding the implications of algorithmic decision-making for startup communities. *Journal of Ethics in Entrepreneurship and Technology*, *2*(1), 23–38. DOI: 10.1108/JEET-07-2022-0011

Rudin, C. (2019). Stop explaining black box machine learning models for high stakes decisions and use interpretable models instead. *Nature Machine Intelligence*, *1*(5), 206–215. DOI: 10.1038/s42256-019-0048-x PMID: 35603010

Sætra, H. S. (2022). The ethics of trading privacy for security: The multifaceted effects of privacy on liberty and security. *Technology in Society*, *68*, 101854. DOI: 10.1016/j.techsoc.2021.101854

Saheb, T., & Saheb, T. (2023). Topical review of artificial intelligence national policies: A mixed method analysis. *Technology in Society*, *74*, 102316. DOI: 10.1016/j.techsoc.2023.102316

ŞAHiN, E., Arslan, N. N., & Özdemir, D.ŞAHiN. (2025). Unlocking the black box: An in-depth review on interpretability, explainability, and reliability in deep learning. *Neural Computing & Applications*, *37*(2), 859–965. DOI: 10.1007/s00521-024-10437-2

Salako, A. O., Fabuyi, J. A., Aideyan, N. T., Selesi-Aina, O., Dapo-Oyewole, D. L., & Olaniyi, O. O. (2024). Advancing information governance in AI-Driven cloud ecosystem: Strategies for enhancing data security and meeting regulatory compliance. *Asian Journal of Research in Computer Science, 17*(12), 66–88. DOI: 10.9734/ajrcos/2024/v17i12530

Samuel, P. K, N. R. A., Rajesh, S., M, N. K., & A, N. K. R. (2023). AI-Based big data algorithms and machine learning techniques for managing data in E-Governance. In *Advances in electronic government, digital divide, and regional development book series* (pp. 19–35). DOI: 10.4018/978-1-6684-7697-0.ch002

Samuels, E. (1988). The idea-expression dichotomy in copyright law. *Tennessee Law Review, 56*, 321.

Sanders, C. K., & Scanlon, E. (2021). The digital divide is a human rights issue: Advancing social inclusion through social work advocacy. *Journal of Human Rights and Social Work, 6*(2), 130–143. DOI: 10.1007/s41134-020-00147-9

Schiff, D. (2022). Education for AI, not AI for education: The role of education and ethics in national AI policy strategies. *International Journal of Artificial Intelligence in Education, 32*(3), 527–563. DOI: 10.1007/s40593-021-00270-2

Schmidt, J., Schutte, N. M., Buttigieg, S., Novillo-Ortiz, D., Sutherland, E., Anderson, M., de Witte, B., Peolsson, M., Unim, B., Pavlova, M., Stern, A. D., Mossialos, E., & Van Kessel, R. (2024). Mapping the regulatory landscape for artificial intelligence in health within the European Union. *NPJ Digital Medicine, 7*(1), 229. DOI: 10.1038/s41746-024-01221-6 PMID: 39191937

Segal, M. (2025). Social workers' evaluation of ChatGPT for solving ethical dilemmas within the limits of confidentiality. *Journal of Social Work Practice*, •••, 1–14. DOI: 10.1080/02650533.2025.2480092

Senftleben, M. (2023). Generative AI and Author Remuneration. IIC - International Review of Intellectual Property and Competition Law, 54, 1535–1560. DOI: 10.1007/s40319-023-01399-4

Sessa, F., Esposito, M., Cocimano, G., Sablone, S., Karaboue, M. A. A., Chisari, M., Albano, D. G., & Salerno, M. (2024). Artificial intelligence and forensic genetics: Current applications and future perspectives. *Applied Sciences (Basel, Switzerland)*, *14*(5), 2113. DOI: 10.3390/app14052113

Shaban, O. S., & Omoush, A. (2025). AI-driven financial transparency and corporate governance: Enhancing accounting practices with evidence from Jordan. *Sustainability (Basel)*, *17*(9), 3818. Advance online publication. DOI: 10.3390/su17093818

Shandilya, S. K., Datta, A., Kartik, Y., & Nagar, A. (2024). Navigating the regulatory landscape. In *EAI/Springer Innovations in Communication and Computing* (pp. 127–240). DOI: 10.1007/978-3-031-53290-0_3

Sharma, R., & Haralayya, B. (2025). Corporate Governance and AI Ethics: A Strategic Framework for Ethical Decision-Making in business. SSRN *Electronic Journal*. DOI: 10.2139/ssrn.5252708

Sheppard, K. G., Talaugon, A. R., & Hernandez, J. L. (2024). Assessing the feasibility and performance of risk assessment instruments for early intervention and prevention services in Juvenile Justice. *Journal of Criminal Justice*, *94*, 102262. DOI: 10.1016/j.jcrimjus.2024.102262

Simmler, M. (2025). Facial recognition technology in law enforcement. *ScienceDirect*. Retrieved July 20, 2025, from https://www.sciencedirect.com/science/article/pii/S0267364924001572

Simon, D. A. (2025). Copyright's missing personality. *Houston Law Review*, *62*(5), 993–1054. https://houstonlawreview.org/article/138618-copyright-s-missing-personality

Singhania, M., & Saini, N. (2021). Institutional framework of ESG disclosures: Comparative analysis of developed and developing countries. *Journal of Sustainable Finance & Investment*, *13*(1), 516–559. DOI: 10.1080/20430795.2021.1964810

Sinha, A. (2024, March 13). The landscape of facial recognition technologies in India. TechPolicy.Press. Retrieved July 20, 2025, from https://techpolicy.press/the-landscape-of-facial-recognition-technologies-in-india/

Sklavos, G., Theodossiou, G., Papanikolaou, Z., Karelakis, C., & Ragazou, K. (2024). Environmental, Social, and Governance-Based Artificial Intelligence Governance: Digitalizing firms' leadership and human resources management. *Sustainability (Basel)*, *16*(16), 7154. DOI: 10.3390/su16167154

Slobogin, C., & Stevenson, M. T. (2018). Algoirithmic Risk Assessment and the Double Edged Sword of Youth. *Washington University Law Review, 96.*

Smriti, D. (2024). *A Framework for Artificial Intelligence (AI) Design to Support Emotion Work of Informal Caregivers* (Doctoral dissertation, Drexel University).

Software Freedom Law Center. India. (2024, November 12). Deployment of facial recognition technology for state surveillance and monitoring. Retrieved July 20, 2025, from https://sflc.in/deployment-of-facial-recognition-technology-for-state-surveillance/

Solaiman, B., & Malik, A. (2025). Regulating algorithmic care in the European Union: Evolving doctor–patient models through the Artificial Intelligence Act (AI Act) and the liability directives. *Medical Law Review*, *33*(1), fwae033. DOI: 10.1093/medlaw/fwae033 PMID: 39257157

Solanki, P., Grundy, J., & Hussain, W. (2023). Operationalising ethics in artificial intelligence for healthcare: A framework for AI developers. *AI and Ethics*, *3*(1), 223–240. DOI: 10.1007/s43681-022-00195-z

South Wales Police. (2025). Live facial recognition technology: Everything you need to know. Retrieved July 20, 2025, from https://www.south-wales.police.uk/news/south-wales/news/2025/live-facial-recognition-technology-everything-you-need-to-know/

Southerland, V. M. (2023). The Master's Tool and a Mission: Using Community Control and Oversight Laws to Resist and Abolish Police Surveillance Technologies. *UCLA Law Review. University of California, Los Angeles. School of Law*, *70*, 2.

Spivack, J., & Garvie, C. (2020). A taxonomy of legislative approaches to face recognition in the United States. In A. Kak (Ed.), Regulating biometrics: Global approaches and urgent questions. AI Now Institute. Retrieved July 20, 2025, from https://ainowinstitute.org/regulating-biometrics.html

Stephen Thaler vs Shira Perlmutter. (2025). US Court of Appeals (District of Columbia Circuit), No. 23-5233, 18 March 2025.

Stim, R. (2013, April 4). Measuring fair use: The four factors. *Stanford Copyright and Fair Use Center*. https://fairuse.stanford.edu/overview/fair-use/four-factors/

Strowel, A., & Ducato, R. (2021). Artificial intelligence and text and data mining: a copyright carol. In *The Routledge handbook of EU copyright law* (pp. 299–316). Routledge.

Sundara Rajan, M. T. (2025). *The moral rights of authors and artists: From the birth of copyright to the age of artificial intelligence* (2nd ed.). Oxford University Press. DOI: 10.1093/law/9780198791850.001.0001

Taetzsch, E. S. (2024). Privacy Purgatory: Why the United States Needs a Comprehensive Federal Data Privacy Law. *Journal of Legislation*, *50*, 121.

Tang, D., Xi, X., Li, Y., & Hu, M. (2025). Regulatory approaches towards AI medical devices: A comparative study of the United States, the European Union and China. *Health Policy (Amsterdam)*, *153*, 105260. DOI: 10.1016/j.healthpol.2025.105260 PMID: 39951854

Technische Universität Darmstadt v. Eugen Ulmer KG. (2014). Court of Justice of the European Union, C-117/13, 11 September 2014, ECLI:EU:C:2014:2196.

The American Civil Liberties Union of Illinois. (2024). Biometric Information Privacy Act (BIPA). Retrieved July 20, 2025, from https://www.aclu-il.org/en/cases/biometric-information-privacy-act-bipa

The American Civil Liberties Union of Minnesota. (2021, June 9). Biased technology: The automated discrimination of facial recognition. Retrieved July 20, 2025, from https://www.aclu-mn.org/en/news/biased-technology-automated-discrimination-facial-recognition

The American Civil Liberties Union. (n.d.). ACLU v. Clearview AI. Retrieved July 20, 2025, from https://www.aclu.org/cases/aclu-v-clearview-ai

The New Indian Express. (2018, August 3). TSCOP app to use facial recognition. The New Indian Express Retrieved July 20, 2025, from. https://www.newindianexpress.com/cities/hyderabad/2018/Aug/03/tscop-app-to-use-facial-recognition-1852485.html

The New Indian Express. (2024, June 8). Second major data breach hits Telangana police as TSCOP app hacked. Retrieved July 20, 2025, from https://www.newindianexpress.com/states/telangana/2024/jun/08/second-major-data-breach-hits-telangana-police-as-tscop-app-hacked

Thinking Neuron. (2025). Convolutional neural networks (CNN) - Face recognition case study - Algorithm & full code explained [Video]. YouTube. Retrieved July 20, 2025, from https://www.youtube.com/watch?v=[VideoID]

Thomas, A., Denis, A., Robert, W., Kabiito, S. P., Morish, Z., Samuel, A., Sallam, M., & Adamopoulos, I. (2025). Artificial Intelligence-Powered Robotic Technology for Transforming Palliative Care. *Mesopotamian Journal of Artificial Intelligence in Healthcare, 2025*, 58–84. DOI: 10.58496/MJAIH/2025/007

Thomas, J. M. (1990). Willful Copyright Infringement: In Search of a Standard. *Washington Law Review (Seattle, Wash.), 65*, 903.

Tilala, M. H., Chenchala, P. K., Choppadandi, A., Kaur, J., Naguri, S., & Saoji, R., & Devaguptapu. (2024). Ethical considerations in the use of artificial intelligence and machine learning in health care: A comprehensive review. *Cureus, 16*(6), e62443.

Turkkan Zencirli, B., & Altin, M. (2025). The impact of artificial intelligence on workplace dehumanization: A critical review. *Journal of Hospitality and Tourism Horizons*, *1*(2), 128–149. DOI: 10.1108/JHTH-01-2025-0014

Ulnicane, I. (2024). When code isn't law: Rethinking regulation for artificial intelligence. *Policy and Society*, *43*(2), 194–206. DOI: 10.1093/polsoc/puae020

University of Michigan Law School. (2025, Winter). Flawed facial recognition technology leads to wrongful arrest and historic settlement. Law Quadrangle. Retrieved July 20, 2025, from https://quadrangle.law.umich.edu/winter2025/flawed-facial-recognition-technology/

Urantia Foundation v. Maaherra. (1995). United States District Court for the District of Arizona, 895 F. Supp. 1347.

Vadlapati, P. (2023). Does Seed Matter? Investigating the Effect of Random Seeds on LLM Accuracy. [IJSAT]. *International Journal on Science and Technology*, *14*(3).

Van Kolfschooten, H., & Van Oirschot, J. (2024). The EU Artificial Intelligence Act (2024): Implications for healthcare. *Health Policy (Amsterdam)*, *149*, 105152. DOI: 10.1016/j.healthpol.2024.105152 PMID: 39244818

Various class action lawsuits. (2023). [Multiple pending cases including Author Guild v. OpenAI; Getty Images v. Stability AI; Sarah Andersen et al. v. Stability AI et al.]

Vettriselvan, R., Velmurugan, P. R., Regins, J. C., Maheswari, S. U., & Joyce, R. (2025a). Best practices, ethical challenges, and regulatory frameworks for AI integration in banking. In *Advances in computational intelligence and robotics book series* (pp. 377–410). DOI: 10.4018/979-8-3693-9356-7.ch015

Villasenor, J., & Foggo, V. (2020). Artificial intelligence, due process and criminal sentencing. *Mich. St. L. Rev.*, 295.

Vujicic, J. (2024). Algorithmic accountability and ethical oversight: Legal challenges in transatlantic AI regulation. *International Journal of Scientific Research Archives, 13*(2).

Walter, Y. (2024). Managing the race to the moon: Global policy and governance in Artificial Intelligence regulation—A contemporary overview and an analysis of socioeconomic consequences. *Discover Artificial Intelligence, 4*(1), 14. Advance online publication. DOI: 10.1007/s44163-024-00109-4

Wang, Y., & Zhang, J. (2024, February 2). Beijing Internet Court grants copyright to AI-generated image for the first time. Kluwer Copyright Blog. https://copyrightblog.kluweriplaw.com/2024/02/02/beijing-internet-court-grants-copyright-to-ai-generated-image-for-the-first-time

Wang, X., Wu, Y. C., Zhou, M., & Fu, H. (2024). Beyond surveillance: Privacy, ethics, and regulations in facial recognition technology. *Frontiers in Big Data, 7*, 1337465. Retrieved July 20, 2025, from https://www.frontiersin.org/journals/big-data/articles/10.3389/fdata.2024.1337465/full. DOI: 10.3389/fdata.2024.1337465 PMID: 39027377

Wassal, K., Ashurst, C., Hron, J., & Zilka, M. (2024). Reimagining AI in social work: Practitioner perspectives on incorporating technology in their practice. *arXiv preprint arXiv:2407.10244.*

Waterloo News. (2024). *Can you tell AI-generated people from real ones?* Waterloo News.

Weiss, D. A. (2025). INHUMAN REASON: Predictive Policing Algorithms and the Fourth Amendment. *Criminal Justice, 39*(4), 15–20.

Whetzel, J., Cornish, T., Anders, S., LaFratta, J., & Poulos, C. (2025). Looking Back, Looking Forward: The First Step Act and the Art of the Possible. *Federal Sentencing Reporter, 37*(1), 41–53. DOI: 10.1215/10539867-11484730

Wiertz, S., & Boldt, J. (2022). Evaluating models of consent in changing health research environments. *Medicine, Health Care, and Philosophy, 25*(2), 269–280. DOI: 10.1007/s11019-022-10074-3

Williamson, S. M., & Prybutok, V. (2024). Balancing privacy and progress: A review of privacy challenges, systemic oversight, and patient perceptions in AI-driven healthcare. *Applied Sciences (Basel, Switzerland)*, *14*(2), 675. DOI: 10.3390/app14020675

Wong, K. L. Y., Hung, L., Wong, J., Park, J., Alfares, H., Zhao, Y., Mousavinejad, A., Soni, A., & Zhao, H. (2024). Adoption of artificial intelligence–enabled robots in long-term care homes by health care providers: Scoping review. *JMIR Aging*, *7*(1), e55257. DOI: 10.2196/55257

Wu, F., Dixon-Woods, M., Aveling, E. L., Campbell, A., Willars, J., Tarrant, C., Bates, D. W., Dankcrs, C., Mitchell, I., Pronovost, P., & Martin, G. P. (2021). The role of the informal and formal organisation in voice about concerns in healthcare: A qualitative interview study. *Social Science & Medicine*, *280*, 114050. DOI: 10.1016/j.socscimed.2021.114050

Xu, H., Xie, B., & Chang, C. H. (2024). Empowering the care of older adults through the use of technology. *Work, Aging and Retirement*, *10*(1), 1–5. DOI: 10.1093/workar/waad030

Yee, D. G. (2025). Artificial Intelligence: An Impetus to Amend the ABA Model Code of Judicial Conduct. *Mary's J. on Legal Malpractice & Ethics*, *15*, 2.

Yoo, C. S., & Jagasia, A. (2024). Identifying Fourth Amendment Values: An Evidence-Based Approach. *Wake Forest Law Review*, *59*, 1219. DOI: 10.2139/ssrn.4867896

Ystgaard, K. F., & De Moor, K. (2023). Envisioning the future: A multidisciplinary approach to human-centered intelligent environments. *Quality and User Experience*, *8*(1), 11. DOI: 10.1007/s41233-023-00064-5

Yu, P. K. (2014). Moral Rights 2.0. *Texas A&M. Law Review*, *1*(4), 873–900. DOI: 10.37419/LR.V1.I4.3

Zahra, Y. (2025). Regulating AI in legal practice: Challenges and opportunities. [JOSAPEN]. *Journal of Computer Science Application and Engineering*, *3*(1), 10–15. DOI: 10.70356/josapen.v3i1.47

Zens, J. (2021). Face It: Only Congress Can Preserve Privacy from the Pervasive Use of Facial Recognition Technology by Police. *The San Diego Law Review*, *58*, 143.

Zhao, J., & Fariñas, B. G. (2022). Artificial intelligence and sustainable decisions. *European Business Organization Law Review*, *24*(1), 1–39. DOI: 10.1007/s40804-022-00262-2

Zhu, Y., Yang, Q., & Mao, X. (2023). Global trends in the study of smart healthcare systems for the elderly: Artificial intelligence solutions. *International Journal of Computational Intelligence Systems*, *16*(1), 105. DOI: 10.1007/s44196-023-00283-w

Zick, T. (2023). *Managed dissent: The law of public protest*. Cambridge University Press. Retrieved July 20, 2025, from https://www.cambridge.org/core/books/managed-dissent/12A7E4D9035D78C4A5BF24B1D81B0746

About the Contributors

Konstantinos Kouroupis is an associate professor of European and IT Law and vice head of the Department of Law at Frederick University in Cyprus. His area of expertise is online protection of privacy, security and data rights, artificial intelligence, digital law, human rights and European Law. He has participated in numerous international conferences as a speaker and keynote lecturer on data rights, privacy and EU issues. Some of his studies have been uploaded to the digital library of EUROJUST, in Hague and are accessible from a large number of prosecutors, judicial officers and administrative staff of the European agency. In 2018, he delivered a speech on "National and European legal framework on Cybersecurity and data protection" as an expert and on behalf of the Republic of Cyprus, during an international exercise under the supervision of European Defence Agency, held at Zenon Coordination Centre, in Larnaka, in Cyprus. He has participated in European projects and actions funded by the EU concerning the consolidation of a European area of justice and human rights. He has served as a Management Committee Delegate, representing Cyprus, in the framework of the European Cost action entitled "Global Digital Human Rights Network", under the auspices of the European Cooperation in Science and Technology (COST). He is a member of the editorial board of esteemed legal journals. He is also a member of the pool of experts of the European Data Protection Board in the field of Data Protection and New Technologies, upon evaluation. Since August 2023, he has been appointed as a member of the Cyprus National Bioethics Committee upon a decision of the Council of Ministers of the Republic of Cyprus for a period of 4 years.

Iris Efthymiou is a thought leader, university lecturer, and author of 17 books, specialising in AI ethics and behavioural health economics. Passionate about bridging technology and humanity, she advocates for ethical AI and user-centred design to enhance well-being and education in the digital age. She has served as a college director, founded a Public Affairs consultancy, worked with global leaders, and spoken at the UN in Geneva. She serves as an Academic Board Member of the LabHEM at the University of Piraeus, a Board Member of HAPSc and Guildhouse School in London, and a Member of the Business Intelligence Committee (BIC) of the All-Party Parliamentary Group on Artificial Intelligence (APPG AI) in the UK. She has published over 17 books, 40 articles, and book chapters in peer-reviewed journals, and she is the chief editor of the Journal of Politics and Ethics in New Technologies and AI. She believes in equal opportunities, uniqueness, and the normality of imperfection! Iris has a Ph.D. in Behavioural Economics, a Master's in Health Economics and Management, and a Bachelor's in Economics.

S. M. Aamir Ali is presently Assistant Professor at Symbiosis Law School Pune, Symbiosis International (Deemed University), Pune. He is currently pursuing his PhD from West Bengal National University of Juridical Sciences (WBNUJS), Kolkata, and has completed his LL.M from National Law School of India University (NLSIU), Bengaluru, with a specialization in Human Rights Law. Mr Ali has been teaching across specializations in Constitutional Law, Human Rights and Criminal Law at UG and PG levels since 2019.

Angelo Brown received his master's at Arizona State University and his Ph.D. Criminal Justice and Criminology at Washington State University. His research and teaching in criminal justice and criminology are primarily on policy and policing from a comparative and intersectional perspective.

Anuttama Ghose is an Assistant Professor of Law and Program Co-ordinator of BA LLB (Hons.) Program at the School of Law, Dr. Vishwanath Karad MIT World Peace University, Pune, India. She is also presently Heading the Centre for Innovation Incubation and Intellectual Property Laws (CIIIPL) at MIT WPU School of Law. She has completed her B.A LL.B (IPR Hons.) from the School of Law, KIIT University, Bhubaneshwar and LL.M with specialisation in the field of Intellectual Property Laws from Symbiosis Law School, Pune, India. She has completed her PhD in the field of Protection of Non-Conventional Trademarks from School of Law and Justice, Adamas University, Kolkata. She has previously worked as Vice-Principal and Assistant Professor of Law at Indian Institute of Legal Studies, Darjeeling, West Bengal. Apart from being an IPR enthusiast, she is a very keen researcher and has over 25 academic publications in National and International Journals to her credit.

Philippe Jougleux is a Professor at the Law School of the European University Cyprus, where he teaches Cypriot civil wrongs and contract law, EU copyright law, and EU Internet law. He has authored numerous articles in French, Greek, and English, primarily focusing on topics related to the regulation of new technologies, such as online copyright law, data protection, regulation of AI, and cybercrime. Additionally, he has published several monographs in Greek covering various topics, including 'Elements of Cypriot Law of Obligations,' 'Civil Liability of the State in Cyprus,' 'European Law of the Internet,' and 'European Law of Intellectual Property.' Most recently, he published 'Facebook and the (EU) Law' in English in 2022 and 'Open Justice in the Digital age' in 2024 with Editions Springer. In the field of Intellectual property, he has completed numerous studies (monographies – such as the book "EU Intellectual property law" in Greek, at editions Sakkoulas-, chapters, articles), presented papers in international conferences, and participated to various European programmes. He is one of the founding members of the Cypriot branch of the famous International Copyright law association "ALAI". He teaches this topic for more than a decade to law students.

Mayank Kapila is an Assistant Professor (Senior Scale) in the Department of Law at M.S. College, Motihari, under Babasaheb Bhimrao Ambedkar Bihar University, Muzaffarpur, Bihar, India, and can be reached at kapilalegal.brabu@gmail.com; he is registered as a researcher with the ORCID identifier 0009-0001-4874-8283, reflecting his engagement in academic and scholarly activities in the field of law.

Pallav is a Junior Research Fellow (UGC) and Ph.D Scholar at The West Bengal National University of Judicial Sciences (NUJS), Kolkata. He has completed a PG Diploma in Media Laws from NALSAR, Hyderabad. He has qualified Prestigious UGC NET with JRF. He has practical experience as an Advocate at the Patna High Court. He has also completed an LLM. He has completed BBA LL.B. (Constitutional Law Hons.) from the School of Law, KIIT University, Bhubaneswar.

Vijaishree Dubey Pandey, a distinguished academician and legal professional, serves as the President of the Artificial Intelligence for Women's Empowerment and Representation Council, spearheading initiatives at the intersection of law, technology, and gender equality. Experienced and accomplished academician with a demonstrated history of working in the legal services industry and a passion for research and publication. Her expertise in Human Rights and IPRs and had undergone trainings related to Artificial Intelligence. She has worked in collaboration with jails, orphanages, schools, and RWAs, aiming to provide legal aid and basic legal rights. Her leadership skills, coupled with her dedication to professional ethics and academic excellence, have earned her the respect of her peers and students alike. Her dedication to social causes is evident through her involvement in legal aid programs, advocacy efforts, and community outreach initiatives. Beyond academia, Dr. Pandey is a sought-after resource person and guest speaker, lending her expertise to various institutions and organizations. Her expertise spans across various domains, coupled with her leadership acumen and commitment to women's empowerment. As the President of the Artificial Intelligence for Women's Empowerment and Representation Council, Dr. Pandey spearheads initiatives aimed at bridging the gender gap in AI and fostering inclusivity. Her research prowess is evidenced by a prolific publication record, comprising numerous papers, chapters, and books on diverse legal topics. She has also been an active participant in conferences, seminars, and webinars, contributing to the advancement of legal scholarship and continuously expanding her knowledge and professional network. With an extensive portfolio including multiple paper publications in reputed national and international journals, workshops, book chapters in edited books, and conference presentations, she has established a strong presence in the academic community. Experienced Legal Professional with a strong background in Web 4.0 and Artificial Intelligence. She is skilled in analysing complex legal cases and providing innovative solutions. Proficient in applying cutting-edge technology to the legal field, effectively utilizing AI tools to streamline processes and enhance efficiency. She has developed a deep understanding of the intersection between technology and law, with a focus on leveraging AI advancements to improve access to justice. Looking ahead, her goal is to continue making significant contributions to the legal field and to establish myself as a leading expert and thought leader in the field of law while also mentoring and inspiring the next generation of scholars. She is driven, meticulous, and committed to fostering academic excellence.

Parlalis K. Stavros received both his Masters Degree in Policy Studies (2003) and his Doctorate in Social Work (2008) by the University of Edinburgh, Scotland. He obtained his BA in Social Work in 2002 by the ATEI of Crete, Greece. He currently works as Associate Professor in Psychology and Social Sciences at Frederick University. He is lecturing at both the undergraduate and graduate levels; he is also lecturing in the Distance Learning Program of Special Education. He has published one monograph titled as "De-institutionalisation of Persons with Intellectual Disabilities in the Republic of Cyprus" (Power Publishing 2012, p.210) and he has edited the publication of the book titled as "Social Work Applications in Greece and Cyprus" (Pedio Publications 2011, p.368). In addition, he has published articles in international scientific journals and has authored chapters for collective volumes.

Kalpna Sharma is an Assistant Professor at Law Centre-II, Faculty of Law, University of Delhi, India. She holds a Ph.D. in Law and a Post Graduate Diploma in Personnel Management & Labour Welfare (PGDPM & LW) from Himachal Pradesh University, Shimla. Her areas of interest and specialization include Human Rights and Humanitarian Law, Refugee Law, Information Technology Law, Women & Children Law, and Criminal Law.

Sheetal Singh is a seasoned legal academic with over 15 years of experience in teaching, research, and academic administration. Currently serving as Assistant Professor at the School of Law, CHRIST (Deemed to be University), Delhi NCR Campus, she previously held senior faculty roles at Amity Law School, Noida, where she also founded the Amity Legal Aid Cell. She holds a Ph.D. in Law from Amity University and is UGC-NET qualified, with expertise spanning Family Law, Criminal Law, Constitutional Law, Property Law, and Human Rights. Dr. Singh has guided more than 150 LLB and LLM dissertations and supervises Ph.D. research on gender justice and victimology. Her scholarly contributions include chapters in edited volumes published by Thomson Reuters, CRC Press, Springer, and Cambridge Scholars Publishing, covering topics such as media law, reproductive rights, cybersecurity, and comparative constitutional analysis. She has presented papers at national and international conferences, delivered guest lectures, and organized seminars and workshops on legal education, gender sensitization, and human rights. Her administrative roles include serving as Head of Department, Program Coordinator, and member of various university committees such as IQAC, Moot Court, and Placement. Widely recognized for her commitment to legal education and interdisciplinary research, Dr. Singh continues to contribute meaningfully to academia and social justice initiatives.

Rituraj Sinha is an Assistant Professor at the School of Law, CHRIST (Deemed to be University), Delhi NCR. He holds a Ph.D. from Guru Gobind Singh Indraprastha University and an LL.M. from NALSAR. With prior teaching experience at Amity Law School and IMS Unison University, he also practiced as an advocate in Delhi. His academic interests include Corporate Law, gender justice, intellectual property rights, and the legal dimensions of emerging technologies. He has contributed to reputed journals and international conference volumes and actively mentors students in research and legal scholarship.

Shashank Solanki is a B.B.A. LL.B (Hons.) student at Christ University. With a strong academic foundation and a keen interest in Arbitration, Securities, Corporate Law, and Banking & Finance, Shashank has actively contributed to legal scholarship. His research works have been accepted for publication in esteemed Scopus-indexed platforms, addressing critical areas such as medical big data, digital healthcare ethics, and the Metaverse. Beyond academics, he has demonstrated excellence through multiple internships, gaining hands-on experience in dispute resolution, corporate law, and judicial research. Shashank's dedication to academic pursuits and practical legal applications reflects his commitment to contributing meaningfully to the legal domain.

Muhammad Usman Tariq is a strategic higher education leader and scholar with more than 17 years of international experience across academia, research, and industry. He holds dual doctorates, a PhD in Artificial Intelligence and a Doctorate in Business Administration and has published extensively as the author of research articles, case studies, book chapters, and academic texts. His contributions also include several patents, reflecting his applied research in technology, business, and education. He is the Founder and CEO of TheCaseHQ.com, a global hub for professional certification programmes, narrative and video case studies, and digital learning innovation. In addition, he serves as President of the Gulf Higher Education Network (Gulf HE), an initiative dedicated to advancing academic practice, faculty development, and institutional collaboration across the region. He is a Principal Fellow of Advance HE (UK), Chartered Fellow of the CIPD (UK), Senior Fellow of SEDA (UK), and a Senior Member of IEEE, reflecting his standing as both an academic innovator and a global professional leader.

Vijeta Verma is an Assistant Professor at the School of Law, CHRIST (Deemed to be University), Delhi NCR. She holds a Ph.D. in Law from Mewar University and an LL.M. from Amity University, Noida. With over a decade of academic experience, she has previously served as an Assistant Professor at JIMS Engineering Management & Technical Campus and Ideal Institute of Management & Technology. Her research interests lie in Constitutional Law, HumanRights, and Gender Justice. At CHRIST, she actively contributes as the Faculty Convenor for various academic committees and has been a key organizer of national and international legal conferences.

Index

A

C

D

E

F

www.ingramcontent.com/pod-product-compliance
Lightning Source LLC
LaVergne TN
LVHW081524300926
849161LV00006B/1288